PLUMBING FOR OLD AND NEW HOUSES

PLUMBING
FOR OLD AND NEW HOUSES

JAY HEDDEN

CREATIVE HOMEOWNER PRESS®

A DIVISION OF FEDERAL MARKETING CORPORATION,
24 PARK WAY, UPPER SADDLE RIVER, NEW JERSEY 07458

Manufactured in United States of America

Current Printing (last digit)
10 9   8   7

Editor: Shirley M. Horowitz
Art Director: Léone Lewensohn
Proofreader: Marilyn M. Auer
Additional Drawings: Norman Nuding

Cover: American Standard, New Brunswick, NJ 08903

Library of Congress Cataloging in Publication Data

Hedden, Jay W
  Modern plumbing for old and new homes

  Includes index.
  1. Plumbing — Amateurs' manuals.   1.   Title.
TH6124.H42   696'.1   81-67297
ISBN 0-932944-45-0
ISBN 0-932944-46-9 pbk.

CREATIVE HOMEOWNER PRESS®
BOOK SERIES

A DIVISION OF FEDERAL
MARKETING CORPORATION
24 PARK WAY,
UPPER SADDLE RIVER, NJ 07458

THIRTY-SIX SELECTED PROJECTS

Adding a bathroom   125-140
Aerators for faucets   69, 76
Air chamber installation   48
Bathtub additions   86-89
Conversion of separate hot/cold faucets to mixed, single control   54
Cross-connection of plumbing, preventing/correcting   56
Dishwasher repairs and installation   91-94
Drains, unplugging   37
Emergency pipe fixups   58-60
Faucet repairs and replacements   65-86
Flares for pipes   21-22
Frozen pipes, prevention and thawing   62-63
Flush-handle assemblies   83
Hot water tanks, replacing   97
Hot water heater leaks   61
Insulation for hot water tank   98-99
Leaks in valves   57
New piping, installing   16-35
Noisy pipes, correcting   48-49
Plastic pipe connection   32-33
Septic tank addition   102-107
Shower pans   87
Shutoff valves   45-47
Sillcock installation   114
Solar collectors   116-121
Soldering copper pipe   22-24
Spray hoses   76
Sprinkler systems   110-113
Sump pumps   99-101
Threading steel pipe   16-17
Toilet replacement and repairs   77-86
Washing machine repairs   90-91
Water-saving devices   50-53, 56
Vent stack cleanout   41
Washing machines, levelling   90-91
Wells, drilling   107

Contents

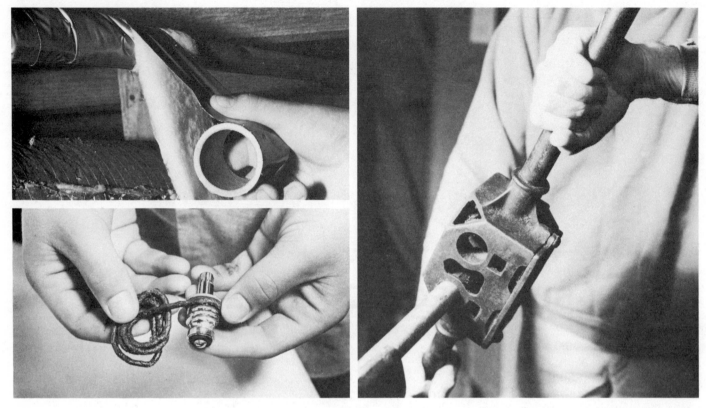

1   **The Plumbing System**   10
Pipe and Valve Alternatives, Component Layout

2   **Working with Steel Pipe**   16
Replacement, Unions, Safety

3   **Working with Copper Pipe**   21
Type of Tubing, Tools and Special Joints, Flux and Soldering

4   **Working with Cast Iron Pipe**   26
Types and Sizes, Cutting the Pipe, Supporting the Pipe, Joints and Calking Irons

5   **Working with Plastic Pipe**   31
Types, Fittings, Meeting Code, Cost Tradeoffs

6   **Repairing Clogged Drains**   36
Pressure Devices, Snakes, Sinks, Vanities, Toilets, Bathtub Drains

7   **Updating the System and Installing Shutoff Valves**   47
Shutoff Valves, Water Hammer, Other Noises, Low or Excess Pressure,
Extending Plumbing, Converting Separate Hot/Cold Faucets,
Water-Saving Fixtures

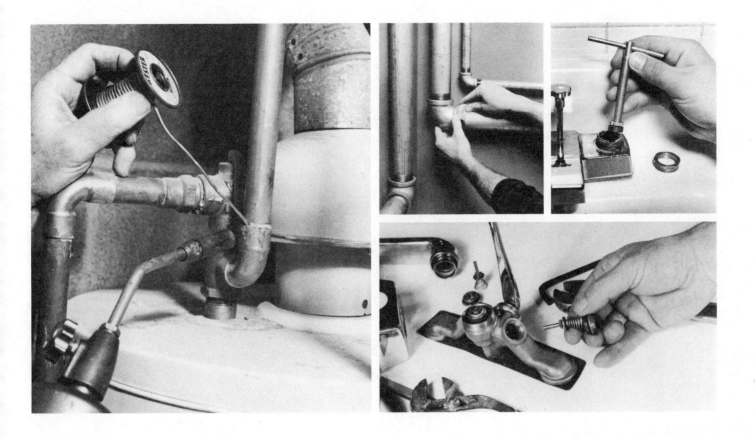

8   **Leaks and Other Pipe Repairs**   57
Leaks, Thawing Pipes, Wrapping Pipes to Prevent Freezing

9   **Replacing and Repairing Fixtures**   65
Faucets, Toilets, Tubs, Aerators

10   **Plumbing Breakdowns in Appliances**   90
Water Heaters, Clothes Washers, Dishwashers, Disposals, Sump Pumps

11   **Outdoor Plumbing and Private Systems**   102
Septic Tanks, Wells, Composting Toilets, Underground Sprinklers, Sillcocks

12   **How to Build Your Own Solar Collector**   115
Liquid or Air-Cooled? Construction Steps, Manufactured Components

13   **Plumbing for a New Bathroom**   125
Soil Stack, Hot and Cold Lines, Adding a Vanity, Bathroom in Basement

Appendices: **A** Glossary 143   **B** Where to Write for Appliance Parts 146
C Metric Conversion Charts 150   **D** Helpful Government
Publications 153   **E** Manufacturers' Addresses 155
Index 156

FOREWORD

This plumbing book is for anyone who is interested in saving hundreds of dollars by handling his or her home's plumbing problems without calling in a contractor.

Nowhere in this book are we going to say that plumbing is easy, and that anyone can do a plumbing job and have it always work the first time they try. Plumbing can be hard work; you can cut your fingers on the sharp threads of steel pipe, or burn your hands on hot copper tubing right after you have made a sweat joint. It can be frustrating to have a threaded joint in brass or steel pipe leak after you have spent an hour threading the pipe, applying pipe-joint compound, and sweating and groaning to tighten the connection. A soldered joint in a copper tube can look just fine but still spray water when the pressure is turned on. Even a glued joint in plastic pipe can leak—even though you know the job was done correctly!

The author has had all these things happen to him, both as a professional steam fitter and as a do-it-yourself homeowner years later, when he figured that the knowledge of such skills, like riding a bicycle, was something you never lose. It is true that you don't lose the skills; you just forget the problems and how to solve them.

So the main thrust of this book will be not only how to carry out plumbing projects and repairs, but how to correct the mistakes you are bound to make, and how to stop seemingly unstoppable leaks. The latter are the kind that occur on Sunday evening with guests coming for dinner and no way to prevent a flood except to shut the main valve—which means there is no water to the kitchen and none to the bathrooms. You might get by in the kitchen by some miracle, but asking your guests to go to the corner gas station to use the bathroom could make you an outcast among your friends and cause family arguments. This is a situation where a little knowledge or skill could save you many miserable hours.

What is the answer? Install a shut-off valve under each faucet so that any leak can be isolated to that fixture and repaired later.

MODERN MATERIALS

Most do-it-yourself plumbing in this day and age is done with plastic pipe and fittings. This space-age material is used for hot and cold water and for drain, waste, and vent lines. It can be used to replace both steel pipe and rigid or flexible copper tubing, or to run extensions from the metal pipes.

The fact remains, however, that there are thousands of miles of threaded steel pipe and sweat-soldered copper tubing in millions of homes in this country; they will undoubtedly be repaired or replaced in kind. Because plastic is a petrochemical, a look down the road indicates that plastic plumbing could become scarce in the future; this is another reason that skills with metal plumbing pipe and fittings could become very valuable.

Tools

You will need some tools that you might not have now, like pipe wrenches, tubing cutters, pipe taps and dies. It is quite likely you already have a propane torch to use for sweat-soldering copper tubing, and the water-pump pliers found in many tool boxes are ideal for working with threaded pipe up to ¾-inch size. Tools for the various types of pipes and projects will be given in the first part of each chapter. The most important consideration in selecting tools is their quality. Quality tools not only make any job easier, but will last a lifetime. Good pipe wrenches grip steel pipe firmly, even through galvanizing. Cheap ones slip because the serrations in the jaws become dull—and they slip just when your hand is where it will bash against a concrete wall. The savings in doctor bills alone make the price of quality tools a bargain.

Considering that plumbers charge $20 an hour or more, the first job you do will pay for this book. Over the years as a homeowner you will save hundreds, if not thousands, of dollars in repairs and maintenance of the plumbing system in your home.

Here's to clean running water and a dry house. You are the do-it-yourselfer who will make that possible.

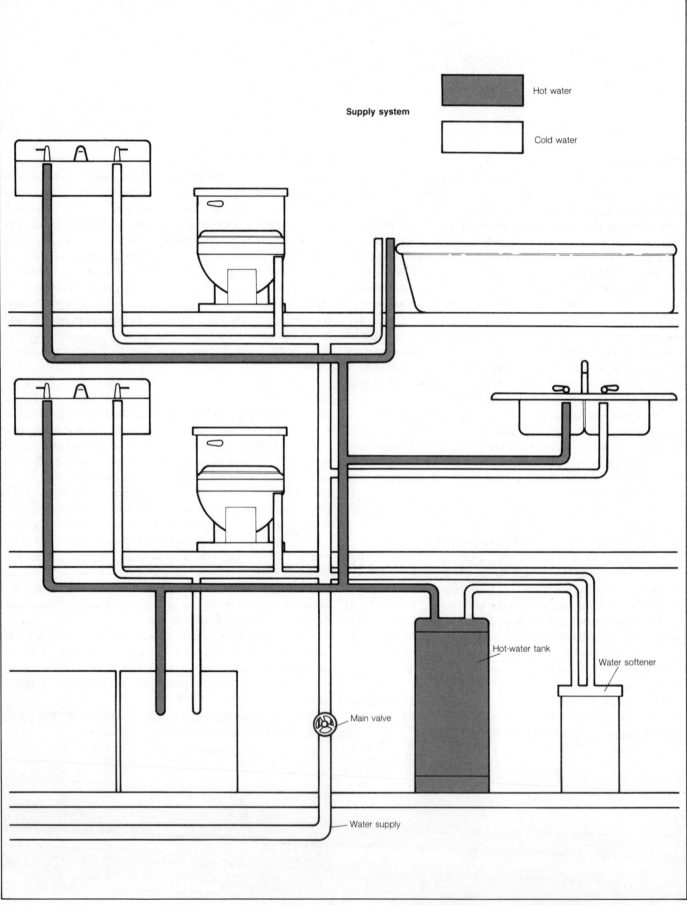

Supply system

Hot water

Cold water

Hot-water tank

Water softener

Main valve

Water supply

This diagram of a typical water supply system for a two-story house with basement shows how water enters through the main valve and is routed to the hot water tank and to various fixtures.

1 The Plumbing System

A home's plumbing system probably seems mysterious to many homeowners because most of it is hidden in walls and floors. The highly visible points are where the water supply ends—in kitchen sinks, in bathroom fixtures and even in bar sinks; drain lines begin at all these places.

The water supply will enter a house either from a city main or, in rural and some suburban areas, from a line from a well. If the supply is from a city main, the water first passes through a meter valve, then a water meter and then a stop valve. In colder parts of the country the water meter will be in the basement or crawl space, while in more moderate climates the meter will be in a "dry well" out in the yard. It is the stop valve (also called "main water shutoff" and similar names) that you would shut off when all water to the house must be stopped. Never turn off the meter valve, which is on the street side of the meter. There are two reasons for this latter caution. First, you are responsible for all water lines from the meter to the house, while the water company retains responsibility for the lines starting with the meter, running to the street and all the way to the water-treatment plant that supplies the water. Second, it is possible to damage the meter if the water is turned on suddenly. It is always better to avoid conflicts with bureaucrats, even those from the water company.

SHUT-OFF VALVES

If the plumbing in your home is properly designed, you should rarely need to shut off the main water valve. All water-using appliances and fixtures in a home should have separate shut-off valves, one for the hot and one for the cold. This includes water softeners, hot-water tanks, dishwashers, toilets, sinks and basins; there should be no exceptions. Unfortunately, even in new homes there are seldom valves under the various fixtures, because not installing them saves money and the house can be sold at lower cost. This is a foolish economy, as every homeowner finds out sooner or later, because eventually these shut-off valves need to be installed.

If the water for your home is supplied from a well, the situation is only a little different. You will still want shut-off valves at every fixture so that someone can still take a bath while you repair the faucet in the kitchen sink. But in this case, shutting off the main valve is more a matter of shutting off the pump that supplies water under pressure. Various types of pumps are used for private water systems, and they are described more completely in Chapter 10.

PIPE ALTERNATIVES

The supply line that enters the house, from either a city system or a well, should be no smaller than ¾ inch pipe; 1 inch pipe is even better. The smaller the pipe the less water it supplies, and the more friction there will be. Both these factors are involved when water pressure becomes low during hot summer months as water usage reaches a peak.

Shortly after the main supply line enters a house it splits into two lines. One runs to the hot water tank, while the other is routed directly to the cold water faucets in the various sinks and basins, and the toilets. If there is a water softener required because the water is very hard, one line will run to it, and from it to the hot water tank. In this setup only the hot water will be softened, while all cold water will remain hard because treated water is generally bland and does not make good coffee, tea or other beverage; also, running treated water out through an outside faucet to sprinkle a lawn or garden can be expensive.

If you don't mind your plumbing system becoming somewhat complicated, you can provide untreated water to the kitchen sink and perhaps a bar, while supplying softened water—both hot and cold—to the bathroom.

For either a city or private water system, the plumbing lines can be of galvanized-steel or cast iron piping, rigid copper tubing or plastic. Very often, local plumbing codes will be very specific as to the type of plumbing lines that must be used. Generally, where the code has not been brought up to date, steel pipe will be required. More progressive codes will call for copper tubing, while the very up-to-date codes will accept plastic piping.

Plastic piping can be used for both hot and cold water, and for drain, waste and vent (DWV) piping. Plastic piping can be used with other types of piping by means of adapters. Because plastic piping is "inert," meaning that it does not interact with other types of materials, there is never the problem of galvanic action that can occur when two dissimilar metals are included in a piping system.

LAYOUT AND COMPONENTS

Water lines that run vertically—from the basement or crawl space to the first and second floor, for example — are called risers. Lines that run horizontally from the risers are called branches. Not always included in a home plumbing system, although they should be, are air chambers. These are vertical lengths of pipe fitted into the walls behind fixtures. Air in these vertical chambers acts similar to shock absorbers when the water is turned off suddenly. Instead of banging and shaking when the water pressure is suddenly stopped, the piping pushes the pressure into the air chamber where the air compresses and absorbs the water hammer. Eliminating the water hammer not only makes for a quiet and peaceful house, it also prevents damage to the piping. Constant hammering on a joint can cause it to leak, and that same hammering can cause leaking at a faucet.

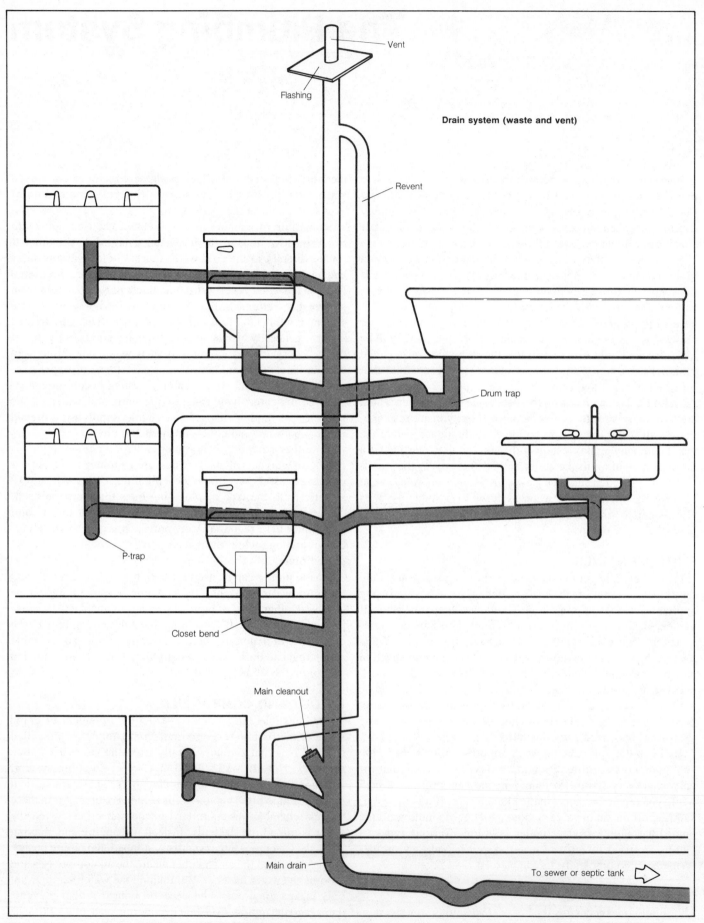

Drain system (waste and vent)

Vent

Flashing

Revent

Drum trap

P-trap

Closet bend

Main cleanout

Main drain

To sewer or septic tank

The drain system includes waste and vent lines. Note that toilets must drain directly into the main stack, which is generally 3 or 4 inches in diameter, while sinks and vanities can drain into smaller waste lines that run to the main stack.

In order to use the shortest possible water lines and therefore assure the most economical installation, as well as a minimum of line friction, fixtures (sinks, vanities, bathtubs, toilets) should be located as close together as possible. This is not always possible, as in the case of adding a new bathroom or wet bar at some distance from the existing bathroom or kitchen. The ideal situation is to have rooms with fixtures back-to-back, so the plumbing in one wall supplies both rooms. Such an arrangement also makes it possible for one main drain line to handle the waste water from both rooms. Note that toilets must empty directly into a main drain line, while bathtubs, basins and other fixtures can drain indirectly through smaller lines. Usually these smaller lines are 1½ or 2-inch pipes. They empty into a much larger vertical drain line which is called a "stack." This will be a line that measures 3, 3½, 4 inches or larger, and it will run vertically from the basement or crawl space right up through the roof. Although the vertical stack may be plastic, rigid copper tubing or cast iron soil pipe, the line that enters the ground and empties into the city sewer system, or into a septic tank in the case of a private system, will be cast iron. The main reason for this is that cast iron pipe is stronger than other types and so resists crushing and soil pressures.

Traps

All fixtures that drain into the stack are fitted with traps. These traps consist of curved sections of piping under each fixture so that there is always a water seal to keep out sewer gases, which can be unhealthy as well as causing very unpleasant odors. The

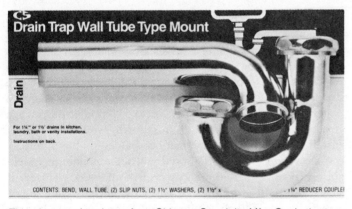

This chrome-plated trap from Chicago Specialty Mfg. Co. is the type that runs to the drain located in the wall. The U-shape section retains water to seal out sewer gas and insects.

water seal also discourages "strange creatures" from crawling into a fixture from the sewer line. You will see the chrome-plated traps in the shape of a "P" or a "J" or even an "S." Toilets have a built-in trap. Bathtubs generally will have a "drum trap," which will be located under the floor beneath the tub. It has a screw-on cover that must be removed when the trap needs to be cleaned.

Vents

The main drain line will not only have a trap in it just before it leaves the building, it will also have a vent stack. There are three reasons that a plumbing drain line must be vented.

(1) It allows atmospheric pressure into the drains, which assures that water drains easily with no partial vacuum in any of the lines—when you hear a "glug-glug" in a drain line, it generally means the stack is at least partly plugged and atmospheric pressure is not flowing into the vent behind the dropping water.

(2) The opening in the vent on the roof lets dangerous sewer gases escape into the air, well above any people; if you have ever worked on a roof and come close to a vent, you know what a stench is expelled from it.

(3) The venting prevents draining water from backing up into a fixture below it that also is draining; if you note that a downstairs basin has water backing up into it when a basin is draining upstairs, you can be pretty sure the vent stack is plugged—it is not unheard of to have a bird build a nest on top of a stack.

At the lower end of every vent stack there is a cleanout. This is in the form of a plug that unscrews. If you cannot clean the drain from a fixture, very often you can get below it by running a "snake" up from the cleanout to reach the stoppage. These cleanout plugs do tend to rust shut, which makes them difficult to open. We will describe the methods to free these plugs in another chapter.

Besides the main vent there also are "revents." The drain line from a sink or basin will run directly to the main vent, but there will be a smaller vent that runs up from the fixture, then across to the main vent. Such an arrangement assures that air is pulled into the drain line as the waste water runs out the drain. This keeps the water seal in the trap from being syphoned out and creating a health hazard.

Valves

There are three main types of valves used in the water supply system of a house: globe, gate and check. There also are variations of these valves, as will be explained.

Right-angle shut-off globe valve from Genova has pressure under the disk because of its configuration. It is used under sinks and toilets to shut off water to the fixture.

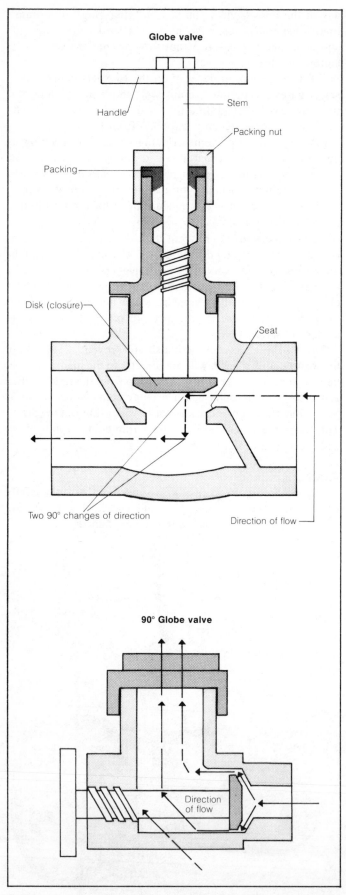

Globe valve

Handle

Stem

Packing nut

Packing

Disk (closure)

Seat

Two 90° changes of direction

Direction of flow

90° Globe valve

Direction
of flow

A globe valve is used to control the flow of water. Note, however, that there are two 90-degree direction changes in flow of water, creating friction in the water flow The valve should be installed so that water pressure is on top of the disk closure when the valve is closed.

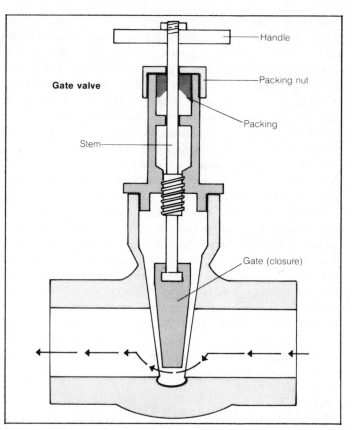

Handle

Packing nut

Packing

Gate valve

Stem

Gate (closure)

Gate valves are not often used in home plumbing, as they must be either all the way open or all the way closed. They sometimes are used as shut-off valves where main supply line enters the basement after the meter.

The globe valve is used to shut off the water to fixtures and appliances, and is also the type used for the meter valve and main shut-off valve. Globe valves are found where the water supply needs to be reduced or controlled, as in the case of sill cocks used to supply water to garden hoses. Note in the drawing that a globe valve does offer considerable resistance to water flow, as the water must make two right-angle turns when it passes through the valve—this is why you should never install a smaller valve than can be handled by the piping.

Gate valves are not often used in a home plumbing system since they are either all the way open or all the way closed. If you try to reduce the flow of water by partly closing a gate valve, the gate is likely to vibrate and quickly wear itself to the point where it will no longer stop the flow of water when closed. In some gate valves the stem will rise (like a globe valve) when it is opened; in others the gate rises but the stem does not. There is no real difference in the operation of either kind of gate valve, but in a restricted location the nonrising stem might be required.

The third type of valve is the check valve. As in the drawing, it is designed with a flap so that the flap opens when water flows through the valve in one direction. If the water tries to reverse its flow, the flap shuts. Often there is an arrow on the body of a check valve, indicating in which direction the water should flow through it. If there is no arrow, check that the valve is installed so that the water flow will lift the flap of the valve. When a check valve is installed in a vertical line (riser), the flap should always lift upwards so that gravity will help keep it closed when water starts to flow back through the pipe.

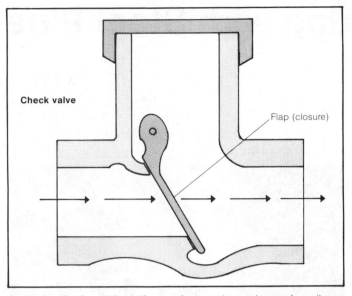

Check valve

Flap (closure)

A check valve is used mostly on private water systems where it prevents backflow of water from house when pump shuts off. Check valves are also used in lines at bottom of wells (called a "foot valve" in that application) to prevent lines emptying when pump shuts off.

Check valves are seldom used in homes in an area where the water supply is provided by the city. They might be used in a line from the pump in a well system. The check valve would prevent the water in the tank and the lines in the house from flowing back to the well.

SPECIAL SUPPORT FOR PIPES

Pipes must pass through walls both horizontally and vertically; the most important consideration is maintaining the integrity of the structure so that it will be as strong after it has been modified for passage of the pipes as it was previously.

If the wall is load-bearing, provide additional strength by spiking a stud to the notched one, at right angles. This is important for load-bearing walls to which you have made cuts.

When notching joists for pipes, they must be reinforced more strongly than vertical studs. Notches should be no more than one-fourth the depth of the joists, and near joists ends.

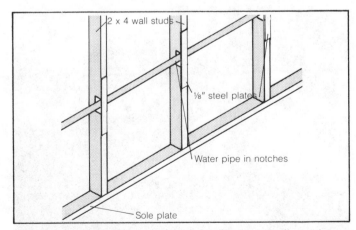

2 x 4 wall studs

⅛" steel plates

Water pipe in notches

Sole plate

Where pipes must be run through a stud wall, you can make notches up to 2½ inches square but no larger. Or, bore round holes to within 1½ inches of the edge of a stud; the problem here is that the pipe must be "threaded" through round holes, which requires access to an exposed end stud. After the studs have been notched, reinforce the openings with lengths of ⅛ x 1½-inch steel flats nailed or screwed across the notches.

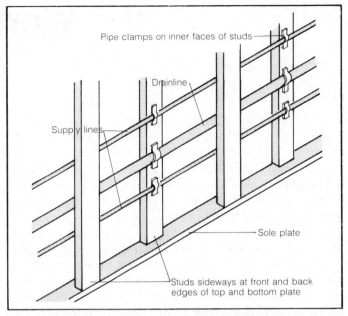

Pipe clamps on inner faces of studs

Drainline

Supply lines

Sole plate

Studs sideways at front and back edges of top and bottom plate

A wall in a kitchen, bathroom or bar can provide space for supply and drain lines if studs are turned edgewise and spiked to the edges of the sole and top plates. Studs are staggered as shown, and the pipes are fastened to the inside faces of the studs with clamps.

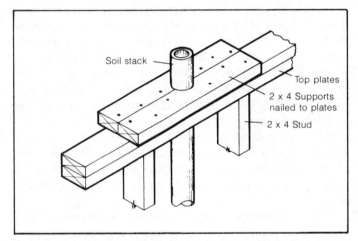

Soil stack

Top plates

2 x 4 Supports nailed to plates

2 x 4 Stud

Where a pipe must run vertically (as for a vent or stack) through the top plates of stud wall, the plates must be reinforced with lengths of 2 x 4 (notched to fit around pipe) nailed to the plates on their inner edges. The 2 x 4s will project beyond the edges of the plates. The top plates are bored just a little larger than the pipe while the reinforcing pieces have a half-round cut in each one.

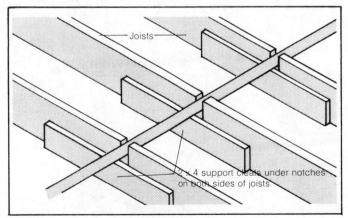

Joists

2 x 4 support cleats under notches on both sides of joists

Where it is necessary to notch floor joists to permit running a pipe through them, they are reinforced with 2 x 4 cleats spiked to *both* sides of the joists, under the notches.

2   Working with Steel Pipe

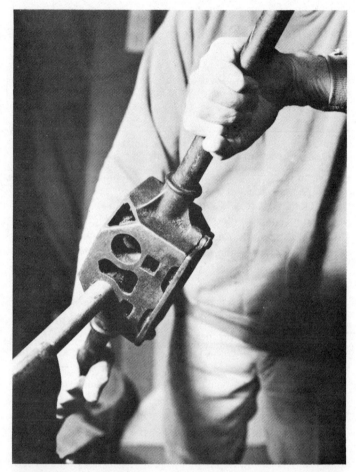

The piping system in any home ten years old or older (and in a few newer homes where cost is a major factor, or in areas where copper tubing is in short supply) will have threaded steel pipe and fittings. Repairs to this type of pipe, which is also called "iron," call for more tools and somewhat more skill than when dealing with either copper tubing or plastic pipe.

One of the main problems with steel pipe is the lack of flexibility in making up a system. You must be quite accurate with your measurements. If the made-up length is too short, you have to replace it with a longer one; if it is too long, you have to cut it off and rethread it. The second problem is that after many years, steel pipe tends to become plugged with mineral deposits.

On the plus side, steel pipe has a lifespan of 20 to 25 or more years, as proven by the piping in homes built at the turn of the century and now being restored. Some of the piping has to be replaced, of course, but much of it is still serviceable.

One note of caution for a house that has steel pipe: if your system has shown few if any leaks, but you install a water-softening system, there is a good chance leaks will appear. The author has had personal experience with this problem. It seems that the softened water removes the deposits which over a number of years not only plug the pipes somewhat but also seal slight leaks in threaded joints. Luckily, the leaks seem to occur in horizontal runs in the basement or crawl space, rather than in risers.

To sum up about steel pipe: it has been used in more homes than any other kind of pipe, and unless your home is brand new it is likely there will be threaded steel pipe in the system.

Steel pipe is easy to recognize when used for water or gas. Gas pipe generally is "black" pipe without galvanizing, since the gas does not create the corrosion problem that occurs with water pipe.

Die is used to cut threads on steel pipe. The tool can have a fixed die, or can have ratchet handle that makes it usable in restricted locations.

PIPE THREADS

Steel pipe requires the use of dies in order to cut threads on the ends. Although not free, a set of standard pipe dies is not too expensive and the dies are a must to work with steel pipe.

The basic instrument is a round or square block of steel in which there is an opening with hardened teeth that cut threads into the relatively soft steel of the pipe. Most such dies come in sets with pipe sizes of ⅜, ½, ¾, and 1 inch. The latter size generally is the largest size that will be used in the water-supply line of a home. Larger pipes would, of course, be used in commercial and industrial applications, but the homeowner seldom has need for tools to handle the larger sizes of 1¼, 1½, 2, 2½ or 3 inches.

Steel pipe in sizes of 1¼ and 1½ inches are used for drain lines from sinks and some vents, but when you get to this kind of a job, it's best to go to a local hardware store and have them thread the larger sizes of pipe with their threading machine. A well-stocked hardware can cut and thread pipe to the lengths you want, and also will have bins full of pipe "nipples," which are short lengths of pipe threaded at both ends and ready for use. The nipples vary in length from 1½ inches (called a "close nipple," which is so short that the threads at each end meet in the middle) to 6 inches. The lengths are in ½-inch increments: 1½, 2, 2½, 3 inches and so on. While the 6-inch nipple is the longest "standard" size, you can often find nipples that are 8, 10 and 12 inches long to suit the requirements of do-it-yourself homeowners. Professional plumbers also find these "over-long" nipples very handy too, and sometimes make them up while on the job if they are not readily available.

Once pipe has been threaded, oil must be applied to the die to lubricate the cutters. Quite a bit of metal is removed by the cutters. After making one turn with the die, you must then back up about a half turn to clear out the metal shavings. Repeat this until the thread is completely cut. In most cases a full length of thread is completed when the pipe just starts to project from the edge of the die. Be careful when handling steel pipe that has just been threaded; the threads will not only be knife sharp, but there may be some small shavings still in the threads that can cut your hands quite badly.

When buying new lengths of steel pipe, the threads will be protected by straight couplings that are put on at the factory. To prevent damage to the threads, and to your hands, leave the couplings on until you are ready to work with the pipe. Also, if you are in a situation where you need to run consecutive lengths of pipe that must be joined by a straight coupling, be sure to remove the coupling and apply joint compound. The coupling then is snugly turned onto the pipe with a pipe wrench.

Fittings

A complete hardware store will have bins full of fittings, such as elbows, tees, couplings and unions. These fittings come in one size, as well as in a "reducing" size. That is, while the fitting will have one size to accommodate the pipe you are using, there will be one or more connections that are smaller. An example would be a ½-inch tee fitting that has a "straight-through" size of ¾ inch, while the connection at right angles would be ½ or ⅜ inch for the connection that supplies water to a sink or basin.

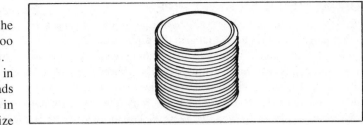

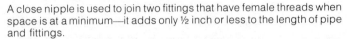

A close nipple is used to join two fittings that have female threads when space is at a minimum—it adds only ½ inch or less to the length of pipe and fittings.

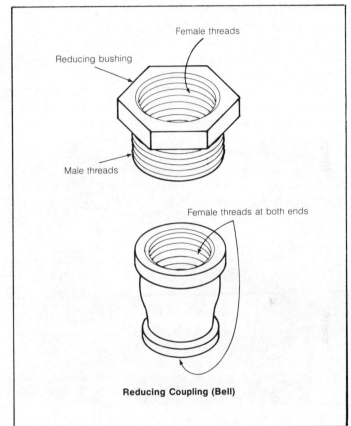

Reducing bushings and reducing couplings are a common way of going from one pipe size to another in a run of pipe, as opposed to a turn in the pipe.

Another way to "reduce" pipe size is with "reducing bushings" and "reducing couplings" (sometimes called "reducing bells" after their shape). The bushings have "male" threads that twist into the "female" threads, with a smaller opening that has female threads into which a smaller pipe is turned. The term "male" means the threads are on the outside of a pipe or fitting, while "female" refers to interior threads.

One fitting that has both male and female threads is a "street elbow," commonly called a "street ell." All elbows, whether 90 degree, 45 degree, or street (which comes as both 90 and 45 degree fittings) are commonly called "ells."

Fittings in steel pipe provide right-angle or 45-degree changes of direction, but you can create a "swing joint" by using two street ells. These fittings come in either a 90- or a 45-degree angle. They can be angled in a combination of two (or more), sometimes along with a standard 90- or 45-degree elbow which has female threads in both ends, rather than the combination of male and female found in a street ell.

USING TOOLS ON STEEL PIPE

Tools needed for working with steel pipe include a pipe vise, which has jaws with teeth that grip the pipe. Some machinists' (bench) vises can be fitted with removable jaws for pipe work. Pipe wrenches also have gripping teeth in their jaws. A pipe wrench is designed with one jaw that is spring-loaded; as you apply turning force to the wrench, the movable spring-loaded jaw tends to bite or tighten on the pipe. The more you turn the wrench, the tighter the jaw will clamp.

Most steel pipe is galvanized. The zinc plating that helps prevent rusting also can cause a pipe wrench to slip and to scrape off the plating. When working with galvanized pipe, avoid putting tremendous strain on a pipe wrench or it will slip as the galvanizing peels away under the pressure of the jaws. Since you cut through galvanizing when threading pipe, the threads are usually the first place to rust on steel pipe.

After steel pipe has been cut with a cutter, or even a hacksaw, there will be a burr inside. This must be removed to prevent its creating resistance to water flow and becoming a

place where mineral deposits can collect and build up. A reamer is used to remove it; and most pipe cutters will have one as part of the tool. As an alternative, you can purchase a pipe reamer as a separate tool.

A pipe thread is tapered, rather than being straight as on a bolt. This taper creates a wedging action that produces tremendous pressure as the threads turn into a fitting. When working with steel pipe, always use two wrenches. One wrench holds the fitting, while the other turns the pipe into it. Conversely, a

Pipe cutter is the preferred tool because it makes a square cut so that pipe is easier to thread.

Most steel water pipe is galvanized inside and out, and this coating can cause a pipe wrench to slip — especially if the wrench is a cheap model with dull teeth in the jaws (photo courtesy of Ridge Tools).

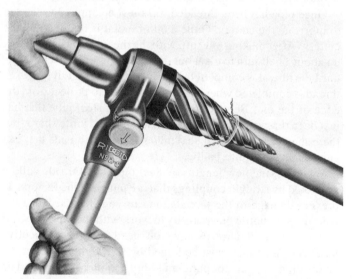

Even when pipe cutter is used, there is a burr inside steel pipe that must be removed with reamer. Otherwise the burr will cause restriction in the pipe, and encourage mineral buildup.

Pipe vise, or pipe jaws in machinists' vise, are required to hold pipe when it is threaded or when pipe and joints are "made up."

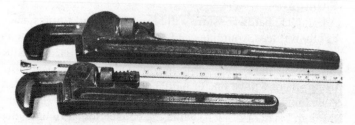

The largest pipe wrench a homeowner will need is 24-inch size, and for most jobs a 14-inch model is adequate.

wrench can hold pipe while a fitting is turned onto it. The use of two wrenches is especially important when working on pipe that is already installed. If you do not hold the existing pipe against turning pressure, you could turn a fitting somewhere inside a wall and cause a leak — and a lot of trouble.

For most work in a home, a pipe wrench need not be larger than the 14-inch size, and an 18-inch size will handle almost everything you will ever need turned. Be cautious when working with a pipe wrench on smaller sizes of pipe; you can

Thread on the end of pipe is tapered, as opposed to the thread on a bolt, which is straight. This taper creates a wedging effect that makes joint watertight, but also can split the fitting if overtightened.

Always use two wrenches when working with steel pipe. One wrench holds pipe while fitting is turned onto it, or vice versa. Pipe vise takes the place of one wrench when it is used for making up pipe and fittings.

overtighten a fitting. This causes the fitting to expand, and not only will the threads probably leak but the fitting may crack.

Once again, the importance of the quality of your tools cannot be overemphasized. Using a pipe wrench with dull or soft teeth in the jaws could easily cause muscle strain.

PIPE REPLACEMENT

One common repair of steel pipe is replacement of a section that has rusted or corroded and has begun to leak. The first step, as with any kind of repair on any kind of pipe, is to shut off the water supply. The next step is to measure the length of the pipe between the fittings — the "exposed" length. Write that length down somewhere; it is too easy to forget it.

Next, locate the leaking section and cut it out, making the

cut several inches away from the leak. This is to assure that you leave only good pipe. You can use a hacksaw, which almost every homeowner has, or a pipe cutter. The latter is easier to use and makes a clean cut that is exactly at right angles to the length of the pipe. Few of us can make a right-angle cut with a hacksaw. If you are going to do any amount of plumbing, or work on various types of piping, a pipe cutter will quickly pay for itself. You can buy quality cutters that will handle steel pipe, copper tubing (rigid or flexible) and plastic pipe.

Unscrew the damaged section of pipe from the fitting, then look at the end of the piece of pipe still in place. If it looks rusted or corroded inside, or is plugged with "lime," you would do well to remove it and replace the complete length. If you don't, it will leak in the near future and/or slow the flow of water to the fixture it supplies.

If the remaining pipe does look good, it still must be unscrewed from its fitting in order to be threaded. Thread it yourself, or take it to the hardware store where you will be buying the new piece of pipe and the union you will need. If replacing the complete length of pipe, the damaged piece of pipe plus the length of the good pipe will tell the hardware man (or you) how long the replacement piece must be — you must then subtract the length that will be taken up by the union. In any instance it is better for the pipe/union assembly to be just a fraction too long than too short. You can almost always turn the pipe into a fitting one additional turn, which will shorten the overall length.

Union

A union consists of three parts: there is a piece at each end that turns onto the pipe, and there is a large "nut" at the center that draws the two end pieces together. The mating surfaces of the two end pieces are polished concave and convex surfaces that create a kind of "ball joint." Be careful when making up a joint

Union allows replacement of a section of pipe. Mating faces of union are left clean, but each end of the union, and the large nut that joins the halves, are coated with pipe joint compound.   (Photo Courtesy Genova, Inc.)

with a union not to drag one polished surface over another. This could cause a scratch or gouge that would make the joint leak. Because of the ball-joint effect, a union can even make up for some misalignment in the pipe. The misalignment should be very slight, however; too much could cause a leak.

No joint compound is applied to the meeting faces of a union. Compound is used, however, on the threads at the ends of the fitting that turn onto pipe, and also to the nut that pulls the two halves of the union together. A substitute for pipe-joint compound is Teflon™ applied as a strip around the threads of the male connection. The plastic provides a lubrication that eases tightening of the threads and also makes the joint watertight.

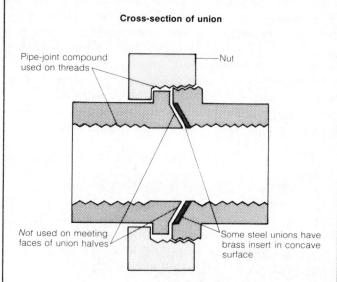

ELECTRICAL SAFETY
Look for the electrical ground connection on any steel pipe you work on; it will be on the cold water side. If you see such a ground wire, replace it immediately after making your repair or connection. If it is heavy wire, it will be from your main electrical supply and is an absolutely necessary connection to assure safe and complete electrical service (it will have no electric current in it). If it is a small ground wire, it will probably be from your telephone, and it is likely that your phone will not work properly until it is reconnected. The cold water line is used as a ground connection because it runs directly into the earth and provides a positive ground to earth. A hot water line should never be used because it is interrupted through a heating tank, and is possibly even an insulated "dielectric" fitting intended to prevent galvanic action. This fitting could also insulate the electric current from passing to the earth in case of a fault in the electrical system. It will not work even if a ground fault interrupter is included in the wiring system; the GFI still needs to direct current to ground, if only for a mere fraction of a second.

Despite the difficulties noted here, you should not be afraid to try working with threaded steel pipe. The best example of why you should not be concerned is one homeowner we know who tore out a whole piping system in a basement when he

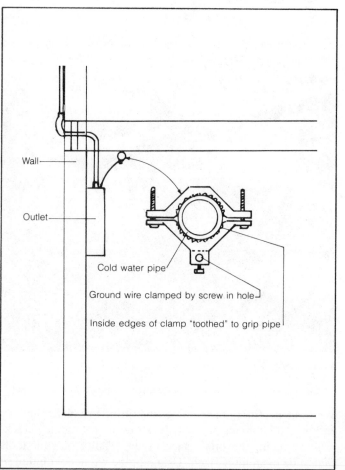

This is one of several sizes and types of ground clamps used on cold water lines. When working on steel pipe (also copper tubing) replace any ground wire you must remove while doing the job. Heavy wire will be from main electric service, small wire will be for telephone. Neither should have any current in it.

remodeled it for living space. He had had no previous experience with plumbing, but he used the old pipe and fittings plus a few new ones, and did an almost professional job of replumbing. When people commented on it, he expressed surprise that anyone should consider working with steel pipe difficult!

3 Working with Copper Pipe

Copper tubing is relatively expensive, but it has become the material most used in homes today for both the water supply and drain, waste and vent systems. It offers several advantages, being light in weight, readily available and easily fabricated. It is also quite strong, noncorrosive and resistant to high temperatures, and therefore can be used not only for hot water but even for hot-water heating systems. While most homeowners have forced-air heat rather than hot water (hydronic), those who do have hot-water heating should be relieved to learn do-it-yourself plumbers can make repairs to their systems.

TYPES OF TUBING

Copper tubing comes in 10- and 20-foot lengths and in three weights: Type M has a thin wall, Type L has a medium wall and Type K has a thick wall. Unless otherwise specified by local code, Type M is sufficiently strong for the water supply system in a home. Copper tubing is always ⅛ inch larger than the nominal size, meaning that, for example, ½ inch copper tubing measures ⅝ inch in outside diameter. The actual inside diameter varies with the thickness of the pipe wall; the thicker the wall, the smaller the inside diameter.

In the 10 and 20 feet lengths Types K, L and M are available in "drawn temper," which is a rigid form of tubing. In the piping trades this is usually referred to as "hard" tubing because it is rigid. The three types of tubing are also made in annealed (soft) temper in pretty much the same sizes as the hard tubing, and in the same lengths. However, the soft tubing comes packaged in rolls rather than being in straight lengths as is hard tubing.

The Copper Development Association, Inc. — a trade association dedicated to promoting the proper use of copper tubing — recommends hard temper Type M or soft temper Type L for underground water services, although local codes may call for the thick-walled Type K for this service. In most instances, Type M with thin walls is adequate for the water supply system of a home, as previously stated.

Another class of copper tubing, called DWV (drain, waste and vent), is available only as rigid tubing in larger sizes. As the name implies, this tubing is used for waste, drain and vent lines in the drainage system of a home. Because the tubing is quite large, it may be necessary to use an extra large tip on your propane torch.

Tubing in sizes of ⅜, ½, ¾ and 1 inch are suitable for home water supply systems, while 1¼, 1½, 3 and 4 inch sizes are for drain, waste and vent.

The other main class of copper tubing, designated ACR, is intended for air conditioning and refrigeration field service. An average homeowner will not encounter this type of tubing unless he installs his own air conditioner. Such an undertaking is not unknown in this day and age; in this case then he will work with it in sealed lengths that are precharged with refrigerant. ACR tubing is designated by the *actual outside* diameter, as opposed to other types of copper tubing. Available in uncharged lengths of 20 feet in drawn temper (hard) and 50 feet coils of soft temper, ACR tubing is suitable even for solar collectors. This is true even if temperatures get up to 400 degrees F. or higher when the collector is not being cooled by water or antifreeze circulation, as in the summer when heating for the home is not required. (More about solar collectors and how to build them will be described in the chapter devoted to this subject.)

Tools and Special Joints

An ordinary propane torch will handle pipe and tubing up to about 1 or 1¼ inches in diameter. Above that size you'd better work with a "Mapp" gas torch or an oxy-acetylene torch. You can buy or rent the latter in a modified type, with small tanks of oxygen that are the size of standard propane tanks. The torch uses a tank of oxygen and a tank of propane to create an extremely hot flame.

When you are working with copper tubing smaller than ½ inch, as for connecting faucets under sinks and basins, flexible soft tempered tubing is easiest to handle. It can be bent and shaped to go around obstacles and up into tight places. The soft tubing is not usually soldered, but is joined with flare fittings. Flared fittings are mechanical connections created with a special tool that grips the tubing in a sort of vise. An anvil then is forced into the end of the tubing by turning a screw, to spread

Join soft-temper copper tubing in small sizes using flare fittings. Ends of tubing are clamped in flaring tool and the cone-shape "anvil" is turned into end of tubing to flare it out. Note that the nut is already on the tubing before flare is made.

the end of the tubing out to form a flare or flange. The main thing to remember when using this flaring tool is to always slip the connector onto the tubing before making the flare. If you don't, you'll have to cut off the flare with a tubing cutter, slip on the connector, and then remake the flare.

Once the flare has been made on the end of the tubing, the metal should be almost as thick as it was originally. If you overtighten the flaring tool, the edge of the metal is too thin and may crack. Such a flare should be cut off and remade to assure a tight joint.

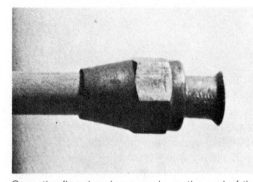

Surface of flare must be smooth to match perfectly with polished surface of fitting to which it is mated. Fitting shown is adapter from copper tubing to steel pipe fitting.

Do not overtighten the flaring tool, as this will make the flare thin at the edges and will cause splits. It then is necessary to cut off the flare and remake it. Examine the flare after you make it to be sure there are no burrs or scratches. The flare must be smooth to mate snugly with the connector and to create a watertight joint.

Soft temper tubing could be used for a full run in a water supply system because it can be bent around corners, eliminating the need for elbows or other connectors. The drawback is that flare fittings are quite expensive as compared to solder fittings. The same is true of compression fittings, which are made by slipping a ball-shape ferrule onto the tubing — after first slipping on the connector nut — then tightening the connection. The tightening action causes the ferrule to bite into the tubing to create a watertight joint between it and the tubing. The fitting then bears tightly on the ferrule so that connection is watertight.

The ferrule compression joint is quick and easy to make, but again it is quite expensive. If the joint for some reason must be remade, the tubing must be cut off behind the ferrule and that part of the tubing and the ferrule discarded.

There are tubing-to-pipe adapters available, with one end of the fitting designed to be soldered to copper tubing, and the other end threaded to turn onto steel pipe. As previously stated, however, it is not recommended that copper pipe or tubing and steel pipe be used in the same system because of galvanic action. There are "dielectric" fittings with an insulator in them to minimize galvanic action, but the fittings simply cannot prevent the slight but constant flow of electricity between the unlike metals; the copper gradually will be deposited on the steel, and leaks will occur in the copper. This is especially true at fittings, where brass or copper threads offer a knife edge that deteriorates rapidly.

The Exceptions

There are a few cases in which copper tubing and steel pipe are connected in the same system: ice makers for kitchen freezers, and furnace humidifiers. No matter what kind of piping you have in the home, the "kits" that come with these appliances will be soft-temper copper tubing, joined with flare or ferrule fittings. Connection to a water line generally is by a "saddle valve." This kind of valve requires that you drill a ⅛ or ¼-inch hole in the cold water line (after shutting off the pressure, of course) then clamping the valve to the water line so that the closure needle of the valve is centered in the hole.

If you have a humidifier or ice maker with this kind of hookup, it is a good idea every couple of years to shut off the water and disassemble the valve and clean it. Because the opening and the tubing are small, it takes only a little corrosion or debris to block, or partly block, the line to the appliance. This is especially true where the copper saddle valve is on a steel pipe, and galvanic action is bound to occur.

This saddle valve on a galvanized steel water line supplies water to furnace humidifier. Light color on compression nut is sign that corrosion already is occurring due to galvanic action.

SOLDER AND FLUX

Rigid copper tubing in a home plumbing system is assembled with sweat-soldered fittings, using "soft" solder. This solder is a combination of tin and lead; "50-50" (half tin, half lead) solder is most commonly used, but 60-40 is sometimes used. The higher percentage of tin causes the 60-40 to melt at a lower

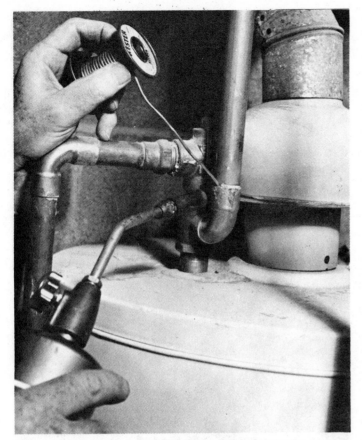

Wire solder must be added to a joint made with solder/flux in paste form. This assures the band that shows completely around edge of fitting.

Paste solder/flux must be mixed thoroughly if it has been on the shelf for a while, and every few minutes while it is being used. The heavy particles of solder tend to quickly settle to the bottom of the container.

temperature; however this also makes it more difficult to use than the 50-50.

Solder generally is used in wire form, but paste-type solders also are available (do not use acid-core solder with copper pipes). They consist of finely ground solder in a suspension of paste flux. You must follow four rules when using paste-type solders:

(1) Wire solder must be applied in addition to the paste. The wire helps fill voids and aids in displacing the flux, and if it is not used you may have nicely tinned surfaces with a poor joint resulting from a lack of continuous solder bond.

(2) The paste solder must be thoroughly mixed if it has been standing in the container for more than a short time. The heavy solder has a tendency to settle to the bottom of the container, and taking material from the upper portion of the container will result in a mixture that is mostly flux.

(3) Do not depend on the flux to clean the end of the tubing — clean the tubing manually with steel wool or fine sandpaper. Emery cloth is sometimes used but is more expensive than sandpaper, and metal particles can become deposited in the joint; steel wool actually is best as it readily conforms to the shape of the tubing or the inside of a fitting.

(4) Remove any excess flux — only enough flux should be used to lightly coat the areas to be joined with solder.

The functions of flux are to remove any residue of oxide from the surfaces of the tubing and fittings, to promote "wetting" of the solder so it flows easily, and to prevent the heated

surfaces from becoming oxidized. Because copper is an "active" metal, an oxide will quickly reform on its surface after it has been cleaned, so a flux should be applied to the metal as soon as possible after cleaning.

The fluxes that are best suited for 50-50 and 60-40 solders are mildly corrosive liquids, or petroleum-based pastes containing chlorides of zinc and ammonium. Some liquid fluxes are claimed to be "self-cleaning," as are some paste-type fluxes, but there is a moderate risk involved in using these fluxes. While there is no doubt that a corrosive flux does remove some oxides and dirt films, it is uncertain whether or not it provides a uniform cleaning of the surfaces. Also, if the flux is not completely dissipated by the heat of the torch, it may continue its corrosive action after the soldering has been completed and at some future time cause a leak.

End of rigid copper tubing must be cleaned thoroughly to remove any corrosion, oxidation or oil. Emery cloth or sandpaper is often used, but steel wool cleans well and leaves a smoother surface.

How to Solder

Solder joints on copper tubing are made with the following simple steps.

(1) Measure the length of the tube, figuring the distance between fittings plus the necessary lengths to fit into the fittings.

(2) Cut the tubing square; because copper is quite soft, even a "pocket-size" cutter can be used.

(3) Ream the cut end; a smaller tubing cutter will have a reamer on the handle that pivots out for use.

(4) Clean the end of the tubing.

(5) Clean the inside of the fitting.

(6) Apply flux to the end of the tube.

(7) Apply flux inside the fitting; be sparing.

(8) Slip the tubing into the fitting until it contacts the shoulder inside; some tubing does not have the shoulder, and the tubing is simply inserted approximately ½ inch.

(9) Use a cloth to wipe away any flux that squeezes out, or is on the tubing outside the fitting.

(10) Apply heat with a propane torch, playing the flame first on the fitting, which is the thicker metal, then on the tubing.

(11) Apply wire solder to the joint between tubing and fitting; do not play the flame on the solder — the heat of the tubing should melt the solder, and capillary action will pull the solder into the small opening between tubing and fitting.

(12) Keep applying solder until a small fillet (band) of solder shows all around the fitting.

(13) Allow the joint to cool completely before you move the assembly; any movement can fracture the cooling solder.

As heat from propane torch is applied you can see the flux bubble up, allowing solder to migrate to surface of copper.

As heat is continued, the flux melts and drops off tubing (or out of fitting if in use) leaving only clean, shiny solder. Shown is the activity that would take place inside the fitting.

Excess flux should be removed. Here solder/flux is applied to illustrate the excess that would be forced out by the fitting.

Tubing is cut quickly, cleanly and square with tubing cutter. This compact unit can be carried in a pocket or even in a small tool box. Reamer is in back and pivots out for use.

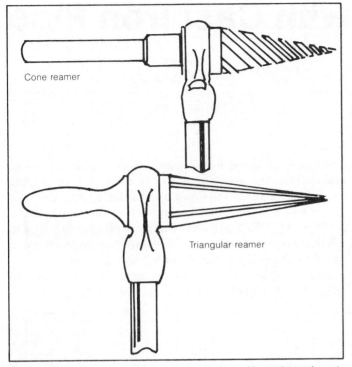

Reamer is a triangular or cone-shape device with cutting edges to remove the burr inside pipe or tubing that results from cutting.

When you first start making solder joints in copper tubing, you may have a couple that leak just a little after the tubing has been installed and the water turned on. To correct this, shut off the water and open a connection near the joint. This can be a union, or a valve. Loosen the union or valve and, in the case of the valve, unscrew the bonnet. The point is to provide an escape for the steam that will be created when you heat the joint to melt the solder; the water in the line boils. If there is not an escape route for the steam, it will blow the solder out at you when it liquifies. Use caution!

Heat the leaking joint and pull it apart after the solder has melted. Heat the tubing and wipe off the molten solder with a clean cloth until there is just a thin, shiny coating of solder. Also heat and wipe out the inside of the fitting. Apply fresh flux, slip the tubing into the fittings and heat the joint. You will need a little less solder this time because both the tubing and fitting have been "tinned" with solder from the first attempt.

If you are making up new tubing and fittings that will be installed in the system and you are working at a vise in the shop, separate flux and solder are fine. However, the author has found that when making joints in copper tubing, especially with tubing and fitting already installed, using paste-solder/flux is a time saver. The problem with working on joints in an installed system seems to be that the mass of tubing (with some water in it) pulls away the heat of the torch. It therefore takes a long time to heat the tubing and fitting sufficiently so the solder is pulled into the joint by capillary action. The flux/solder material heats up as you heat the tubing and fitting, and flows in a much shorter time.

This is strictly a personal observation, of course, and some do-it-yourself homeowners stick with the separate solder and flux and have no problems. Also, the paste flux/solder is relatively expensive, costing several dollars for a small jar. In a matter of several years, and only making a few joints or repairs

each year, my jar of solder/flux still is half full. I will say that if you are having problems making joints in copper tubing, the flux/solder might be your answer.

While soldering of copper tubing and fittings is done with a relatively low temperature — and the metal never changes color — there still is enough heat to burn you severely if you put a bare hand on the metal soon after a joint has been made. It is good practice, therefore, to wear gloves when soldering joints. It is not good practice to pour cold water on a newly soldered joint; this could cause too rapid shrinking of the solder which could cause a leak or, in extreme cases, could cause a fitting to crack. Let the joint cool normally.

Copper Plus Plastic

Copper tubing can be connected to plastic pipe, as described in the chapter on plastic piping. Because plastic is inert and does not react with any metal, no problems occur when mixing plastic and copper in a water supply or drain system.

Fittings are attached to plastic pipe with cement. One end of the plastic fitting is threaded and it is turned into a threaded fitting that has been soldered to the copper.

Valves and other plastic fittings that have compression nuts at the ends can also be used on copper tubing (and sometimes steel pipe). Just cut out a section of the pipe to allow insertion of the fitting, then put it on the line and tighten the nuts. You will usually need to retighten the nuts about three times over a matter of several days in order to prevent any leaks and still not stress and break the plastic fittings.

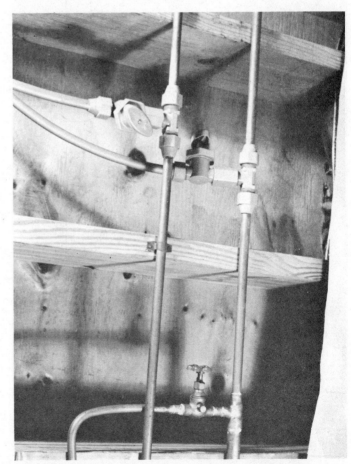

Plastic valves at top are attached to rigid copper pipe by compression nuts on T-fittings. Valve at bottom is soldered to reducing tee.

4   Working with Cast Iron Pipe

Cast iron still has an edge for many applications, although large copper tubing with soldered joints or plastic pipe is often used for drain, waste and vent lines in modern homes. Cast iron is tremendously strong and will withstand heavy pressures, as for example when grading equipment is run over the ground to backfill around a new foundation. Alternative materials would collapse under the weight.

It is true that cast iron pipe is heavy and difficult to handle. Nor can you join it with threaded fittings. Instead, the pipe and its fittings are joined by tamping oakum (a treated ropelike material) into the bell-shape end of cast iron pipe, or tamping into the hub of a cast-iron fitting using a calking iron. Once the oakum has been solidly packed in, melted lead is poured into the joint. After the lead has cooled, it is worked until it is quite dense and is packed tightly into the joint by means of a hammer and the calking iron, also called a "yarning" iron.

Note in the sketches that oakum is tamped into the joint until it fills about half the depth of the space. The molten lead then is

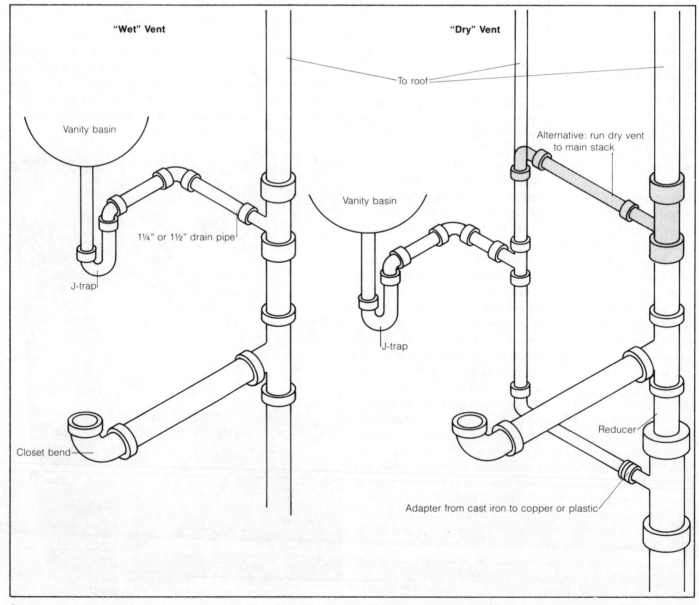

One way to use cast iron for drain, waste and vent in half-bath is a "wet vent," shown at left in sketch. This is not allowed by all plumbing codes, which may require a "dry vent," that allows passage only of air, not liquid, as in right of sketch.

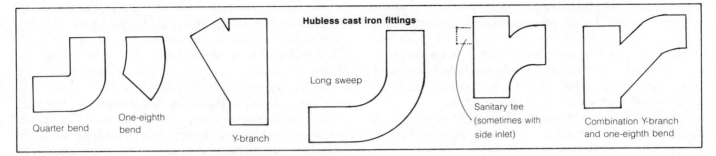

Hubless cast iron fittings

Quarter bend

One-eighth bend

Y-branch

Long sweep

Sanitary tee (sometimes with side inlet)

Combination Y-branch and one-eighth bend

poured over the oakum. It takes about 800 degrees of heat to melt lead, so if you work with cast iron pipe it is a good idea to rent a plumbers furnace that is heated by a fairly large tank of propane. Included with the furnace is a heavy ladle with a long handle.

Use caution and common sense when working with molten lead. Wear heavy work gloves and long sleeves. Don't slop the lead into the joint; pour it slowly to keep it from splashing. Make sure there is no moisture in the joint before you pour in the lead. The molten lead can turn the moisture to steam instantly, and it will "explode" hot lead right out of the joint. Which means you should wear safety glasses as additional protection, to allow for such an occurrence.

Pouring lead into the joint in a horizontal run of pipe is done with a special tool called a joint runner. This device has a collar that keeps the lead from running out as it is poured. As with a vertical joint, oakum first is packed into the joint with a calking iron. Don't be afraid to hammer on the oakum; you want it as solid as you can pack it. As shown in the drawing, the joint

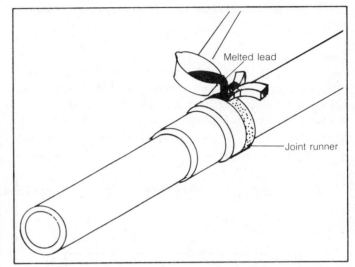

When horizontal joint is made in cast iron, "joint runner" is required. Clamp it on pipe and push firmly against end of hub, pour lead into opening at the top.

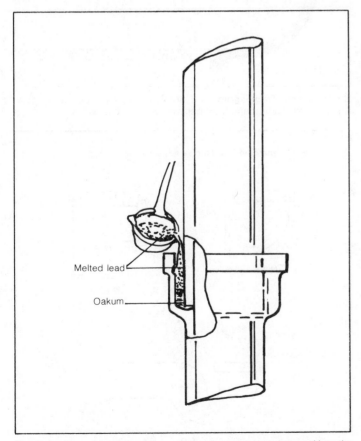

The hub of a cast iron pipe always is up, then oakum is tamped into the joint between pipe and hub and melted lead is poured in on top of the oakum.

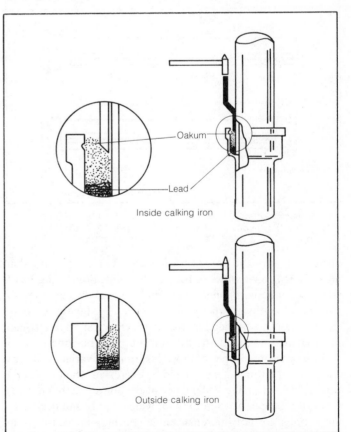

Inside calking iron

Outside calking iron

After the lead has cooled and is solid, calking irons — called "inside" and "outside" irons — are used to force the lead against the pipe and the inside of the hub.

runner is clamped around the pipe, then fitted snugly against the hub of the pipe. Lead is poured into the opening at the top of the pipe. Pour very slowly to avoid pouring in too much lead, or it will spill over — possibly onto your feet. Allow the lead to cool, then calk with the irons. Note that one iron has an inside bevel, the other an outside bevel. Each is used as indicated to force the soft lead against the pipe and the hub.

The caution about moisture is just as important when using the joint runner as when making a vertical joint. If you have the slightest suspicion that moisture might be in the joint, use a regular propane torch to heat the joint and dry it out before you pour in the lead.

Types and Sizes

Cast iron pipe comes in five-foot lengths, although some ten-footers occasionally can be found. One end of the pipe has a hub or bell, while the other end is smooth or has a ridge. The latter end is called the "spigot" end and it is sized to fit snugly into the bell end. Soil pipe is always positioned with the hub

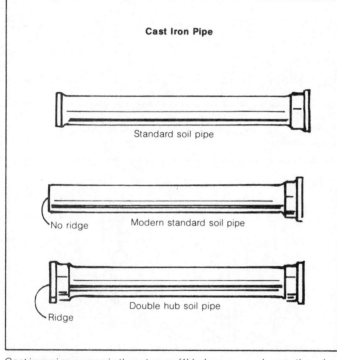

Cast Iron Pipe

Standard soil pipe

No ridge — Modern standard soil pipe

Ridge — Double hub soil pipe

Cast iron pipe comes in three types: (1) hub on one end, smooth end on other (spigot); (2) hub on one end, ridge on spigot end; (3) double-hub pipe that can be cut into two usable shorter lengths.

upward, against the flow of waste water. This is to assure that no solid waste becomes lodged in the joint. Some lengths of soil pipe come with hubs at each end. This allows creation of two short lengths of pipe from one section in situations where short lengths are needed to finish a run. Only a short length can be created from standard cast iron pipe that has one hub.

Similar to other types of pipe, cast iron has variety of kinds and sizes of fittings. Care should be exercised when selecting fittings for a drainage system, because while some (but not all) types of pipe can be used for both water supply and drainage, the fittings are not interchangeable. Fittings made for drain lines are designed to have smooth inside surfaces with no projections at the fittings that would interfere with the passage of solid materials. If regular fittings are included in a drain,

waste and vent piping system, the fittings must be used only in vent lines through which air passes, but no liquid.

The newest innovation in cast iron pipe is the "no-hub" joint. For pipe without hubs the joint is made with a fitting that consists of an inner sleeve manufactured from a synthetic rubber. The inside of the sleeve has a ridge that keeps the ends of the pipe separated. Over the rubber sleeve a stainless steel sleeve is fitted and two clamps, much like hose clamps, are tightened around the two sleeves. This kind of joint is easy to make, and is easily taken apart for repairs or for addition of another drain. Unfortunately this kind of no-hub joining of cast iron pipe is not allowed by the plumbing codes in some localities, so check before you decide to use the system.

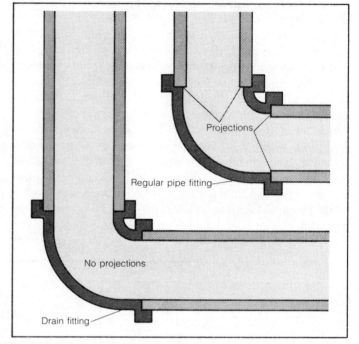

Projections

Regular pipe fitting

No projections

Drain fitting

Cross-section of regular pipe and elbow, and cast iron pipe and elbow, illustrates smooth connection between pipe and fitting.

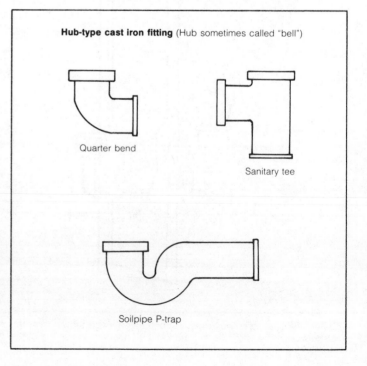

Hub-type cast iron fitting (Hub sometimes called "bell")

Quarter bend

Sanitary tee

Soilpipe P-trap

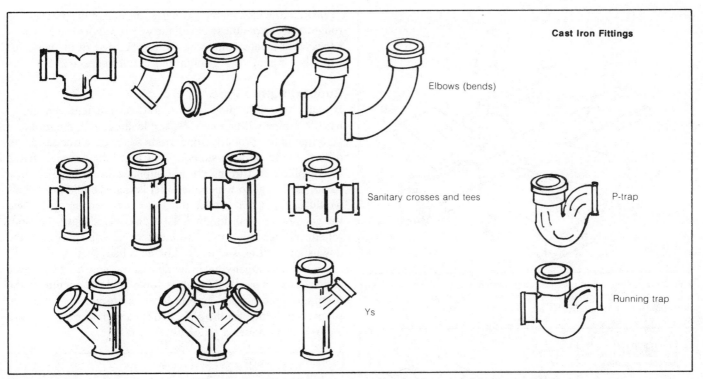

Cast Iron Fittings

Elbows (bends)

Sanitary crosses and tees

P-trap

Running trap

Ys

Special iron fittings create smooth joints with pipe, eliminating projections that could catch solid waste materials.

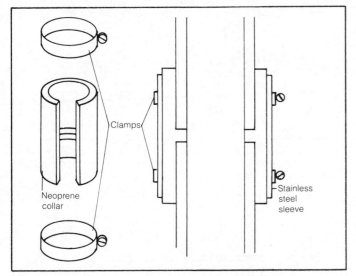

Clamps

Neoprene collar

Stainless steel sleeve

"No-hub" joints made with clamps and stainless steel sleeves are easy to assemble. They can also be taken apart for service or to add other connections. All you need for this joint is a screwdriver.

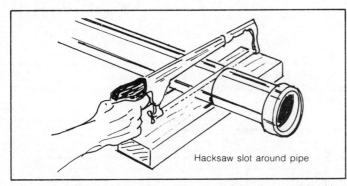

Hacksaw slot around pipe

One method ,of cutting cast iron pipe is to cut all around it with a hacksaw, making a cut about ¹/₁₆ in. deep. Try to keep the cut square, but a slight angle can be sealed in the hub of the next pipe, or in the fitting.

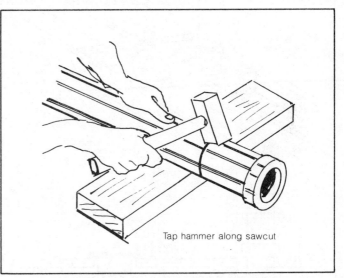

Tap hammer along sawcut

After cutting with a hacksaw, go around the pipe, tapping with a fairly heavy hammer along the cut line until the pipe breaks.

Cutting the Pipe

Professional plumbers have powered devices for cutting cast iron pipe, but their cost is so high that it is not even feasible to rent them. Rather, the occasional plumber such as the do-it-yourself homeowner can cut the heavy pipe in one of two ways.

(1) Use a hacksaw to cut a groove completely around the pipe, making it approximately ¹/₁₆-inch deep. Next, place the pipe on a piece of scrap lumber, with the cut line projecting as indicated. Go around the pipe, tapping with a heavy hammer or light sledge, until the pipe cracks off along the cut line.

(2) Make the cut with the hacksaw, then tap around and around the pipe using a hammer and cold chisel on the cut line until the pipe breaks off.

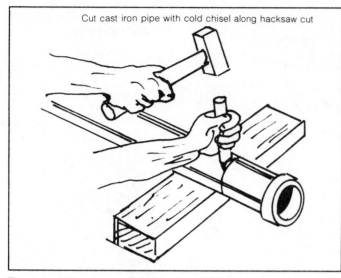

The second way to cut cast iron pipe is to make a cut with hacksaw, then go around the cut with a cold chisel and hammer at it. Hammer and rotate the pipe until it breaks along the cut line.

No matter which method you use, the end of the pipe will be rough. You can of course cut all the way through the pipe with a hacksaw to create a smooth end, but because of the way cast iron pipe is joined, a smooth end is not necessary.

Supporting the Pipe

Because cast iron pipe is so heavy, an amateur can get in trouble if pipe within the walls and leading up to the roof as a vent line is not properly supported. Also, closet bends under toilets should be well supported in the floor framing. If the heavy pipe and fittings are not supported and were to drop some, the flange to which the toilet is sealed could drop. This would cause a leak under the floor between the toilet and flange. Such a leak might not be discovered until the floor rotted through into the basement or crawl space, or the downstairs ceiling suddenly showed a bad, wet stain.

As the accompanying drawings show, you treat any area which cast iron passes through as you would any opening in the framing of the house. Double headers are used, with added supports provided for the pipe, and for any branches such as to a closet bend under a toilet.

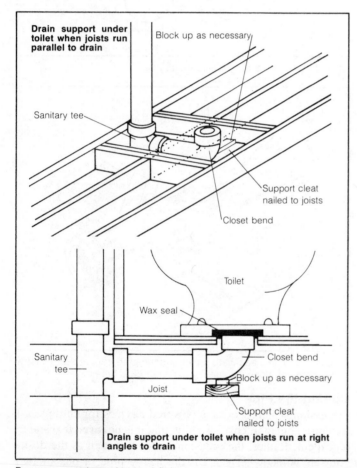

Because cast iron pipe and fittings are so heavy, they need added support in the house framing. The closet bend in particular must be solidly supported so the toilet does not leak.

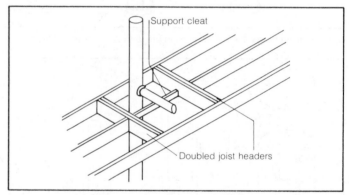

Where soil pipe passes through the floor framing, an opening must be beefed up with double headers, as for any opening. Support must also be provided for horizontal runs of pipe.

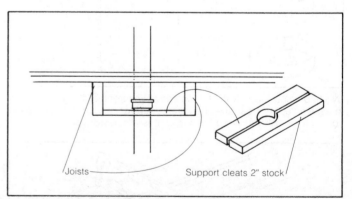

One method of supporting vertical cast iron soil pipe is a "split collar" made of 2-inch lumber, fitted around pipe against hub, then spiked to floor joists.

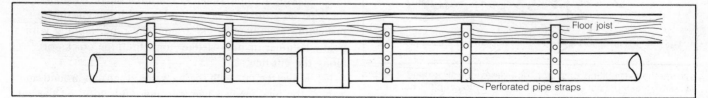

Drain lines must always slope toward the main drain line, and must be strongly supported to maintain the slope and prevent sagging pipes.

5 Working with Plastic Pipe

Plastic pipe and fittings now are being used by professional plumbers, and plastic is definitely the easiest option for the do-it-yourself homeowner. While plastic is a petrochemical, and does use some of our precious and dwindling supply of oil, in the long-run plastic pipe will *save* energy.

How can that be? Plastic pipe lasts for a hundred years or more, which means that no energy will be needed to make more plastic pipe to replace it — and no steel pipe or copper tubing will be needed for replacement of the plastic. Instead, the energy can be used to process steel and copper into solar collectors that will capture "free" energy, energy that will not need to be provided by oil.

If you have owned a home that is 30 or more years old, you know what happens to steel pipe in that time: It has to be replaced because it either rusts out, or is so plugged with mineral deposits that the flow of water becomes restricted or completely stopped. If you replace all or part of the pipe with plastic, it will still be in excellent condition a hundred years from now because it is inert and does not rust or corrode. In addition, when the United States begins to produce oil from shale, plastic pipe can be made from coal along with other synthetic substitutes — once it is made worth the while of industry and inventors.

TYPES OF PLASTIC PIPE

There are four basic types of plastic pipe: polyvinyl chloride (PVC), chlorinated polyvinyl chloride (CPVC), polybutylene (PB) which is the newest member of the family, and

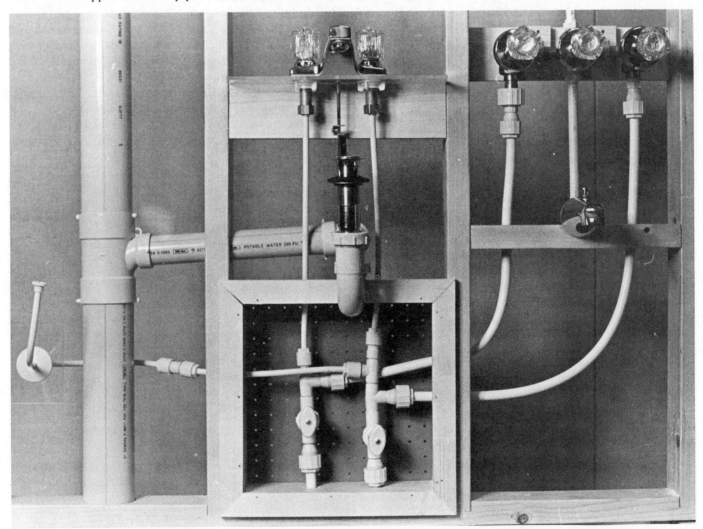

Complete line of pipe, valves and other fittings to "rough in" bathroom, including toilet, vanity basin and tub/shower, are available in plastic. Shown here are CPVC pipe for DWV, along with PB flexible pipe in smaller sizes to supply water (photo courtesy Genova).

acrylonitrile-butadiene-styrene (ABS). The latter is used for drain, waste and vent systems. Polyethylene plastic pipe (PE) is no longer used, as this pioneer in plastic pipe does not have the resistance to pressure and heat that newer plastics such as PB have.

As well as being very easy to handle, plastic pipe offers several other advantages: the inside of the pipes are so smooth that they offer much less resistance to the flow of water than metal pipes. In many instances the plastic pipes permit a smaller size of pipe to supply the same volume of water, as compared to some metal pipes. This is obviously a savings in money and material. Plastic also resists the passage of heat much better than metal, so there is less heat loss in hot water lines. In cold water lines the insulating effect works to reduce "sweating" that occurs in summer weather.

Three of the types of plastic pipe require the use of solvent adhesives; the fourth, PB, cannot be solvent welded and is joined with compression fittings. The one disadvantage of PB pipe is its higher cost, and we have encountered some hardware stores and home centers who do not even carry it because of the higher price tag. For most jobs the solvent-welded plastic pipe is fine, and easy to work.

PB

We have found the added cost of PB to be worthwhile when plumbing in hard-to-reach locations, and when replacing other types of pipe inside a wall where your visibility and space are limited.

PB pipe can be worked very easily; we have pulled a length

PB plastic pipe is joined with compression fittings; it cannot be solvent-welded. One method (Qest products) utilizes nut, stainless steel lock ring, sealing ring and fitting. These components also can be used on CPVC plastic tube or pipe, and also on copper tubing to make watertight connections.

The nut first is slipped onto pipe or tubing; it must be the proper size (photo courtesy Qest Products).

The locking ring is next and then the sealing ring, which must be flush with the end of pipe or tubing. This requires a square cut on pipe or tubing (photo courtesy Qest Products).

of it up through a wall with the aid of a "fish wire," much as you would pull a length of electric wire through a wall. The pipe can be used for hot water, as it is rated well above any temperature that will be encountered with an ordinary hot water tank. It also offers a safety factor of several times the pressure that will ever be produced in a normal water supply system, whether from a municipal line or a private pump.

Solvent-welded pipe

All solvent-welded pipe is handled in much the same manner. You first cut it off cleanly at right angles. This can be done with any fine-toothed saw, including a hacksaw. A good sharp knife will also do the job. A simple miter box will aid in cutting the pipe at a neat right angle. You can also use a tubing cutter designed to cut plastic pipe; this is the easiest, most accurate way to cut it. Cutters intended for copper tubing or steel pipe usually will not give a clean edge because the cutting wheels are not sharp enough, and tend to only crease the plastic pipe rather than cut it.

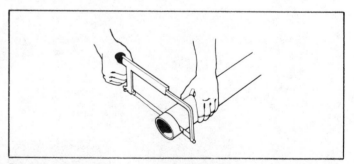

Plastic pipe or tubing must be cut squarely. While hacksaw can be used successfully, a tubing cutter made especially for the job is best (drawing courtesy Genova).

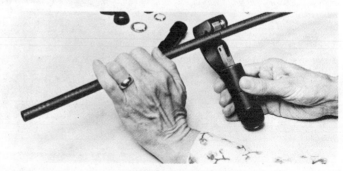

A cutter designed to cut plastic pipe is convenient to use and is small enough to carry in your pocket (photo courtesy Qest Products).

The next step is to remove any burr on the cut end of the pipe, using a sharp knife or sandpaper. A recommended procedure, although not mandatory, is to use a clean rag to wipe some cleaner around the outside of the fitting and the pipe. This will remove any grease, oil or foreign material that would prevent the solvent from reaching the plastic surface. Some craftsmen skip this step, taking a chance that the pipe will clean up by just rubbing it lightly with fine sandpaper. This is not a good idea; the moment or two it takes to clean the plastic is good insurance against a leak later on.

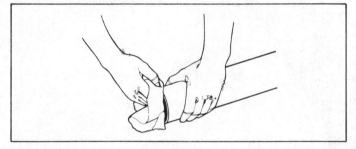

After cutting plastic pipe, remove burrs inside and out with a sharp knife or medium-grit sandpaper (drawing courtesy Genova).

Immediately after cleaning the pipe, and the inside of the fitting as well, apply the solvent adhesive liberally on the pipe and lightly in the socket. Quickly push the pipe into the socket of the fitting, using a slight twisting motion to spread the adhesive. Be sure to align the fitting within a few seconds, as the solvent adhesive begins to set up almost as soon as it is applied. Do not be stingy with the adhesive; any excess will be squeezed out of the fitting when you insert the pipe. The occasional leaks that occur in plastic type are often due to a lack of the adhesive. Try not to overdo it, of course, because the excess cement does not look good, and is almost impossible to remove. Be generous, not sloppy.

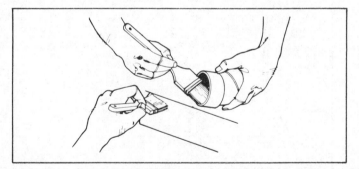

Immediately after cleaning, use a brush to apply adhesive liberally on pipe and sparingly in socket of fitting (drawing courtesy Genova).

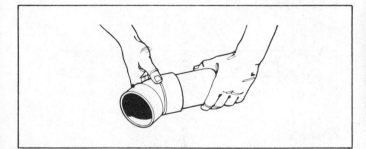

Quickly push pipe into socket of fitting with a slight twisting motion until it bottoms in fitting. Adjust alignment of fitting while twisting since adhesive sets up quickly (drawing courtesy Genova).

Specialty Pipe

While ABS pipe generally is used for drain, waste and vent (DWV) line, one company (Genova Plastic) has a line of PVC fittings and pipe for this application. It is solvent welded in the same manner as the smaller water supply pipe previously described. Genova also has two types of DWV pipe. Their "Schedule 30" pipe will just fit inside a 2 x 4 wall, while their "Schedule 40" will not. The advantage of the Schedule 30 is that you do not have to build the wall out using 2 x 6s, as is ordinarily done in a bathroom and kitchen to provide room for the larger pipe. Both types of pipe have the same inside diameter; the difference between the two types is in the thickness of the pipe wall. Because the Schedule 30 "in-the-wall" pipe is so easy to install, it is accepted by many plumbing codes.

DWV plastic pipe from Genova comes in "Series 30" with thin wall so it will fit inside standard 2 x 4 stud wall. "Series 40" has a thicker wall and requires a 1-inch shim on 2 x 4 to permit installation. In most other cases, 2 x 6s are used to create the thicker wall (photo courtesy Genova).

FITTINGS

Compression fittings used for joining PB pipe consist of a nut, a stainless steel locking ring, and a sealing washer that makes a watertight connection with the fitting — very simple. There is one caution with these fittings: the stainless steel locking ring has a razor-sharp edge, so handle it with care. Your author learned this fact the hard way, with some loss of blood.

Flare fittings

Most brands of PB and CPVC come in the same sizes as copper tubing, and can be flared to accept standard flare fittings. Using the flare fittings makes it convenient to connect to faucets and other fixtures and appliances. A standard flaring

Most brands of PB and CPVC plastic pipe can be flared to accept standard flare fittings as used for copper tubing. Tubing is warmed in water, then flared with standard flaring tool. Don't forget to slip on flare nut before making the flare (photo courtesy Genova).

tool is employed after the end of the pipe has been softened in warm water to prevent its cracking when flared. It is necessary to make an absolutely square cut for a flared end, otherwise the flare will not seal in the flare fitting. As with copper tubing, remember to slip on the flare nut *before* making the flare on the pipe.

MEETING CODE
Plastic pipe and fittings are accepted by most national Plumbing Codes, but some local codes will not accept it. Plumbing codes, sometimes called sanitary codes, are necessary to protect the health of homeowners. But the restriction on plastic pipe usually is a result of pressure from professional groups because plastic pipe is so quick and simple to install that anyone can do it. There is no mystery to it, no apprenticeship and no special tools are required.

Plastic pipe also can be used in private sewer systems. There are perforated pipes for seepage or septic fields, and the solvent-welded pipe can be used from the house to the septic tank or cesspool. Designing and building a septic system is explained in more detail in later chapter.

COST TRADEOFFS
As stated earlier in this chapter, PB pipe and fittings are more expensive than other types of plastic. This additional cost is worthwhile in the savings of time and trouble when connecting plastic pipe to steel or copper. All that is required is to simply remove a section of the metal pipe and slide on the PB fitting. The components fit the metal pipe, and by tightening the nuts at the ends of the fitting (tees in the photograph) the fitting will clamp onto the pipe to make a watertight seal. A variety of adapters are available to enable connection of PB pipe and fittings (or other types of plastic) to the connectors. The accompanying photo shows PB pipe after it has been run to a wet bar in a newly added room, and also to an outside faucet. The flexible PB pipe was easily run up through the stud wall for connection to the bar sink. The pipe to the outside faucet was run along inside the garage wall, and was supported every few feet by plastic pipe clamps.

PB fittings offer a quick and easy changeover from copper or steel to plastic. Here hot and cold water lines are run to a wet bar in a new room, as well as the cold line to an outside faucet.

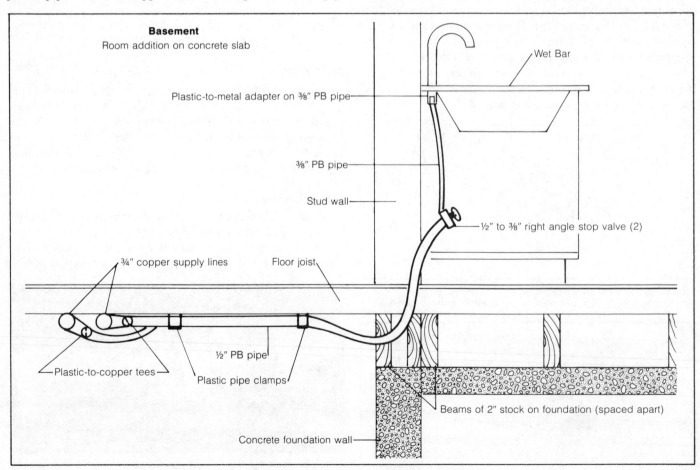

PB supply lines for hot and cold water were run from T-fittings clamped on ¾-inch copper pipe — with a shutoff valve installed in PB line — and clamped to floor joist in basement. Flexible PB pipe was snaked up through a hole in 2-inch beam on the foundation wall, up between beams into the bar cabinet. Right-angle shut-off valves have ½-inch intake, ⅜-inch outlet to supply faucets in sink.

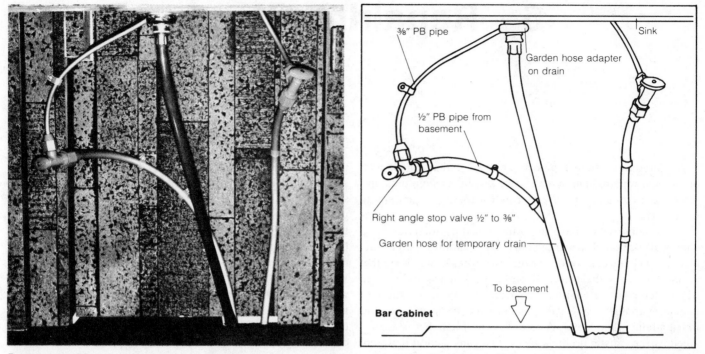

Polybutylene (PB) pipe was snaked up through wall from basement to the wet bar in this room addition. Right-angle stop valves were installed and pipe clamped to back wall of cabinet. Installing 1¼-inch ABS drain line took considerable time; a knowledgeable salesperson at the plumbing-supply house suggested use of a drain adapter to permit using length of graden hose temporarily. It was run-down through wall to basement floor drain.

FITTINGS

DESCRIPTION	NOMINAL TUBE SIZE CONNECTION
Elbow	1/4" x 1/4"
Elbow	3/8" x 3/8"
Elbow	1/2" x 1/2"
Elbow	1/2" x 3/8"
Elbow Adapter	3/8" x 3/8" MPT
Elbow Adapter	1/2" x 1/2" MPT
Street Elbow	1/2" x 1/2" FPT
Tee	1/2" x 1/2" x 1/2"
Tee	1/2" x 1/2" x 1/4"
Tee	1/2" x 1/2" x 3/8"
Female Coupling	1/2" x FPT x 1/2" FPT
Female Coupling	3/4" x FPT x 3/4" FPT
Coupling	1/4" x 1/4"
Coupling	3/8" x 3/8"
Coupling	1/2" x 1/2"
Coupling	1/2" x 3/8"
Coupling Adapter	3/8" x 3/8" MPT
Coupling Adapter	1/2" x 1/2" MPT
Magic Seal Set	1/2"
Magic Seal Set	3/8"

MPT = Male Pipe Thread
FPT = Female Pipe Thread

6   Repairing Clogged Drains

A plumbing system requires continual maintenance, and occasional repairs. The maintenance can be as simple as unstopping a clogged sink drain or as frustrating as snaking a main drain.

Many housewives have a regular schedule for pouring a chemical cleaner down the drains. Application of a caustic cleaner once a week, or once every two weeks, may keep the drain clear, but it also can cause problems. If the drain line and trap under a sink or vanity are the usual thin brass — chrome-plated for appearance — it does not take much corrosive action to eat a hole in the metal. A secondary problem that is aggravated by the caustic drain cleaners is galvanic action between the brass of the trap and drain line, the steel of the sink or vanity, and the cast iron of the drain line (if cast iron is used).

This vulnerability to corrosion and to caustic cleaners is one reason why many homeowners are replacing the drain line and trap with plastic materials. The plastic is unaffected by most chemicals and does not cause galvanic action.

A good starting point in maintenance of drains is to understand how they work and the reason for their configuration. First, there is little or no pressure on drain lines, so that "slip-joint" fittings are used for the drain line running to a sink or a vanity, or even a bathtub. A slip joint consists of a large nut

that is tightened on the threaded end of a pipe (or trap). It squeezes a rubber or plastic gasket so that it grips the smooth surface of the pipe which has been slipped through the nut and gasket. If the connection is new, you often need only hand-tightening in order to make a watertight joint. Most of the time, however, a slight turn with a wrench or slip-joint pliers must be made to stop the leak.

Even when such a joint is tightened enough to make it watertight, it still is possible to pull the smooth pipe out of the nut and gasket. This is why great caution should be used when trying to clear a drain with one of the new "pressure can" devices developed for clearing drain stoppages. These pressurized containers are inverted over the drain, then pushed down to release the air or other gas in order to blow the stoppage down the drain.

We tried using one of these devices for a blockage in a garbage disposal, packing rags around the end of the container to create a seal against the drain. We apparently had not arranged the rags just right, and blew dirty water all over the kitchen — including the ceiling. A second try was more successful, and we did blow out the plugged line. The dirty water stained the walls and ceiling, of course, and a certain wife had some harsh things to say about the device (and the user). The point is, if there is that much pressure and you blow into a drain that has slip-joint fittings, or is possibly afflicted by some thin spots about to corrode through, the chances are very good that you will end up with a mess. The slip joints will slip, the weak spots will blow out. Since most kitchen sinks are used for

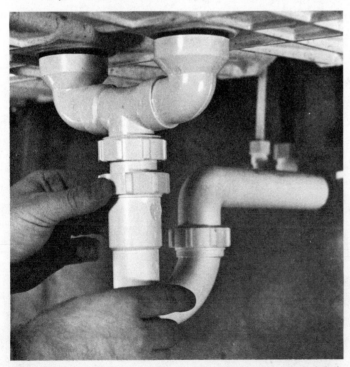

Many homeowners are replacing chrome-plate brass traps and drain lines under sinks with plastic because it does not corrode, nor is it affected by harsh drain cleaners (photo courtesy Chicago Specialty Mfg. Co.).

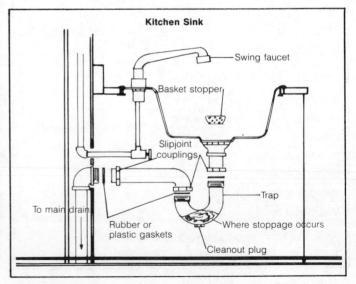

Drain lines under typical kitchen sink have slip joints. This sink has a J-trap that runs the drain back to the wall. A P-trap would be used if the drain ran straight down through the floor. Note that the bottom of the trap is where debris usually settles to plug your drain.

storage beneath, the detergents and other materials underneath can end up a water-soaked loss. If you do try using such a device, first remove anything located below the drain. It also is suggested that a generous quantity of paper towels or rags be placed on the floor of the cabinet to catch the water.

Most often a clogged sink or vanity is the result of material piling up in the bottom of the trap. The debris eventually completely fills the pipe and the water either drains very slowly or not at all. The first step is to try the old-fashioned

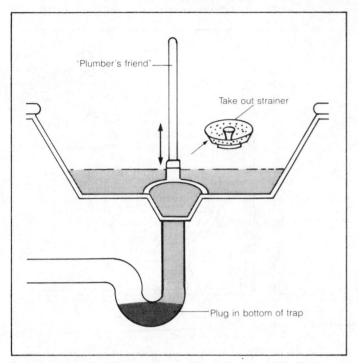

To assure pressure, plug overflow opening with a wet cloth. Tip the cup slightly to force air out, place cup over drain. For a tighter seal, apply petroleum jelly to the bottom of the cup.

This long snake comes in lengths of 25, 50, 75 and 100 feet, and is used for cleaning long drains such as those in basement floor.

"plumber's helper," otherwise known as a force cup or plunger. You first make sure there is enough standing water to seal the edge of the cup, then you move the handle up and down briskly. The alternate pressure and suction created by this action churns up the plug, and if it is not too tightly packed, it breaks up and goes down the drain.

WHEN TO USE A SNAKE

If the stoppage is solid, a plunger will not do the job. This is the kind of blockage that occurs when hot, liquid grease is poured into the drain and then cold water is run into it. The grease congeals into a ball and everything that is poured down the drain afterward sticks to it. After a time the ball becomes a solid mass and must be removed by mechanical action. This means the use of a "snake," which is a flat ribbon of flexible steel that is slipped into the drain and rotated like a drill.

There are plain snakes, those with crank handles, and even some with an electric motor to drive them. Although they will work effectively to remove a blockage in a drain, they also entail some risk. If the slip-joint pipe and fittings under the sink or vanity are not in good condition, the snake might punch a hole in a corroded section of the pipe or even push apart a slip-joint connection.

Try Easier Alternative First

The first step should be to examine the trap under the sink or vanity. As in the drawing on the facing page, there may be a cleanout plug. If there is, place a pan or bucket under the plug and remove it. If no water runs out, poke a wire (or small, lightweight snake) up into the opening and try to break up the plug (use caution). Quite possibly you will be able to push the wire in both directions — up toward the basin and up toward the drain — to clear the obstruction. Carefully pour water into the basin and let if flush the debris from the trap out the opening of the cleanout. When you think you have the drain cleared, replace the cleanout plug and run water into the sink. Slowly, to see if it will drain.

Gaskets

If there is no cleanout plug in the trap, then you will have to remove the trap. Do this by loosening the nuts at the slip joints. Almost invariably you will have to replace the rubber or plastic gaskets in the joints. Buy a half-dozen of the gaskets at a hardware store and keep them on hand. The drain will be either 1¼ or 1½ inches. If your house has both drain sizes, the kitchen sink probably will have the larger 1½-inch drain, while bathroom vanities will have the smaller 1¼-inch size. Get gaskets

This is a small power auger which has motor somewhat like an electric drill. Versions of this device can be rented (photo courtesy Ridge Tool Co.).

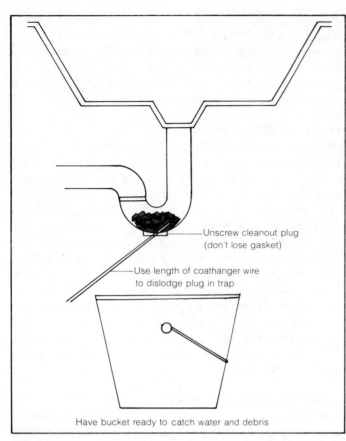

If the trap has a cleanout plug it can be removed and a wire or snake slipped into the drain to unplug the clog.

for both sizes. If you do not, it is likely that you will have to run back to the hardware store at the most delicate stage of your operation.

If you have only one drain size, take an old gasket with you and find a size that matches. Note which bin you take the gaskets from to determine what the size is, and so you know what size to buy the next time gaskets are needed.

The drains for kitchen sinks are uncomplicated in that they have a strainer basket that is used to close the drain. Turned one way, the basket strains the material such as trimmings from vegetables and prevents it dropping into the drain. When turned a bit more, the basket drops down into the drain opening so a rubber or plastic gasket on the basket provides a water-tight seal.

Bathroom vanities are somewhat different. Unless, of course, you have an old-fashioned basin (and they are in style in restored homes) where a simple rubber stopper closes the drain. More modern vanities will have one of several types of "pop-up" drain closers.

Two of the pop-up types shown close by pulling up on the button on the top of a rod, while the third is closed by pushing down. In the latter mechanism the lever under the sink reverses the motion of the closing rod when you push down.

Toilet Problems

Toilet bowls can plug up and overflow, especially if a toddler flushes a toy or teddy bear down the drain and it never makes it through.

There are special toilet augers for this job. They are short and more flexible than larger, longer augers used for most drains. Toilet bowls have a built-in trap, which makes a very short-radius turn, and thus they need a very flexible auger. In extreme cases even the toilet auger will not remove the clog. The toilet must be removed from the floor and turned upside down. If your toilet is the type that has the tank bolted to the rear of it, do not remove it. Instead, drain the bowl and the tank and get help in raising and inverting the unit. Be cautious because toilets are porcelain, which is a form of glass, and they are easily broken.

Toilets are fastened down in two ways: the older method is

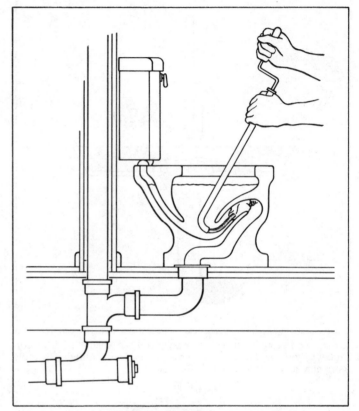

The drain auger can be used for vanity drains, but is specifically designed for cleaning toilets. The flexible, springlike end portion will bend around the sharp trap in a toilet.

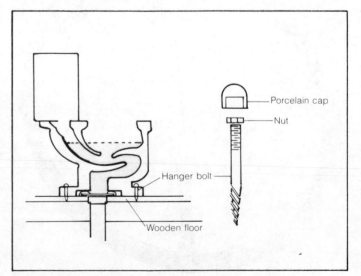

The toilet bowl can be fastened with hanger bolts into a wooden floor or subfloor, or by bolting directly to the flange on closet bend in drain. Plastic closet bends have provision for flanges into which the tie-down bolts fit.

with "hanger bolts." These are devices ¼ inch in diameter and about 3 inches long, with wood-screw threads on one end, machine-screw threads on the other. The wood-screw end is turned into the wood of the floor, then a nut is turned on the machine-screw end to force the flange of the toilet bowl down. The seal for the bowl is a ring of plumber's putty around the opening in the bowl, or the modern replacement — a wax ring. As the bowl is tightened down, the wax or putty oozes out and seals the bowl to the special flange on the drain line.

Modern installations (especially plastic drain lines) have the bowl bolted directly to the flange for a more positive seal. If you must remove the toilet from the floor to unplug a stoppage, first get a wax ring from the hardware store. The sealing material must be replaced when the toilet is removed and reinstalled.

Incidentally, if you notice that the floor around the toilet is wet, and you can see a water stain or leak on the underside of the floor in the basement or crawl space, this also indicates that a new wax seal is required.

In some instances the hanger bolts in the floor have become loosened because moisture from condensation over the years has caused the wooden floor to rot. In extreme cases it will be necessary to replace part of the floor. If it is just the hole into which the bolt is turned that is rotted, you sometimes can pack wood putty in the hole. The hanger bolt is immediately turned into the soft putty and the putty is allowed to set for at least a day. The toilet — with a new wax ring — can then be replaced.

Closing Mechanisms

If a vanity basin is only draining slowly, rather then being completely plugged, check the action of the closer mechanism. On two of the pop-ups you may simply need to adjust the height of the push or pull button to make the stopper rise higher for faster drainage of the water. It also can happen that the ball-shape in the raise-lower mechanism is plastic, and the metal pin that projects to raise and lower the drain closer is loose. We found this in one drain mechanism on a Sunday afternoon, and corrected it "temporarily" by sealing the rod into the ball with epoxy glue. The supposedly short-term solution has lasted three years, but should be replaced before it causes problems again. It was necessary to adjust the height of the raising-lowering rod since the repair did not get the projecting short rod completely in line with the rest of the mechanism.

Note that one type of drain has a slot that allows a half-turn to permit lifting the closer out of the drain. This permits you to clean the edges of the stopper (as well as the drain opening) to assure a watertight seal when it is closed. If your basin slowly drains when the stopper is closed, it is possible that the meeting surfaces of the closer should be cleaned — or that the height adjustment of the raising-lowering rod needs to be changed to let the stopper drop down a little more.

Another type of pop-up drain requires that the packing nut be unscrewed and the lift rod pulled out of an "eye" at the bottom of the closer to permit removing it for cleaning, replacement or repair. Each of the several types of pop-up drains also has a gasket (seal) that might after many years of use start to leak. You can easily replace one by disassembling the mechanism, removing the old gasket, and replacing it with a new one.

A plastic toilet flange accepts bolts in serrated slots which allow positioning as necessary. The flange has a plug to prevent dropping anything in the drain until the stool is ready to install. The plug then is knocked out with a hammer (photo courtesy Genova, Inc.).

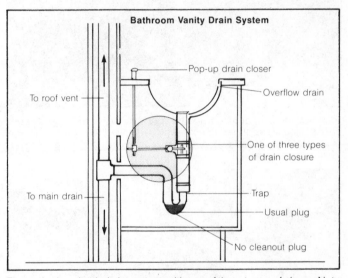

The typical vanity drain has a trap with one of three types of closer. Note that the overflow drain is cast into the sink basin; on rare occasions the overflow drain can plug and cause slow drainage.

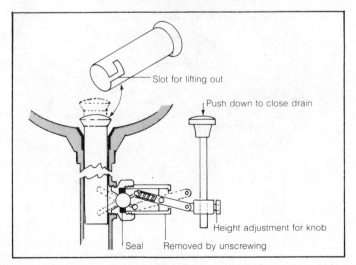

This vanity drain closes when rod is pushed down. Open/close action is reversed by a short lever in "ball joint" inside packing nut. L-shape slot in stopper permits it to be removed by a half twist that disengages the lift lever.

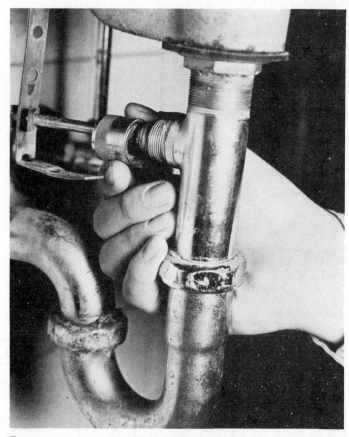

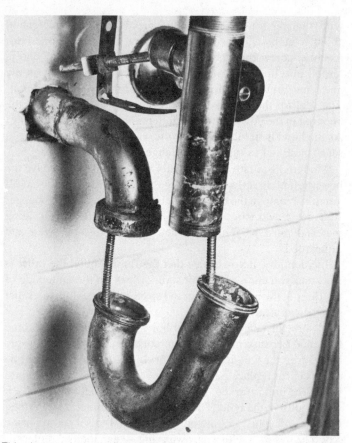

To remove a stopper in a sink or lavatory, first try turning the stopper counterclockwise. If this doesn't work, remove the pivot rod on the tailpipe of the sink or lavatory. It simply unscrews; pull out on the rod.

This simulated setup shows how an auger goes down and through a sink trap to remove debris blocking the trap. Most sink and lavatory stoppage is in the trap area.

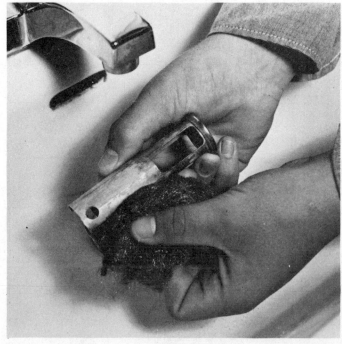

Clean the stopper with steel wool and household detergent. Or use a stiff brush. Stoppers should be cleaned every six weeks or so to remove grease, hair, and debris.

To remove a trap, unscrew the retaining nuts at the top and bottom of the drain pipe. Place a bucket under the trap to catch any water in the pipe and the sink above.

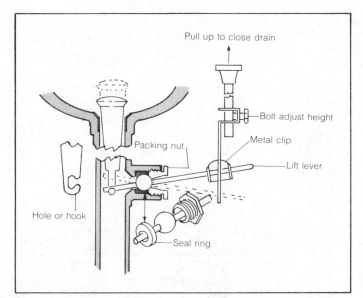

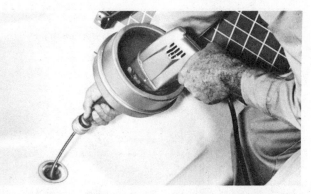

If cleaning weight or spring-type bathroom stopper does not enable water to drain properly, use a drain auger to reach down for the clog. Shown is a power auger, which makes the job easier (photo courtesy Ridge Tool Co.).

This drain also is closed by lifting up on the button on the stem. The stopper will have a hole or hook through which the lift lever fits. If it is a hook, the stopper can be twisted a half turn and removed.

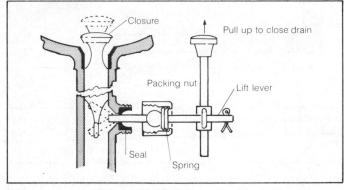

In this type of vanity drain the stopper is closed by pulling up on the stem. The stopper cannot be removed without first unscrewing the packing nut and removing the lift lever.

How To Use A Snake or Auger

If, after you have removed the trap from under a sink or vanity and have tried using a wire or snake to clean the trap, the water sitll does not drain properly, you will have to run a snake into the drain beyond the trap. Push and/or turn the snake until you feel an obstruction, then twist and pull to remove the blockage. In extreme cases you may have to go up on the roof and pass a snake down through the vent in order to reach into the main drain to break up a heavy obstruction. In a situation like this it might pay to rent a power snake, unless you don't mind paying the "rooter" fellow to do the job for you.

BATHTUB DRAINS

Bathtub drains frequently become plugged or drain slowly, and the problem usually is caused by the closing device. It will be one of two types, spring or weight. You can readily tell which one your tub has: if the stopper lifts out, it is a spring model; if there is a small perforated grille over the drain that does not lift out, it is a weight model.

As the drawings indicate, you remove either type by unscrewing two screws in the overflow plate that also contains the lever that opens and closes the drain. These types of stoppers are especially prone to becoming plugged with hair,

In extreme cases it may be necessary to climb onto the roof and pass the drain auger down vent line to reach plugged line. The vent allows you to reach straight down to the main drain line (photo courtesy Ridge Tool Co.).

which then acts like a net to catch everything else and prevent it from going down the drain properly.

You will have to remove the overflow plate, but place a cloth or paper towel over either drain while removing the plate. Murphy's Law states that one or both of the short screws will fall into the drain where they cannot be retrieved. In the case of the spring type, the stopper can be closed while the spring mechanism is removed. But play it safe; otherwise you may drop the mechanism while trying to remove it, which could pop open the stopper and the screws will then disappear down the drain. In both cases, clean the mechanism carefully and let hot water run down the drain while you are doing the cleaning. If the hot water drains properly, then the problem has, indeed, been the closer mechanism.

If the water does not drain quickly, you will have to find the drum trap under the tub. In some older homes the trap will be in the floor, or at least the screw-in cover will be. Some newer homes will have the drum trap under the floor in basement or crawl space. Generally it will be upside down, with the cover on the bottom. We have known of cases where a sadistic or

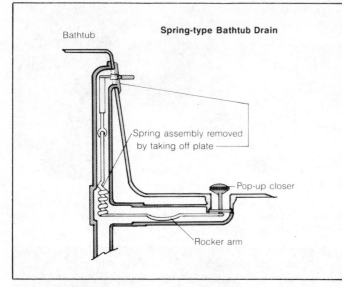

Spring-type bathtub drain has a rocker arm that is actuated when you flip the lever in the overflow plate. Rocker arm and stopper can be pulled out of the drain for cleaning.

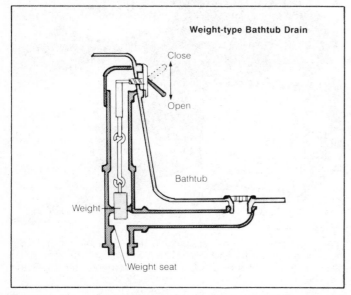

The drain in a bathtub with weight-type stopper cannot be removed. The weight can be removed for cleaning by taking off the overflow plate in which the open/close lever is located.

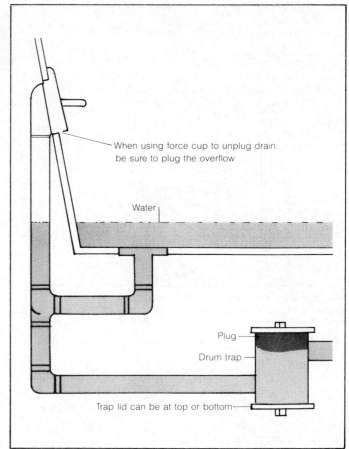

The drum trap for the bathtub can be located by its cap flush with the bathroom floor — or it may be under the floor in basement or crawl space.

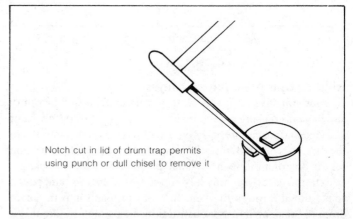

If the cap of a drum trap cannot be removed with a wrench on hexagon projection, try notching the cap's opposite sides and using a hammer and chisel to loosen it.

careless plumber has installed a drum trap with the cover on top, up next to the underside of the joists or floor.

Assuming the drum trap has been installed in a reasonable manner, you will be able to reach a hexagon-shape projection on the screw-on cap. Generally the cap is brass, while the trap itself will be cast iron. There are exceptions; the trap may also be brass. In newer and more modern installations the assembly will be plastic and removing the cap is simply a matter of a half turn and lifting up.

If the trap is cast iron with a brass cap, first go around the edge of the cap tapping lightly with a hammer — or try a wrench with a fairly long handle. Do this for several minutes to loosen the corrosion that is bound to exist between the cap and the trap. A pipe wrench sometimes can be used to grip the hexagon projection.

If all your efforts will not budge the cap, cut a couple of triangular-shape notches in the edge of the cap, spacing them across from each other. Now, try again with a hammer and chisel, gently but firmly banging against the notches.

If all else fails (and the hardware store is open so you can buy a replacement) chisel the cap into pieces, making sure you later get every piece out of the trap. A new cap will have to be installed, of course. Measure the inside diameter of the trap and purchase a cap which has a threaded portion of the same diameter. It will be around 3½ to 4½ inches in size.

Do not get carried away and become careless while bashing the cap; you do not want to loosen any of the joints in the drain line. Also, the cast iron trap could break if you hit it too hard.

PINPOINTING DRAIN STOPPAGES

Bathrooms

Locating a drain blockage in a bathroom is not too difficult. The toilet drains directly into the main drain or stack, while the bathtub and basin drain first into 1¼ or 1½ inch drain lines, which then empty into the main drain.

Most blockages occur in the traps of fixtures. If the toilet and basin both drain well, but the bathtub drains slowly, then the tub trap or drain line is the source of the problem. If only the basin drains slowly, then it is the trap in the basin. If, however, when water drains from the basin it backs up into the tub, then the blockage is between the basin and the toilet, or between the basin and the main drain. This is not common, but can occur if the drain between the basin and the stack slants down toward the basin, perhaps because of settling in an older building.

To correct this blockage, the first step would be to remove the trap under the basin and run a snake into the drain; try to direct it toward the main stack. If there is a T-fitting under the floor you have a 50-50 chance of the snake going in the right direction. Sometimes several tries will bring the correct results. Failing that, you should go downstairs to the basement (if you have one) to see if you can somehow open a connection there. If so, insert the snake into the line at a point that allows you to direct it toward the main drain. Unfortunately, if the drain is on the second floor, between the floor and ceiling, your only choice is to keep trying under the basin in the bathroom.

The drain from the tub and basin may be connected to a larger line that runs from the toilet to the main drain or stack. In an upstairs room the drum trap for the tub will have the top flush with the floor for access to it. If, after you have cleaned the traps for both the tub and basin, one or both still do not drain well, you may then have to remove the toilet to run a snake from the main drain (or drain between toilet and stack) back through the drain line from the tub and basin. Removing and replacing the toilet is explained in Chapter 9, "Replacing and Repairing Fixtures."

Kitchens

If a kitchen sink drains slowly, or not at all, or backs up into another bowl of the sink, it may be related to the disposal under one of the basins (considering a double or triple basin sink). Check to see if the regular sink(s) have drain lines that join with the one from the disposal. In this situation, it would actually be the disposal drain that is plugged.

Your author recently noted that a disposal drained very slowly—so slowly that the sink basin filled partially before the pulverized garbage would drain. The adjacent sink bowl also drained somewhat slowly. An examination of the drain line showed a suspicious spot in the upcurve of the trap where it entered the wall. The first step was to go to the workshop to make sure there were new slip nuts and gaskets if they were needed. The drain then was disassembled, with a pan below to catch the water.

The trap broke off at the suspicious spot, and the drain line as well as the trap were lined with a gooey material the consistency of putty. After cleaning out the rather stinking material, another length of the drain was found to be nearly completely corroded. A trip to the hardware store plumbing department was necessary to replace the drain parts—chrome-plated brass, of course—and several slip nuts and gaskets were also purchased. These replaced the ones that had to be used to replace the corroded and useless units removed from the drain.

While the disposal drain was disassembled, the drain from the sink basin also was cleaned. The dishwasher is adjacent to the sink, and it also drains into the line that drains the disposal. This particular dishwasher is used only a few times a year, when dinner parties create more dirty dishes than can be handled easily by hand washing. However, there is no doubt that the machine would have backed up and made the dishes even dirtier if the disposal drain had not been cleaned and repaired at this time. So, if your dishwasher overflows, check to see if the drain joins that of the disposal, and try to remember whether the disposal has been draining slowly.

In another recent case, the disposal side of a double-bowl sink appeared to be draining, but the other bowl began to fill up with oily water. An examination of the lines under sink showed separate traps for each bowl, joined in the middle by another pipe leading to the waste. Because the flow of water between sinks was not impeded, but the drainage out from them obviously was, the center pipe was removed. The blockage was routed out with a snake, after determining that it was between the first floor and the basement level.

Basements

Basement floor drains are another problem. Very often they receive sawdust and dirt from a workshop, plus lint and soil from an automatic clothes washer. If the line runs the length of the basement and is not slanted sufficiently toward the main drain it will become plugged every few months.

The solution here is to buy a 50-foot snake and run it through the floor drains once a month or so. This is a case where periodic maintenance is a requirement to overcome a built-in problem that existed the moment the house was built.

One homeowner did lengthen the time between cleaning the drain with a snake by weekly treatment with a caustic drain cleaner. The cast iron drain line is more resistant to strong chemicals than the thin brass drains under sinks, tubs and basins. However, to make sure the chemical did not stay in the drain after it had completed its work, the drain was flushed about half an hour afterward with plenty of cold water by means of a length of garden hose inserted about 15 feet. The water was kept running while the hose was inserted.

You cannot use such harsh chemicals in a septic system, so the drain between the house and tank should have a readily accessible cleanout. If there is none in the drain line, then install one; you will need it sooner or later.

Flexible traps can be turned and twisted to match misaligned drain pipes. Traps are subjected to lots of wear from soap and debris; they should be replaced every 5 years.

7 Updating the System
Installing Shutoff Valves

Unless your house is brand new, parts of the plumbing system will require updating. There are various measures you can take to make the system quieter, more convenient, and more dependable.

SHUTOFF VALVES

The very first step in your program should be installation of shutoff valves under — or adjacent to — sinks, vanities, toilets and other fixtures.

Copper or Steel Plus Plastic

The fastest and easiest way to install shutoff valves in either a copper-tubing or steel-pipe system is with a plastic valve that has compression fittings on the ends. You simply cut out a section of the pipe, slide the compression nuts onto the cut ends, and then slide the valve onto one of the cut ends. The pipe must be pushed aside just a little to slide the nut onto the valve. Then align the pipes and slip the valve onto the other pipe. Once the nuts are turned onto the ends of the valve, the installation is complete.

For either copper or steel pipe, the pipe first should be cleaned with steel wool or sandpaper. We also found it necessary to snug up the nuts about ⅛ turn for three or four days after installation in order to completely stop any seepage. Do not try to tighten the nuts too much when you first install the valve, because a plastic component can be stripped or cracked by overtightening. Just turn it a little more each day to avoid this possibility.

Plastic valves can be used without compression fittings with steel pipe that comes out of the wall under a toilet tank and makes a right angle turn upward to the tank.

First cut the small line that runs upward from the elbow (or disconnect the line at the tank) and unscrew it from the elbow.

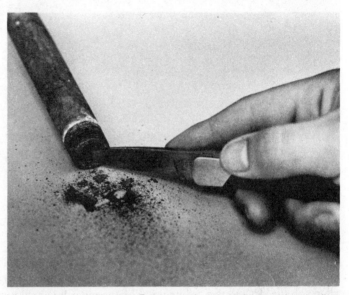
Limed pipes look like this. Do not try a chemical to remove the lime deposit; the pipes probably will have to be replaced with new pipes.

Main water shutoff valves are located near or next to the water meter, usually in the basement or a heated crawl space. Or the water may be turned off at the cold water inlet on the gas or electric water heater.

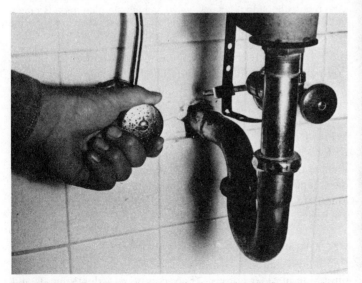
Turn off the water to fixtures at shutoff valves below the fixture — shown is a lavatory. If the fixture doesn't have a shutoff valve, turn off the water at the main meter.

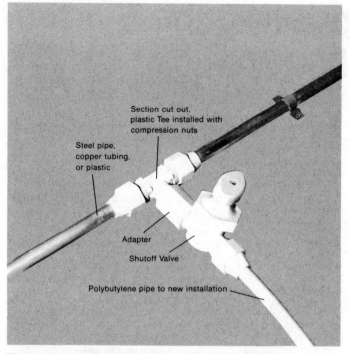

The quickest way to install a valve under a toilet, sink or vanity is to cut out a section of the existing line and install a plastic valve with compression fittings on the end. Compression fittings will make a watertight connection on steel pipe, copper tubing or rigid or flexible plastic piping. This means you can change the existing line from the valve to the fixture by replacing it with flexible plastic, which simplifies connecting up to the fixture.

A right angle plastic valve with pipe threads at one end is now turned onto the pipe coming out of the wall. The opening of the valve that faces upward can be a compression connection for a short length of flexible plastic pipe. The plastic pipe has a ball shape on the top end that is integral with the pipe. It is held by the same nut that originally held the steel pipe (or possibly flexible copper) to the bottom of the tank.

For Steel Pipe

If you have steel pipe, you can cut out a section and replace it with a valve, a nipple and a union. There generally is very little space under a sink or vanity, which means that threading the cut-off pipe in place requires a ratchet pipe die, considerable strength and a great amount of patience.

For Copper Pipe

With copper tubing, you can cut out a section of the pipe and sweat-solder a valve into the line, but here we run into the problem of a hot flame in an enclosed place, and a fire hazard. Yes, it can be done with the proper safeguards: be sure to empty nearby cabinets and place a sheet of metal over any flammable wood. The steps are the same as those given in Chapter 3, "Working with Copper Pipe." Overall, we recommend the plastic valves.

Kits

You can buy "kits" for installing shutoff valves; they actually are for connecting toilets or sinks, and contain all necessary fittings including valves. The next time you are in a hardware store, look over the display of the plastic plumbing parts and installation kits. Most makers of the plastic pipe and fittings

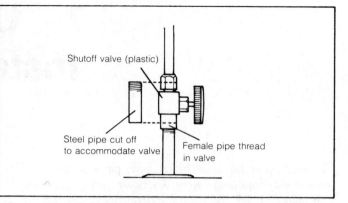

If you do not want to use plastic valves and fittings in steel piping, you must cut out a section and fit in a shutoff valve. No union is required, as pipe-to-tubing adapter provides the same action as a union. A short pipe nipple in the valve allows use of existing pipe-to-tubing adapter, with female threads.

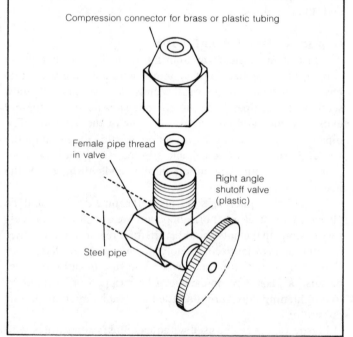

One type of right-angle plastic valve has female pipe threads on the inlet, and a plastic compression fitting on the outlet side that goes to the fixture. In effect, the valve is a steel-to-plastic adapter.

offer free booklets describing how their particular line of components should be handled. The booklets are worth picking up just for information on the latest developments.

Location

While it is very convenient to have shutoff valves directly under sinks and vanities, it is not mandatory that they be located there. A practical alternative is to put the valves in the basement under the fixture. The advantage of such a location is that there is more room to work, and you avoid the mess in the kitchen.

PLUMBING NOISES

Plumbing is subject to strange noises when in use, especially plumbing in older homes. There can be whistles, squeals and bangs; all of them are annoying and some can actually indicate conditions that will damage pipes and fixtures. Fortunately, all

Almost every hardware store and home center will have an extensive display of pipe and fittings of materials in which shutoff valves are included; those shown are plastic (photo courtesy Chicago Specialty Mfg. Co.).

Installation kits, as previously described, contain shutoff valves, and kits can be used to update your plumbing to provide handy shutoff valves at every fixture (photo courtesy Chicago Specialty Mfg. Co.).

the strange sounds can be eliminated by the do-it-yourself plumber, after some detective work to locate the cause.

Water Hammer — The Cause

Probably the worst noise, and the most damaging situation for piping, is "water hammer". This loud bang occurs when a faucet or valve is shut off. The sudden stoppage under pressure of the water in motion is the cause. This is due to water's noncompressible nature; the water cannot stop as quickly or as suddenly as is required.

The elimination of water hammer is accomplished in new homes through the addition of air chambers. These are simply pipe columns fitted vertically in the line behind faucets. Most often, the air chambers are hidden in walls, and so are not a recognized part of plumbing. The function of the air chamber is to provide a cushion of air that absorbs the energy of the suddenly stopped water.

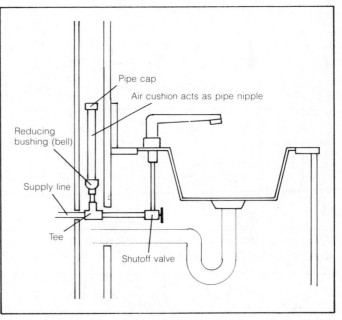

Air chambers to eliminate water hammer generally are hidden inside walls when the plumbing is installed. The air chamber is a vertical length of pipe larger than the line to the fixture, which traps air to provide a shock-absorbing cushion.

The air chamber is a length of pipe about 18 to 24 inches in height which has been filled with air. Over a period of time the air can be absorbed by the water, and thus lose its effectiveness. If this is the case, you simply shut off the main water valve and drain the entire system through a faucet or valve in a low part of the system, such as in the basement. Once the system has drained entirely, you turn on the water again and the whole system will fill with water, except for the air chambers. These dead-end pipes will once again contain air and will offer an air cushion to prevent water hammer.

There is another condtion that will cause water hammer, and that is pipes that are not properly fastened to walls or other surfaces. The inertia of moving water is quite high, and when the water is shut off this inertia can move pipes, even if there is an air chamber in that line. This goes back to the principle that for every action there is an opposite and equal reaction. When the water compresses air in the air chamber, it will reverse its motion after a fraction of a second. If there is any loose pipe, that pipe will jump as the energy of the stopped water passes back along the line.

If your plumbing has air chambers but there still is a hammering at some faucets, even the outside hose connections, check that line for spots where it is slack or loose. It may just be that some pipe clamps have loosened over the years. A larger nail might be the answer, or a wood screw that will hold more securely than a nail.

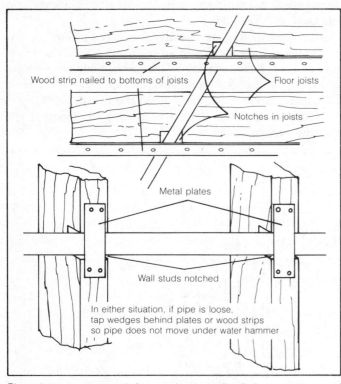

Pipes that are not securely fastened to the wall or (in basement or crawl space) to floor joists can bang when faucets are suddenly shut off.

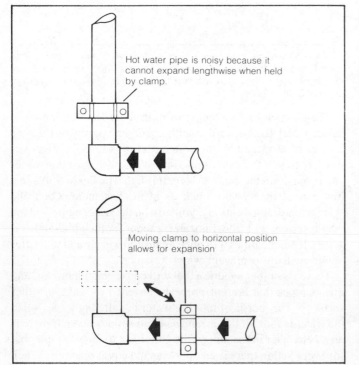

A clamp that is improperly located may keep the pipe from expanding due to hot water, which results in clinking and clanking.

Installation of an Air Chamber

If your plumbing does need an air chamber, you can install one by cutting the supply lines under a sink or vanity and installing a Tee. A short nipple and reducing coupling (bell) is turned into the Tee, and then a length of pipe larger than the line is screwed into the coupling and a cap is turned onto the top of it.

The air chamber must be vertical, and the pipe should be larger than the supply line it cushions. For example, if the supply line is ⅜ or ½ inch, the air cushion should be 1 or 1½ inches respectively. The larger the line, the more air it will contain.

While most air cushions are inside a wall, they can be installed under a sink or a vanity if the supply lines are accessible. In most cases this air cushion would have to be shorter than if it were inside the wall. The largest pipe size practical should be installed. For a homeowner-plumber, that would mean a 1½ inch pipe. An air cushion just 12 inches high would be quite effective for a ⅜ inch line, and probably could be fitted under most sinks.

Alternate Type of Air Chamber

An alternate kind of air cushion is a coil of copper tubing. The coil acts something like a spring, and the spring action combined with the air provides a very effective damping action to reduce or eliminate water hammer.

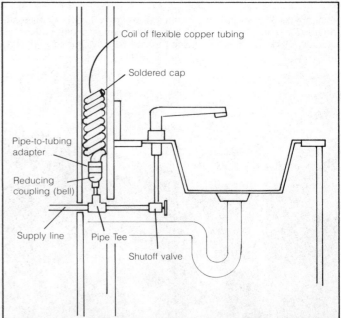

This alternate style of air chamber is coil of copper tubing positioned vertically above the supply line to the fixture. As well as containing air to provide cushion, the coil flexes like a spring to further absorb shock of water hammer. This, or any other type of air chamber, can be installed in the cabinet below to avoid cutting into the wall.

OTHER NOISES

Clunking or Clinking

If there is a clunking or clinking sound in the piping when you first turn on the hot water, this is caused by the cold pipe expanding as the hot water heats it. In this case the pipe needs some slack in it so that it can expand a fraction of an inch. To determine the location of the cold pipe that has this problem, you will have to feel all of the pipes to learn which are cold, then later retouch them to determine which cold pipe has become warm when you turn hot water on for a particular fixture. Next, check along the pipe to see where it might be restricted in movement. It could be as simple as finding that a pipe clamp is holding a vertical pipe near an elbow that connects to a horizontal pipe. Moving the clamp to the horizontal pipe will allow the pipe (horizontal) to expand lengthwise inside the clamp, leaving the vertical pipe to flex slightly and prevent the noise.

Whistling

If you hear an annoying whistling sound in your plumbing it indicates that the water is trying to flow through some kind of restriction. Look for a partly closed valve, which often is the culprit. Someone may have shut off a valve to work on some part of the plumbing and then not re-opened the valve completely.

If a whistling sound comes from a toilet tank, it means that the inlet valve in the flush mechanism is not closing completely. Some mechanisms have a provision for adjustment of the valve to reduce the water flow and stop the noise. If your toilet does not have this provision, just slightly close the stop valve until the whistling stops. In any case, the mechanism needs to be replaced or repaired, which is covered later in Chapter 9.

The Best Way to Open A Valve

When you open a valve, open it all the way and then turn it back a fraction of a turn. This will prevent the valve from "freezing" into the open position. The fraction of a turn back allows for a back-and-forth motion of the valve handle that will free up any stickiness in its action.

Running Water

If you hear water running when the house is very quiet, look for a faucet that is not off completely, or a toilet tank that is "barely" leaking. An enormous amount of water can dribble down the drain through unnoticed leaks like these. In the winter, the sound of running water can be caused by a "self-cleaning" humidifier that lets the water run through and down the drain. These humidifiers do collect less minerals than do other types, but there is no doubt that they waste water. It is a choice between paying for wasted water or occasionally cleaning or replacing the element in the humidifier.

Another source for the sound of running water is an automatic water softener, which usually backflushes on a timed cycle. Be sure that the softener automatically switches from regenerate to soften after it cycles. It if does not, it can waste a lot of water and/or salt. Check to see (or have a plumber do it) whether the timer or valve is malfunctioning (see Chapter 8).

In Drainage System

If noises occur in the drainage system you can suspect faulty venting, or a plugged vent. Clean the vent or, if the vent cannot be reached inside a wall, install an "anti-syphon" trap under the fixture. This type of trap allows air to enter the drain. The air keeps the water in the trap from being pulled out by the slight vacuum created by draining water in the line.

WATER PRESSURE PROBLEMS

Low Pressure

One updating of a plumbing system that should be considered cautiously is the installation of a pump to boost pressure. This often is tempting when you have low — or no — water pressure above the first floor, particularly in the summertime when

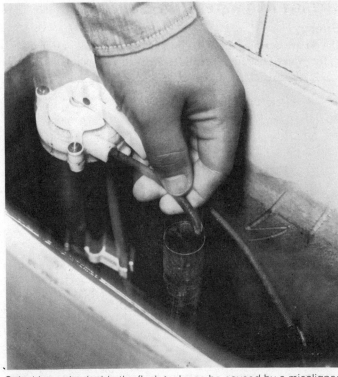

Splashing noise inside the flush tank can be caused by a misaligned refill tube. Make sure the refill tube is connected to the overflow tube, as shown here.

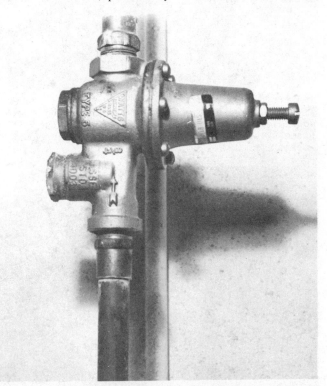

This type of pressure-reducing valve in water supply line is in the author's home. Even in summer there is ample pressure to fixtures on second floor, which means that the unregulated pressure is much too high and could damage pipes and fittings.

water use is heavy. You can get a plumber (or you might do it yourself) to install a pump in the basement that turns on when water pressure reaches a predetermined level.

There is one problem, however. The pump will be pulling water from a line that already has low pressure. The pump will create a slight vacuum in the supply line. This means that previously minor leaks that meant only a tiny loss of water into the ground now become an entry for dirt, contamination and other undesirables into your water supply. If the supply line runs near a sewer line, you really are asking for trouble. In many areas the installation of such a pump is illegal. It might be better to work on your local government to improve quality and quantity and pressure of the whole water system.

Excess Pressure

If, on the other hand, your problem is excess pressure — which is indicated by water hammer even with all pipe securely fastened and all air chambers functioning — you can install a pressure-reducing valve with little hardship.

You can add a sink, vanity, bathroom and not even cut a pipe. Saddle valves require only drilling a hole in a supply line (hot or cold as required), then clamping on the valve and piping from it to the fixture. Be sure the water is shut off before you drill the pipe (photo courtesy Chicago Specialty Mfg. Co.).

A saddle tee lets you tap a pipe to start a new run of pipe. Clamp the tee to the pipe, and drill a hole through the opening into the pipe. Then screw the new pipe into the tee.

Most such valves are factory-preset at about 50 pounds, but you can adjust yours up or down to suit. Excess pressure is a problem that should not be ignored. Just as with constant water hammer, it can break joints, rupture pipes and cause faucets and fixtures to wear out prematurely.

PLUMBING FOR AN ADDITION

If you add a bathroom, powder room or wet bar, you will include shutoff valves in your new plumbing. You need not disconnect any lines for some plumbing additions. Instead you drill a hole in an existing line (after shutting off the water, of course) and clamp on a saddle valve. An elbow or other plastic fitting is screwed into the saddle valve or fitting, and plastic pipe is run from the connection to the new location. As shown in the sample installation, the shutoff valves can be installed just before the ⅜ or ¼ inch risers that go up to the faucets.

CEILING LEAKS

Many desperate homeowners falsely assume that any leak in the ceiling (and the blistering that results) is a plumbing problem. This may be the situation, but in many cases it is caused by gaps in the caulking around tub and shower tiles, or around the escutcheon (fixture metal face plates) or junctures at the floor and the tub or shower. Before you call a plumber — because the average homeowner will have difficulty getting to the plumbing within the wall — recaulk every point where there could be a possible gap in the seal or caulk deterioration. One way to narrow down the location of the gap is to just run water into the tub (if it is a combination tub/shower). If no leaking occurs, then the problem lies higher up — on the wall or around the escutcheon — rather than at the tub/floor surfaces.

ENERGY AND WATER SAVINGS

Energy

If you are serious about saving energy, you might consider a "Hot Water Dispenser." This is an electric flash heater that is

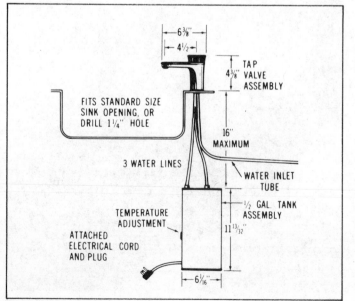

This system by In-Sink-Erator provides up to 60 cups of 190 degree water per hour. It is 750-watt, 6.5 115 volt, and comes with a 3-wire cord and 3-prong plug. A 230 volt export model is available.

installed in the kitchen sink to produce instant hot water at 190 degrees for cooking and other uses. It is said that the device uses 32 percent less energy per day than a 40 watt light bulb, and about 80 percent less energy than a range-top unit used for heating water. This is the same kind of unit suggested as an energy saver in the last chapter of this book, "How to Build Your Own Solar Collector."

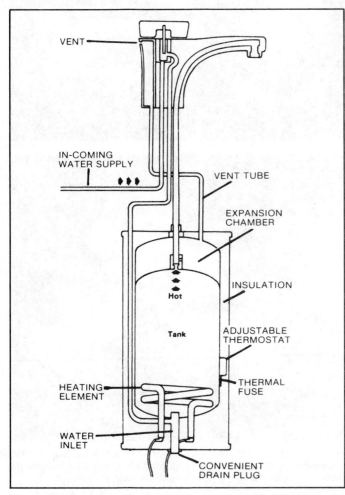

The heating element is thermostatically controlled to keep a particular tank water temperature. A self-closing faucet controls dispensing by allowing cold water to enter the tank at the bottom, forcing the heated water out of the top and through the spout. (art courtesy of In-Sink-Erator).

Water

If you live in an area that experiences water shortages and need to conserve — or you just want to conserve dollars by cutting your water usage — there are a variety of products designed to help you use less water. The chart below indicates home water-usage breakdown, according to EPA data.

This means that nearly all the water usage occurs in the bathroom, which is where you will have to concentrate your efforts to avoid waste. In addition to water-saving toilets, there are also "dams" or "dikes" or other devices that can be inserted into the tank.

This shower head (S-2252-AF Speakman Anystream) is equipped with 2.75 G.P.M. flow control so you can choose your reduced setting.

Shown is an anti-scald shower valve combination (Sentinel Mark II Regency) for protection of the bather even at reduced flow rates (photo courtesy of Speakman Co.).

Household Activity	%
Toilet flushing	39.1%
Bathing	31.3
Laundry	13.7
Dishwashing	5.9
Drinking and cooking	4.7
Oral Hygiene	3.1
Misc. cleaning	2.2

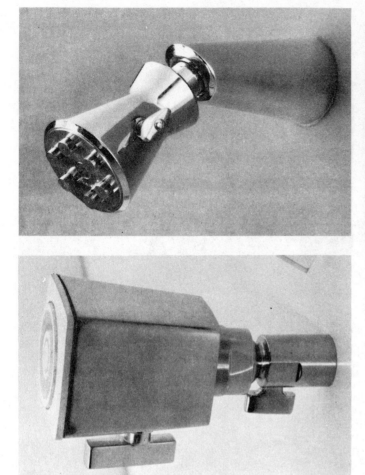

These Water-Guard showerheads reduce flow by 50% — 3 gallons per minute rather than 6 gallons per minute. Since most showers last 5 minutes or more, this can result in a considerable savings. In addition, the lesser amount of hot water supplied can lower hot-water heating bills (photo courtesy Kohler Co.).

At normal water pressures — 40 to 80 psi — Water-Guard faucets have a standard flow rate of 2 to 2.75 gallons per minute; their maximum setting is 3 gallons per minute. (photo courtesy of Kohler Co.).

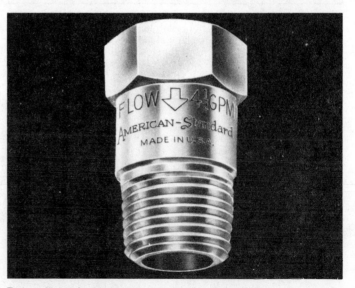

The NOVA showerhead water-saving has undergone many university-conducted tests. Results show that payback of original investment takes 11 to 16 months at current energy costs (photo courtesy Earth Care Co.).

To install the Aquamizer™, unscrew the showerhead, screw on the Aquamizer, and then replace the showerhead using joint compound. This fitting cuts the average shower down from 31 to 13 gallons—a savings of 60% (photo courtesy of American-Standard).

The fittings in the Aquarian II restrict water flow to 3½ gallons per minute. Shown is an exploded view (photo courtesy of American-Standard).

The high-line Water-Guard is an extra-height toilet designed for the special needs of elderly persons and wheelchair patients. The toilet flushes with 3½ gallons of water, which is 36 percent less than most conventional toilets. The model shown above has a special Kohler Lustra supporting arms toilet seat, another aid for the handicapped.

This one-piece water-saver closet (Silhouette II Conserver) flushes no more than 3.5 gallons. It has a 12-inch rough-in and non-overflow features (photo courtesy of Briggs).

CONVERSION OF SEPARATE HOT-COLD FAUCETS

Many older homes — particularly those with attractive pedestal sinks that are again fashionable — have separate hot and cold water faucets. This is not only inconvenient, but the undiluted hot water can be dangerous. Conversion of these types of faucets to a type that mixes the hot and cold water can pose problems, because the distance between the faucets sometimes exceeds the distance allowed for by new faucets. However, there are some models that will handle such a situation. The example shown here is the Delex by Delta. The only problem that was encountered when we installed it was that the copper tubing that had been provided to connect the faucets to the hot and cold water lines were not long enough. It was an easy enough matter to buy two pieces of copper tubing, each about 5 or 6 inches long and of the same diameter. We cut the pieces to the necessary length, using couplings to add them on.

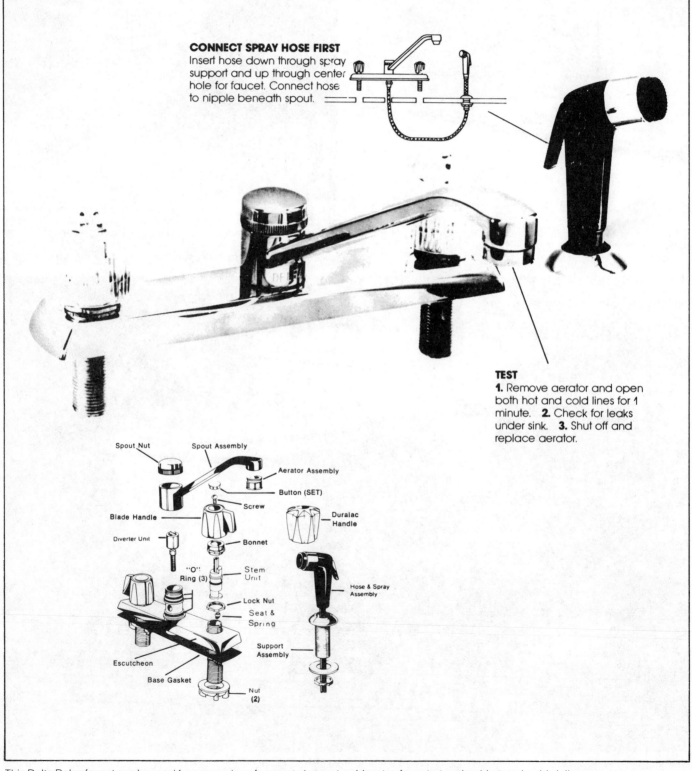

CONNECT SPRAY HOSE FIRST
Insert hose down through spray support and up through center hole for faucet. Connect hose to nipple beneath spout.

TEST
1. Remove aerator and open both hot and cold lines for 1 minute. **2.** Check for leaks under sink. **3.** Shut off and replace aerator.

Spout Nut

Spout Assembly

Aerator Assembly

Button (SET)

Blade Handle

Screw

Duralac Handle

Diverter Unit

Bonnet

"O" Ring (3)

Stem Unit

Lock Nut

Hose & Spray Assembly

Seat & Spring

Support Assembly

Escutcheon

Base Gasket

Nut (2)

This Delta Delex faucet can be used for conversion of separate hot and cold water faucets to mixed hot and cold delivery.

Routine Maintenance Instructions

SHUT OFF WATER SUPPLY

1. Pry off index button, remove screw and lift off handle.

2. Unscrew bonnet.

3. Pull stem straight up and out.

4. Remove seats.

5. Place new seat over spring and push into socket in body.

6. Unscrew spout nut.

7. Lift spout off by rotating back and forth, and pull up gently.

8. Cut "O" rings and remove from body.

9. Stretch new "O" rings and snap into grooves on body.

10. Unscrew diverter using screwdriver. Wash off diverter, and clean and flush out socket of body.

11. Screw diverter tightly in spout socket.

12A. Knob Handle Stem Position — Slip stem unit into body, aligning key with key way, so "stop" on both stems point toward spout.

12B. Blade Handle Stem Position —As you face faucet, slip stem units into body, aligning keys in key way so "stops" on both units point to right

13. Replace bonnet. Tighten securely.

14. Push spout straight down over body, rotating back and forth gently until it rests on faucet base.

15. Screw spout nut on snugly.

16. Replace handle. Tighten screw. Press index button in position.

(A) If the faucet leaks from under the handle or from the spout outlet, replace the stem unit and/or seat as in steps 1, 2, 3, 4 and 5. Reassemble following steps 12, 13, 14, and 15.

(B) If a leak occurs at the top or bottom of the spout body, replace "O" Rings as shown in steps 6, 7, 8, 9, 14, and 15.

(C) If the volume of water from spray models decreases or the spray stops functioning, follow the procedure in steps 6, 10, 11, and 15.

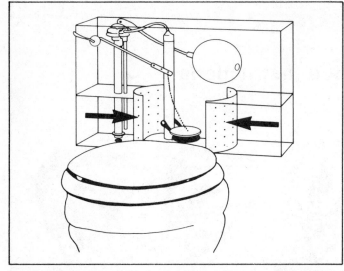

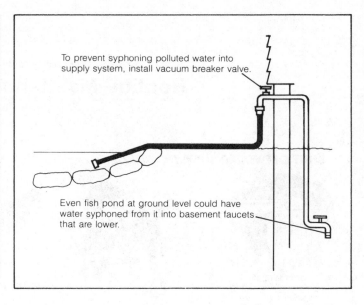

The Flush Tank Water Saver forms a dam at the bottom of the tank to retain most of the water that would otherwise be wasted, saving about 40% of the water used in flushing (drawing courtesy of Earth Care Co.).

Homemade Water Saver

If you are willing to put in a little effort, you can make your own water-saving device. We feel that the safest of the homemade water-saving methods is the plastic-bottle dam; you can create one from a one-gallon plastic bottle.

Cut the neck of the bottle off and put a few stones into the bottle to act as a weight. Then very carefully sink the bottle, being sure that it does not get in the way of the flushing mechanism. Test this arrangement; if the toilet functions well using the one bottle, then consider sinking a second bottle to cut down even further. Flush and check to see how the second bottle affects the toilet system. If it results in an unsatisfactory flush, cut off ½ inch from the top of the bottle. Repeat, and continue to reduce the bottle size until you achieve an acceptable flush.

After installing any device, check that the water in the bowl returns to its normal level. You can test this by using a grease pencil to mark the original level before adding the plastic bottles (or other device).

One result of lowered toilet water usage may be that the toilet does not completely replace the contaminated water. You can check this by adding about one ounce of toilet cleaner to the water. This will dye the water a very noticeable blue. Flush; if the water in the bowl has been completely replaced, the water will be clear or just slightly blue. If there is still a strong blue tinge, you will need to increase the amount of water flushed in by removing or adjusting the water-saving device.

CROSS-CONNECTIONS

Almost every home has some cross-connections in the plumbing system that usually are temporary, as the case shown where a garden hose was used to fill a fish pond, but was not removed when the task was completed. A drop in the water pressure could cause polluted water from the fish pond to be drawn into the water supply line, especially through basement faucets that are below the pond.

Such cross-connections should be avoided, of course, but in some cases this will require the replacement of fixtures. If a sink, basin or bathtub has faucets that could be submerged

when the fixture filled with water in an overflow condition— for example, when the drain plugged—you will have a cross-connection. The polluted water in the fixture could be syphoned into the supply system through one or both faucets.

A cross-connection also would be created if someone used a spray attachment on a hose in a tub or basin, and then left the attachment connected to the faucet(s) with the spray head under water in the fixture. Elsewhere, someone might taste shampoo in the drinking water.

Some older toilets have flush tanks that have a cross-connection. Lift the lid and check to see if the supply valve is below the water when the tank is filled. If the valve does not stay above the waterline in the tank, replace it with a vacuum-breaker inlet from the supply line. Or bend the float rod so the tank does not fill above the inlet valve. In most cases, the tank still will hold enough water for a proper flushing action, and there will be a saving of several gallons a day.

MAKE IT EASIER ON YOURSELF

Here is an aid when making repairs in water supply lines: when installing a stop valve in the basement or at a low point in the system, install one that has a drain in it. This is a small metal plug in the side of the valve that you remove with a screwdriver. This assures a complete draining of the system beyond the valve.

8   Leaks and Other Pipe Repairs

Pipe leaks always seem to occur at night, or on weekends when hardware stores are closed. This means that in most cases the repairs will be of the emergency type, and that later on a permanent repair must be made. This followup is important because too often once an emergency repair seems to be holding and the problem is forgotten until the same leak starts up again, or expands from the original point in the water pipe.

LIKELY LOCATIONS
Drain lines are also susceptible to leaks, as well as pipes under kitchen sinks and bathroom basins. The various items stored in the cabinets under sinks and basins can become soaked with polluted water before you recognize and correct the situation.

Rust and corrosion in steel pipes and copper tubing are the main culprits in problems with these kinds of supply lines. If there is a mixture of steel pipe and copper tubing, you can count on leaks sometime during the life of the house due to galvanic action.

At Packing Nut
One area where a water supply line is likely to develop a leak is around the packing nut on the valve. This happens nearly every time that a valve is shut off, then turned on again. Shutoff valves are used very infrequently, so that just turning the stem disturbs the packing. When the water is turned back on again and pressure is released from under the valve seat and bears against the packing, the leak occurs. The "repair" here is to simply snug up on the packing nut. Turn it to the right (clockwise) a fraction of a turn until the leak stops. Do not overdo it; you want to tighten the nut only enough to compress the packing around the valve stem so the leak will stop.

Saddle valves, as used to supply water to ice makers in freezers and to furnace humidifiers, will exhibit this same tendency to leak when shut off and then turned on again. The packing nuts on these valves are quite small—as is the valve—so even less of a turn is required on the packing nut to stop the leak.

Two-part epoxy materials can be used to stop small leaks in water supply lines, including those around a threaded joint in a steel pipe. The line must be drained, the area cleaned of grease and dirt and wire-brushed to remove rust when necessary. Read instructions to find out how long the epoxy must set up before water can be turned on again (photo courtesy Borden Chemical).

Valves often will leak at the packing nut when turned off and then on again. Small valves such as the saddle type used to supply water to ice makers and humidifiers have small packing nuts, and should be tightened very gently until the leak stops.

Plastic valves do not leak as readily around the packing nut when turned on and off, probably because the slick surface of the plastic slides more easily inside the packing material. These valves may show some leakage, however, which can be stopped in the same manner—by gently tightening the packing nut.

The valve shown has a built-in drain plug. If you install this type of shutoff valve in a low part of the plumbing system, you can eliminate the need to open a connection when draining the line (photo courtesy of Genova).

Leaks In Steel Pipe

One common repair of steel pipe is replacement of a section that has rusted or corroded and has begun to leak. First, locate the leaking section. Water can run a considerable distance down a pipe before it drips off. Run your hand along the pipe in either direction from where the water is dropping and you will be able to pinpoint the direction from which the water is coming.

Next, as with any kind of repair on any kind of pipe, shut off the water supply. Cut out the damaged section several inches away from the leak to assure that you leave only good pipe. Use a hacksaw or a pipe cutter. The latter is easier to use and makes a clean cut that is exactly at right angles to the length of the pipe.

Look at the end of the piece of pipe still in place. If it looks rusted or corroded inside, or is plugged with "lime", remove it and replace the complete length. If the remaining pipe does look good, it still must be unscrewed from its fitting in order to be threaded. If you are replacing only the cut-out section, measure. Subtract the length that will be taken up by the unions. The

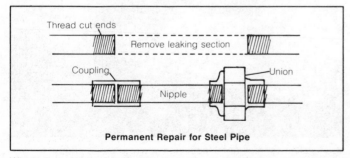

Permanent Repair for Steel Pipe

Where there is a leak in a steel pipe, a section will have to be removed and the cut ends threaded. Then a union, nipple and coupling are installed (described in Chapter 2).

result is the length you need. It is better for the pipe/union assembly to be just a fraction too long than too short.

If replacing the complete length of pipe, the damaged piece of pipe plus the length of the good pipe will tell you how long the replacement piece must be.

If the leak is at a fitting, it might be that turning the pipe a partial turn to tighten it in the fitting will stop the leak. Use two wrenches to tighten the pipe in the fitting. Apply pipe-joint compound or wrap with Teflon tape.

EMERGENCY MEASURES

If the leak in a pipe seems to be just a small hole, you can make an emergency patch in one of the several ways. First, if you have some sheet rubber such as a piece of tire inner tube, wrap it around the pipe, then tape it in place with rubber or plastic tape. Or, if the leak is more than just a pinhole, wrap the rubber around the pipe, then make a clamp from a piece of metal. This can be a piece cut from a food tin. Shape it like the drawing, then drill holes in the flanges and use nuts and bolts to hold it around the rubber.

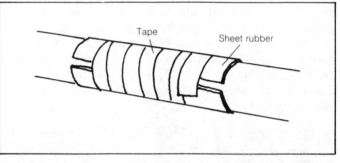

One kind of temporary repair for water pipe is with piece of sheet rubber such as inner tube, wrapped around pipe and held with plastic or rubber tape. This is good for small leaks only.

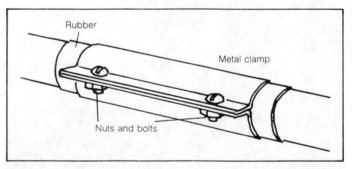

Sheet metal clamp around sheet of rubber works a little bit better than taped rubber. You can make the clamp with metal cut from food tin, plus a couple of nuts and bolts or buy a pipe clamp.

If you do not have time to make the sheet metal clamp, try using an ordinary C-clamp over the rubber, directly on the hole. This can be tricky, since you are trying to hold something onto a curved surface with the flat pads of the clamp. Do not put too much trust in this arrangement. Use it for the short term—to get the dishes washed, or clothes, or to finish the family's baths or showers—then shut off the water until the next day when you can make a permanent repair.

An even less permanent method of making an emergency repair to a leak is an arrangement of sheet rubber with sheet metal on top; a wooden wedge holds this "sandwich" together. The wedge is held to the pipe with a piece of coathanger wire.

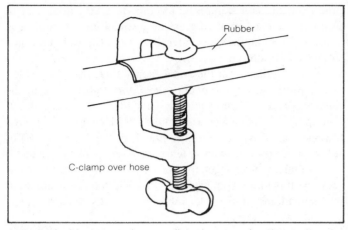

A piece of rubber, or garden or radiator hose can be clamped to pipe with C-clamp. Position pad of the clamp directly over the hole.

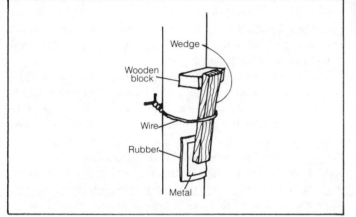

A not-too-effective patch for a leaking pipe—but better than nothing—is a piece of rubber and sheet metal forced against the hole with wired-on wooden wedge.

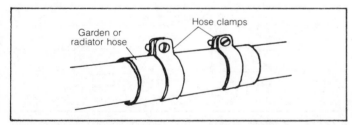

A length of garden hose held with a couple of clamps made from sheet metal and screws (or hose clamps) can create a temporary repair for a small leak in a water pipe.

Again, use the patch just to finish water-related tasks, then shut off the water until you can make a permanent repair.

If a section of pipe several inches long is leaking and obviously is rusted or corroded through, you can cut out the section (with water off first) and slip on a piece of scrap garden hose. Hold the ends on the pipe with hose clamps. This presupposes that you have hose clamps—it's not a bad idea to have a few on hand. There is also a "universal" clamp that can be adjusted to fit from 2 or 3 inches in diameter down to less than an inch. You need such clamps for a number of projects, often including repairing or replacing water hoses in your car, so buy a couple and hang them on a nail in the garage or on the wall of your workshop.

Here is another repair, slightly more permanent, that can be made to a trap using hose and clamps. Take your damaged trap

A screw plug with a rubber gasket is a good temporary repair for large pipes with holes in them. You may have to enlarge the hole slightly so the screw plug will fit in.

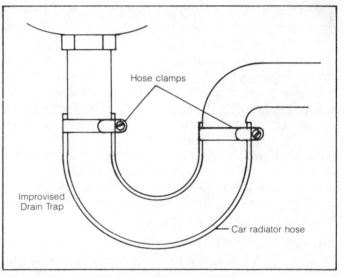

In a situation where the permanent replacement of a trap under a sink or basin must be held up for some time, a U-shape mold auto radiator hose can substitute for the trap.

and match it as closely as possible with a piece of U-shape radiator hose. Also purchase a couple of hose clamps. Clamp the hose to the drain in place of the trap. The repair may last many years, although we do not recommend leaving it for very long as it would certainly not meet plumbing code requirements.

Leaks at Joints

If you note a leak in copper tubing at a fitting, it might be that the joint was subject to vibration, possibly from an automatic clothes washer—or water hammer may have battered the joint often enough to break the solder.

Shut off the water and drain the line. Open the nearest connection, a union or a valve. Remove the valve stem by unscrewing the packing nut and turning out the stem so the washer—if there is one—will not be damaged by the heat. The line must be dry and free of water before the solder will melt and fresh solder can be applied to be pulled into the joint by capillary action. Never try to solder a joint without an opening nearby where the water can drain. This way if the water turns to steam, the pressure can be dissipated. If you heat a solder joint with no place for the steam pressure to escape, you are likely to get a splash of hot solder blasted out by the steam pressure.

Treat the joint as you would a new joint, heating both the copper tubing and fitting until the solder will melt when it contacts the surface of the tubing. (This is covered in Chapter 3 "Working with Copper Pipe.")

If the joint shows signs of having leaked for some time, you should heat the joint until the solder is molten and then pull the joint apart. There will be a streak of dirt and corrosion in the solder, and you will have to heat the tubing and wipe off the solder all the way around. It may be necessary to apply flux to the dirty spot. Then heat it and apply solder. Wipe it off immediately so a clean, shiny "tinned" surface is left. Do the same with the inside of the fitting.

If you find that the tinned surfaces of the inside of the fitting and the outside of the copper tubing will not slide together because of the added thickness of tinning solder, then heat both the fitting and tubing until the solder is molten (wear gloves for this operation). Slide the tubing into the fitting, being careful not to burn yourself with the excess solder that will be forced out of the joint. Keep the heat on the joint as you slide it together. After the tubing has bottomed in the fitting, apply more solder to create a fillet all around the edge of the fitting.

Let the solder cool, then retighten the nearby joint, or reassemble the valve. Turn on the water. Check the joint for any leakage. If you have been thorough, there should be no leak.

As described in Chapter 3, you will need an ordinary propane torch and wire solder, plus flux, to remake the solder joint. Or, after heating and wiping the old solder off the pipe and from inside the fitting, you can apply the flux/solder mixture as described in Chapter 3.

DRAINS

When you get into repairing drains, you will be concerned with two types: (1) the 1¼ or 1½ inch drains under basins and sinks; (2) the larger cast iron, copper or plastic main drains and vents that will be 3 or 4 inches in diameter.

Smaller Lines

If you find a leak in the smaller drain lines under the sink or basin, check the gaskets under the slip nuts. This will require only unscrewing the nuts and sliding the pieces of drain line apart. If the rubber gaskets (or plastic rings) are obviously shriveled and distorted with age, and damaged due to varying hot and cold water temperatures, then replacing the gasket(s) might stop the leak. While you have the drain apart, examine the inside (after flushing with hot water to remove any residue) to see if there are places where the pipe has corroded through, or is about to. Do not take chances. If there is a possible leak, replace the drain. There really are no long-term repairs, just replacements, for the thin chrome-plated brass pipe used from drains under sinks or basins.

Emergency Repair

You can make an emergency repair to a hole by soldering the pipe—but the hole cannot be too big. It is also necessary to grind off the chrome plating, because solder will not adhere to chrome. This requires a grinder, because a file will not touch the very hard chrome.

After grinding, heat the metal, apply flux, then the solder. Use a propane torch and play the flame lightly around the repair spot. You want to puddle the solder and build it up. If you apply too much heat, the molten solder will fall through the opening. It will take a little practice, and perhaps a lot of solder, but you can make a temporary repair in this manner. The minute you can get to the hardware store, buy a new section of the drain and install it. Once a leak has developed, it will spread and your solder job will last only a short time.

Larger Lines

You will probably never see a leak in the pipe of the main drains or vents, since these generally last the life of the house. You will, however, find leaks in the joints. If the pipe is cast iron, you might be able to stop the leak by using calking irons and resetting the lead in the joint. This is described in Chapter 4, "Working with Cast Iron Pipe".

Should the drain or vent be copper pipe, the same situation as occurs with copper supply pipe (discussed above) would be applicable. You will have to heat the joint to make the solder molten, then add flux and solder. Because the joints in most main drains and vents are horizontal, you might be able to "cook" out the foreign material in the solder that is causing the leak. It is best, of course, to melt the solder and disassemble the joint to clean it. This is difficult with a large drain line, and there are no unions to make it easy to remove a section.

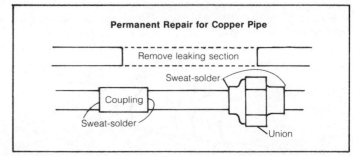

A permanent repair for a leaking section of copper tubing requires cutting out the section and replacing it with a sweat-soldered coupling and a union. (This is described in Chapter 3, "Working with Copper Pipe.")

Where a copper drain line does spring a leak in the pipe itself, you can, in some cases, repair it by soldering. It would be best, however, to replace the section. Cut the leaking length out and install a fresh piece. You can use a straight coupling that will slide up on one pipe, then slide down over the joint so it can be soldered. For an even quicker repair, use neoprene rubber sleeves with stainless steel clamps. While basically made to join plastic drain and vent lines, the sleeves can be used to repair copper tubing and to join plastic and cast iron.

"Plastic Lead"

When plastic pipe first was introduced from drains and vents, adapters were first glued on to the plastic, then the adapter was sealed to the cast iron pipe that ran from the basement to the street using "lead wool". This material looked much like coarse steel wool, but was made of lead. It was packed around the joint between the cast iron pipe and the plastic adapter, then was compacted with calking irons in the same way as poured lead.

For modern applications, however, a "Plastic Lead" material is used. This material also can be used to seal leaks that occur in the joints of cast iron drain line, and in the joints between cast iron and plastic lines. It is applied and smoothed much like putty. When it has set the required amount of time (as per instructions on the container) the drain can be used.

To repair a leaking joint in main drain or vent, "Plastic Lead" can be used instead of poured lead or lead wool. It can be handled like putty, and makes a neat repair of a leaking joint in cast iron, copper or plastic lines (photo courtesy Genova).

Leak at Drains and Drain Connections

The leak is usually caused by worn parts. From underneath the sink, remove the trap, using pipe wrenches or channel lock pliers. Have a bucket handy to catch the water from the bottom of the trap.

Remove the nut that holds the drain assembly in the sink basin. The nut looks something like the connecting nuts on the trap and trap tailpiece. Above this holding nut you will find a metal flange that has small slots around its edge. You will have to position the tip of the screwdriver into these little slots and tap the screwdriver with the rubber hammer to loosen the flange. (*Note:* Older sinks may have a large nut, not a flange, holding the drain assembly. Use a pipe wrench to remove this nut.)

Under the flange may be a metal or rubber washer which would be sandwiched between the flange nut and the bottom of the sink. Inspect this washer for wear and damage and replace the washer if necessary. The washer provides a watertight seal between the metal parts.

You now can remove the drain assembly in the bottom of the sink. Lift out the assembly and clean it and the area around the opening in the bottom of the sink. Use a putty knife and steel wool for this job.

Spread a thin layer of plumber's putty around the hole in the sink and around the bottom of the drain assembly. Now reseat the drain assembly in the putty in the sink. Then reconnect the drain: first flange nut, then the holding nut, then the trap. Let the plumber's putty set for about five days. You now can

remove any excess putty around the drain in the sink with a putty knife and/or steel wool.

HOT WATER TANK LEAK

Any repair you make to a leak in a hot water tank should be considered only temporary, and the tank should be replaced at the first opportunity. If there is one leak in a hot water tank, you shortly will have more. (See Chapter 10 on installing a hot water tank.)

You will discover a leak in a hot water tank by noting water running onto the floor from somewhere in the bottom of the tank. Determine as closely as you can where the leak is, then use tin snips to cut a hole in the sheet metal shell at that point. You will probably have to enlarge the hole—maybe cut two or more holes. Remove the insulation to find the leak. You can make up a "stopper" for the leak by using a toggle bolt, rubber washer and metal washer as indicated. Some hardware stores will carry devices made to plug leaks in tanks, and will be similar to your homemade patching device.

It may be necessary to enlarge the hole in the tank to insert the toggle bolt. If this is necessary, first drain the tank through the valve that is located near the bottom. First shut off the supply line to the tank, of course. You need not drain the tank completely, just lower the water level to below the leak. This will be apparent when water stops running out of the hole. You don't want to waste any more water than you have to.

If the tank is electric, shut off the current by pulling the circuit breaker or fuses. If it is gas or oil, shut off the fuel supply. By the way, if it is apparent that the leak is inside the flue of a gas or oil-fueled hot water tank, and the flame has been doused by the water, you will have to do with cold water until you can replace the tank. There simply is no way to reach down inside the small-diameter flue to make a repair.

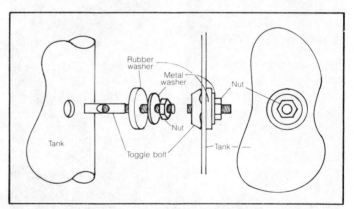

A leak in hot water tank can be temporarily fixed with toggle bolt, flat washer and rubber washer. In a real emergency you can cut the washer from a piece of inner tube, but a large faucet washer is better. Devices for stopping tank leaks are sold in some hardware stores.

LEAKS INSIDE WALLS

A really desperate situation is when you find a leak inside a wall. This will occur mostly in older homes with steel pipe. If you want to tear out the wall in one or two floors, you can replace the damaged pipe. A much more practical repair is to just shut off—and cut off—the pipe and replace (reroute) it with flexible plastic or flexible copper tubing. If it's a short run, say from the basement to the first floor, flexible copper can be threaded up through the wall. If the line is between

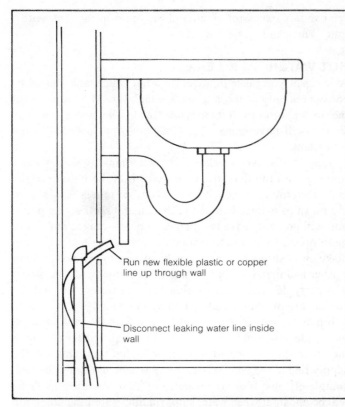

Run new flexible plastic or copper line up through wall

Disconnect leaking water line inside wall

A leaking pipe inside wall is most easily repaired by replacing it with flexible copper or plastic pipe that bypasses it completely.

Wherever vent lines pass through the roof, a flashing is required to seal around it. If this leaks it sometimes can be repaired by brushing on a couple of coats of roofing cement. If the steel or copper flashing has deteriorated too much, it should be replaced. A two-piece plastic unit is easily installed, and will last the life of the house (photo courtesy of Genova).

floors, you will have better luck with flexible plastic. For the latter you can drop a weighted cord down through the wall to which you tie the end of the plastic pipe so it can be pulled up through the wall.

Whether copper tubing or plastic pipe is used, there are adapters to connect it to steel or copper pipe or tubing.

FLASHING (ROOF) LEAKS

One water leak related to plumbing that you will run into sooner or later is a rain leak around the flashing of a vent that passes through the roof. If the galvanized steel or copper flashing has deteriorated it is best to replace it with a plastic unit that comes in two parts. The first part is fitted under the shingles and is nailed to the roof. The second part is a cone-shape piece that slides down over the pipe and snaps onto the first part.

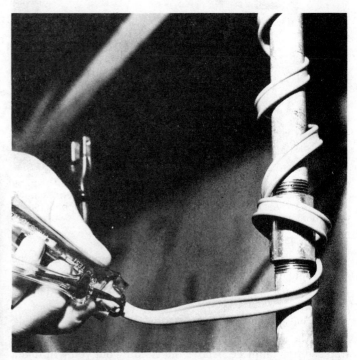

Electric heating tape is the best way to thaw a frozen pipe. It also is the best way to keep pipes from freezing in the first place. Some tapes come with automatic thermostats.

HOW TO THAW FROZEN PIPES

The first step is to determine why the pipe froze. You may have to properly insulate the pipe (described later) or, if the pipe runs through an unheated space or terminates outdoors turn off the water.

If the pipe is exposed, you can try any of these methods:
(1) Wrap the pipe with electric heating tape. Spiral the tape loosely around the pipe and then plug into an electrical outlet. Open the faucet for drainage so the heat will not create steam and break the pipe.
(2) Thaw the pipe with a heat lamp. Be sure to keep a faucet open.
(3) Soak cloth strips with hot water; wrap the cloth strips around the pipe until the pipe is thawed.
(4) Heat the pipe with a propane torch, but be very careful with the fire. Open a faucet and work from the faucet up the pipe to the frozen section.

If the pipe is behind a wall, ceiling, or under a floor, here are some other alternatives.

(1) Try a heat lamp. The heat will penetrate the wall, ceiling or floor covering and thaw the pipe. This is a very slow technique, so be patient. Don't get the heat lamp too close to the covering or the lamp will scorch it.

(2) Open the faucets and let the pipes thaw through normal hot-water heat flow.

If a pipe breaks due to freezing, immediately shut off the water to this water line and replace the pipe when conditions permit. Do not "leave" the pipe as is, since the breaks in the pipe may cause water damage.

HOW TO INSULATE PIPES

Insulation not only prevents pipe freezes, but cuts heat loss in pipes and condensation dripping from cold-water lines.

There are several different types of insulation products sold, both of traditional and updated materials. Most of the traditional types spiral around the pipes and wrap around the fittings such as tees and elbows. Modern materials snap on, although they may not provide as much protection.

Overlap the wrap about ½ inch and pull it fairly tight as you spiral it around the pipe. You probably will have to work in short runs—4 feet or so—since the wrap can become unwieldy in long lengths.

Cut the insulation with scissors or a razor knife. If the insulation is fiberglass, you should wear gloves to protect your hands.

If commercial insulation is not readily available, you can insulate pipes with several layers of newspaper. Tape the newspaper to the pipes, or tie it firmly with a string. This is a stop-gap measure only and can be a fire hazard. Replace the newspapers with insulation as soon as possible.

If no insulation is available and a freeze is expected, leave the faucet open so water trickles out of the spout. This will help prevent freezing. It is not guaranteed, however, so use insulation whenever possible.

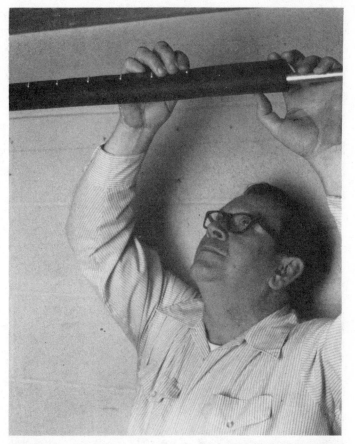

With this Armstrong pipe insulation, the flanged insulation is snapped over the pipe and held in place with clamps.

This insulation can be used on both hot and cold water pipes, and is particularly easy to apply and to remove (photo courtesy of Frelen).

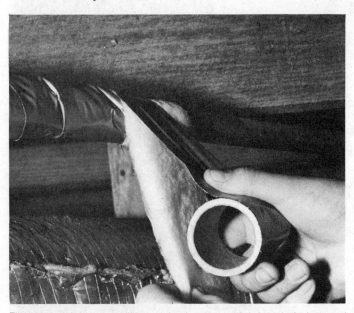

Fiberglass pipe wrap utilizes a plastic tape, which is spiraled around the fiberglass to hold it in position. The plastic then is held on with regular duct tape.

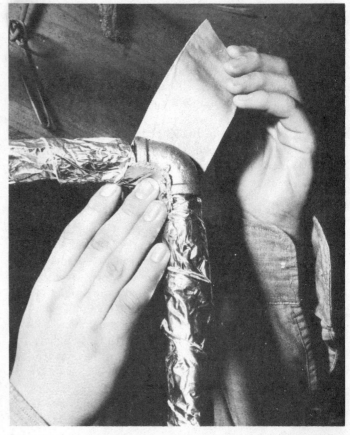

These Foamedge pipe covers have a vinyl skin. The covers are placed over the pipes and then taped down (photo courtesy of Goodyear).

Some pipe wrap has a sticky backing that adheres directly to the pipe. The pipe must be clean and dry. All pipe wrap must be continuous—no gaps—for it to work efficiently.

Although expensive, aluminum faced pipe and duct wrap with an adhesive backing stays where it is put and offers a great amount of insulation. It conforms to most shapes.

9 Replacing and Repairing Fixtures

FAUCET BASICS

Any room in the house that has plumbing and associated fixtures—kitchen, bathroom, laundry room or bar—has faucets. These are devices that require more consistent maintenance and repair than any other plumbing item.

No matter what type, faucets are designed to do just one thing: control the flow of water. Mixing faucets, including a number of the newer one-control types, regulate a mixture of hot and cold water to create the desired temperature.

All faucets have a valve (or valves) of some kind, plus other moving parts that must be sealed to prevent water leaking. Except for cleaning out mineral deposits (usually referred to as "lime") and cleaning out foreign matter, the major part of faucet maintenance is replacement of seals and valve components that have become worn or lost their resiliency.

Typical faucet problems are pinpointed in the "Diagnostic Chart," along with summaries of ways to correct them. The various photos and drawings show how a number of common faucets are assembled, and how you can take them apart for repairs.

There are four basic types of faucets: stem, disc, ball, and cartridge. Stem faucets are the most common. They also need more frequent repair because the washers wear out, and cause leaks. The other faucets, if they leak, simply require an exchange of the washer or cartridge.

Replacements

If you install new faucets in your home, by all means save the installation and maintenance sheets that come with them. Some of the newer types of faucets are quite complex, and the instruction sheets are absolutely necessary if you intend to do your own maintenance and repairs.

These instruction sheets usually have "pull-apart" drawings to show how they are assembled, plus information on obtaining special replacement parts. Sometimes the dealer from whom you purchased the faucets will have the information and special parts. Most well-stocked hardware stores with good plumbing departments will have O-rings, washers, spray hoses and even complete repair kits and replacement "cartridges."

If you have mislaid the instruction sheets, or never had them, take the defective parts to the hardware store and find a knowledgeable clerk to help you find the correct replacement parts. Even without the knowledgeable clerk (a rarity in this day and age) faucet parts are packaged in see-through containers that let you match the old part with a new one.

Even replacement faucet knobs can be purchased, should you have one that is broken or worn. You may, however, have to buy a pair of knobs for a two-knob fixture to get one that matches. It is not probable that you will find a knob to duplicate a knob you own if it is 30 or 40 years old. Even if you could, age changes the color and look of a knob, so that a new pair is the best answer.

A faucet that is damaged or badly worn may require replacement. Measure the center-to-center spacing on the old faucet to make sure the new one will fit. Older faucets may have a wider spacing between the holes than do modern faucets. There are faucets that have adjustable spacing on the supply pipes. Make sure the adjustment is such that it will fit the spacing of the holes in your sink or basin.

Components

Common faucets have a cast body with a removable stem that has coarse threads. There is a washer on one end of the stem and packing fits around the upper portion of the stem to prevent water leaking out around it. The latest types of washer faucets have O-rings that replace the packing around the stem.

One of the modern "metal-to-metal" faucets has a special alloy valve cartridge that is simply replaced when the faucet starts to leak. The cartridge cannot be repaired, it must be replaced as a unit. Another type of modern faucet has a neoprene diaphragm that seals across the seat and also the valve stem.

One-lever mixing faucets may have a lever, turn knob or T-handle that controls both the volume of water and the temperature. There are three general types: (1) a model that has either a ball that swivels in a cup-shape seat, or a cup-shape cap that swivels over a ball-shape seat—spring-loaded cup-like seals are utilized in both types to control water flow; (2) a cam system that is moved by a lever, which contacts the stems of

For panic-free maintenance of a number of faucets, it pays to make up a repair kit with parts that are required most often—as well as sealants, joint compound, valve-seat resurfacer, pipe wrenches and pliers. Keep original instruction sheets in the kit as well.

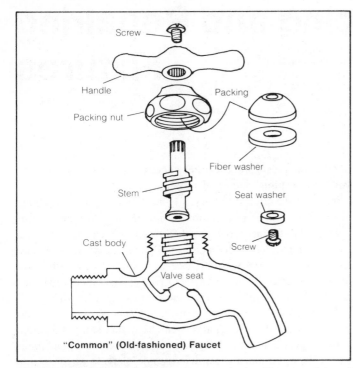

"Common" (Old-fashioned) Faucet

Screw
Handle
Packing nut
Packing
Fiber washer
Stem
Seat washer
Cast body
Screw
Valve seat

"Old-fashioned" (common) faucet has cast body with coarse internal threads into which threaded stem is screwed. Rubber washer at bottom of stem bears against the metal valve seat to shut off water. Packing at the upper end of faucet is squeezed around the stem to create a watertight seal.

The stem here is removed from a common faucet to show its configuration. The washer at right is fixed in place with screw; the one at left is snapped in place and held by friction.

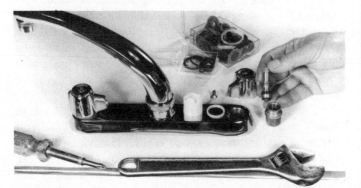

Newer types of faucets with washers may have some plastic parts; an O-ring is used instead of packing to seal the stem.

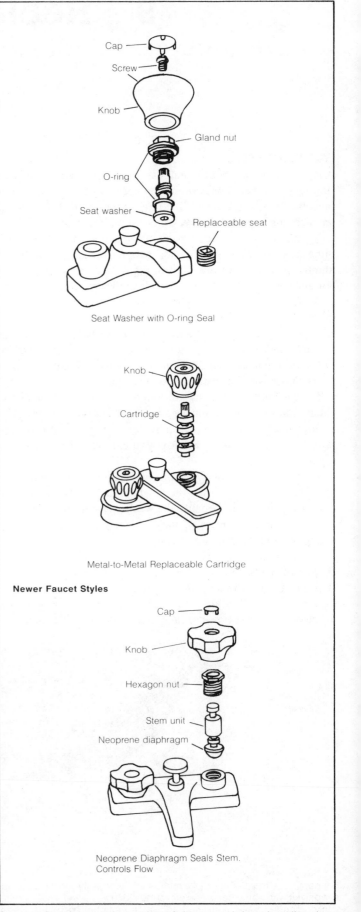

Cap
Screw
Knob
Gland nut
O-ring
Seat washer
Replaceable seat

Seat Washer with O-ring Seal

Knob
Cartridge

Metal-to-Metal Replaceable Cartridge

Newer Faucet Styles

Cap
Knob
Hexagon nut
Stem unit
Neoprene diaphragm

Neoprene Diaphragm Seals Stem.
Controls Flow

Common faucets come in a variety of shapes and sizes, but all work on the same principle of washer bearing against valve seat.

Worn or damaged valve seats that are not the replaceable type can be renewed with a tool that cuts a new face onto seats. The valve shown is cut away to show how tool is used.

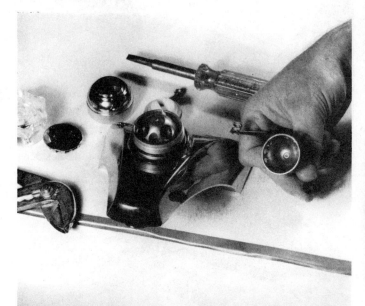

One kind of single-lever faucet has ball that swivels in cup-shape (or cap) seat. The seals are in a dome that is covered by cup, which is moved by the handle. The unit shown is from "Peerless."

Another style of single-handle kitchen faucet operates by having the cam moved by a lever, to contact spring-loaded valves. Valves can be replaced by unscrewing caps that cover them (sold by Sears, Roebuck).

spring-loaded valves; (3) a version with a spool that is sealed by an O-ring—the spool moves laterally and rotates to control the volume of water and the mixture of hot and cold. The usual repair for this faucet is replacement of the spool with its O-ring.

Kitchen faucets that have spray hoses will include a "diverter" valve, which is usually located under the swivel spout. The valve diverts water to the hose, rather than the spout. A slight flow of water from the swivel spout when the spray is being used is normal for most faucets.

If a swing spout leaks around the faucet body, it usually means the O-ring around the spout needs replacing. The O-rings are sold in the plumbing departments of hardware stores. Take along both the old O-ring and the spout; the O-ring may have stretched with age. The new one should fit snugly, yet project enough to create a watertight seal.

This faucet from "Speakman" has a spool (cartridge) that rotates and also moves laterally to control the flow and temperature of water. For quick repair, this faucet takes cartridge replacement.

DISASSEMBLING A FAUCET

Disassembly is similar for all faucets. You first remove the knob or handle. The bonnet, packing or gland nut is removed next. Then the stem is unscrewed to get at the valve seat. Some faucets have removable valve seats, with a square or hexagon opening at the center. An Allen wrench or special square wrench is inserted in the opening and the seat is unscrewed. This generally takes considerable effort, as the seat will be "frozen" in the threads due to corrosion.

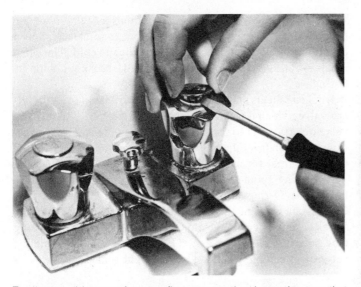

To disassemble most faucets, first remove the decorative cap that hides the screw of the faucet handle. Just pry the cap up and off the handle. Use a screwdriver or pick.

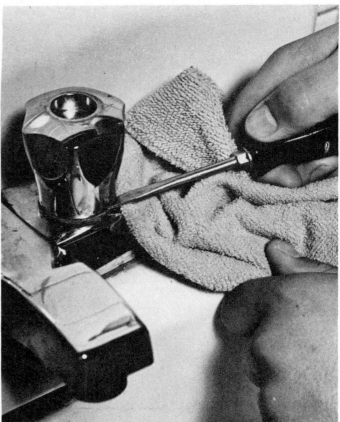

Pry off the faucet handle. Pad the chrome and china parts with an old towel, which also serves as a leverage "block." Some handles don't have screws; you just pry them off.

Remove the faucet handle, held by a standard or Phillips head screw. If the screw is stubborn, coat it with WD-40 penetrating oil. Let it set an hour; then remove it.

Use caution and pieces of rubber on tools (or tape) to prevent scratching chrome plating or damaging delicate parts when disassembling faucets. Remember to close the drain (which this homeowner forgot to do); a dropped part could disappear forever.

Use caution when disassembling faucets (and be sure the water is shut off first) because you will be removing highly polished parts and hidden screws, and some pieces are delicate. The screws that hold handles on faucets usually are hidden under friction-fit caps that can be pried off with a knife blade. Some faucets may have an Allen setscrew near the base of the handle. Before using force to disassemble a faucet, examine it to see if there is a hidden setscrew, or if there is any other reason the part will not come free easily. Avoid damaged to polished, chrome-plated fixtures by wrapping wrenches and pliers with rubber or plastic tape.

O-rings and rubber seals will leak if chafed by rough metal surfaces; always smooth metal surfaces with crocus cloth if the seals show abrasion.

REPAIRS FOR FAUCETS, AERATORS, DIVERTERS

Packing and sealants are handy to seal some faucet leaks. For example, if a new dome packing is not immediately available, a temporary repair can be made by wrapping packing around the stem. Pipe joint compound or sealant can be used on fittings that are removed or replaced to prevent leakage.

Preventive Care

A maintenance chore that is required as frequently as once a week during some periods of the year is the removal and cleaning of aerators on all types of faucets. If the aerator becomes too filled with mineral deposits (lime) it should be replaced. Galvanic action can cause shell of aerator to corrode, and it will leak and spray water sideways.

We will assume that for all these repairs you have already turned off the water, either at the main valve or with a shutoff valve.

Replacing Stem Washers

After turning off the water, remove the handle with a screwdriver—use a Phillips head or standard blade. The handle lifts straight up and off. You may need to encourage it by prying up lightly on the handle.

When the handle is off you will see a hex nut. This nut holds the stem assembly in place. Loosen and remove the nut, using an adjustable wrench or channel lock pliers. If you don't have channel locks, cover the jaws of regular pliers with adhesive bandages. This will protect the metal valve from the serrations of the regular pliers.

Now slip the handle back on the stem and turn the handle. You don't need to screw the handle in position; the handle will loosen the stem in its assembly. Then back out the stem—which is threaded—with your fingers, or with the pliers or adjustable wrench.

At the bottom of the stem is the washer. It is held in place with a screw. Remove the screw and remove the old washer. Be careful not to damage the thin-walled housing that some washers set in.

Fit a new washer on the stem and fasten it in place with the screw. If the screw is damaged, replace it. Most washer assortments contain extra screws in the package. If there is any corrosion on the stem, clean off the corrosion with fine steel wool. Just buff the metal; don't try to remove any.

Re-assemble the faucet—stem, cap, handle. Tighten the

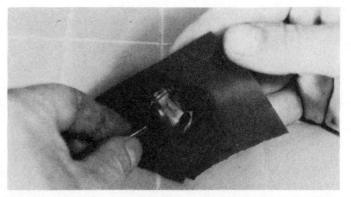

Movable parts (such as this ball from "Peerless" faucet) should be cleaned of mineral deposits and polished with fine crocus cloth. (Crocus cloth is a very fine emery cloth, so fine it appears to have no abrasive coating.)

Remove the packing or cap nut. Then loosen the stem of the faucet, shown, with a wrench. Or place the handle back on the stem, without the screw, and loosen it.

Remove the stem, using your fingers. The stem is threaded, with a packing washer at the top and the faucet washer at the bottom of the stem.

Replace the worn washer at the bottom of the stem. It is held by a brass screw. Since washer assortments are usually packaged with screws, replace the old screw as well.

Clean off any corrosion on the stem by buffing the stem with steel wool. Then wash the part under running water. If the stem is damaged, you will have to replace it.

assembly carefully, using the wrench or pliers; too much pressure can strip the threads and cause the faucet to start leaking again.

Replacing Cap Washers

With a screwdriver, remove the faucet handle, exposing the cap that holds the faucet stem in place. Remove this cap. Under the cap, you will find a flat washer or the remains of a stringlike material.

The string is packing and serves as a washer between the stem and the cap. With the screwdriver, pry out the washer or packing, replace it with new, and re-assemble the faucet. The string is wound around the stem so it forms a seal between the stem and the cap.

Replacing O-Rings

O-ring washers look like tiny rings of rubberlike material. They can be found almost anywhere in a faucet assembly: on the stem, around the cap nut, under the handle, where two different parts are screwed together.

The first step is to remove the handle from the faucet with a screwdriver, then the cap nut with an adjustable wrench or channel lock pliers. Twist or pull out the stem of the faucet to expose the entire assembly.

To replace the washer, remove the old one and slip on the new one, making sure it is properly seated. Re-assemble the faucet.

Regrinding Valve Seats

When a washer becomes worn, you probably try to turn the handle of the faucet tighter to shut off the water. This causes the stem of the faucet to grind into the washer seat at the bottom of the stem. Sometimes a new washer will seal the resulting damage. If not, you will have to regrind the valve seat so the washer seats properly when the faucet handle is closed.

Remove the faucet handle, cap nut, and stem assembly (see "Replacing Washers," this chapter).

Insert the grinding tool into the faucet housing and adjust the guide nut (it moves up and down) of the grinding tool to match the depth of the opening of the faucet housing. This aligns the grinding tool in the faucet housing and provides a turning base.

Now turn the grinding tool with its handle or pliers. Be careful; the metal is soft. You don't need much grinding to smooth the seat in the faucet.

String packing is wrapped around the stem of the faucet just below the packing nut. Or the faucet may have a rubber washer or gasket in place of the string packing.

Insert the faucet seat dressing tool into the faucet housing and turn the handle to smooth the washer seat. Assorted size tools are available.

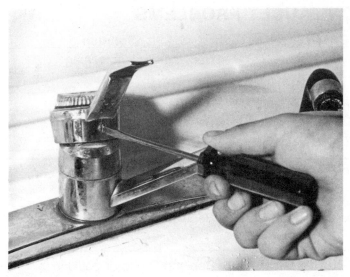

To remove the handle of a tipping valve or handle faucet, back out a set screw under the handle. You may have to remove the decorative cap to expose another holding screw.

Repairing Tipping Valve Faucets

Remove the handle, the faucet spout, and the metal escutcheon covering. This will expose the diverter assembly, bottom cage of the faucet, and the valve stem assembly.

You will see a plug at one side of this assembly. Remove this plug with the screwdriver. Inside will be a gasket and a water strainer. If these parts are clogged with sediment or damaged either clean or replace them.

Leaking can be caused by a worn O-ring that fits between the faucet spout and the diverter assembly. Replace the O-ring with a new one. Also replace any worn gaskets or O-rings in the cam valve assembly. The handle attaches to this unit. If the unit goes bad, which is unlikely, you may be able to buy a replacement. Take the old unit to the store for matching purposes.

Repairing Disc Faucets

Some disc faucets have O-ring seals at the top of the stem; others don't. Remove the handle and the escutcheon covering, which will expose the faucet assembly. The assembly is held together with two screws. Remove these. Below will be the O-ring (if there is one), a top disc, a bottom disc, and inlet and outlet seals.

O-rings and the inlet and outlet seals do need maintenance, and sometimes replacement. Clean the assembly, make any replacements necessary, and re-assemble the faucet. If the discs are worn, you may be able to replace them. Take the worn parts to the store to match them. If not, you will have to install a new faucet.

Repairing Cartridge Faucets

Remove the screw on top of the faucet assembly. This screw may be hidden by a decorative cap; pry it up and off. Push the tip of the screwdriver in the screw hole and press down on the screwdriver. At the same time, lift off the faucet handle and housing or sleeve. The screwdriver holds the cartridge in position while you lift off the handle and housing (sleeve).

If the faucet is dripping, the problem may be the faucet lever. Check that it is properly seated under the lip of the

Unscrew the faucet cap and pull out the handle assembly parts, which are usually manufactured from plastic. If these parts appear worn or broken, replace them.

Gaskets and seals are positioned in a waferlike part at the bottom of the faucet. If worn or damaged, replace these seals and then re-assemble the faucet.

DIAGNOSTIC CHART FOR FAUCET PROBLEMS

Problem	Likely Cause	Solution
Restricted water flow	Aerator or faucet filter screen plugged	Replace or clean screen
Stopper permits water to drain when closed	Drain or valve damaged Lifter misadjusted Pop-up valve dirty	Smooth out or replace Re-adjust to fully close Clean
Leak at spout	Washer has become hard, damaged or worn	Replace washer or seal
Leak at swivel spout	O-ring has become damaged, hard or worn	Replace O-ring
Leak at lever or knob	O-ring or stem packing has become damaged, hard or worn	Replace O-ring or packing
Stopper lever leak	Loose lever nut Defective packing Damaged or worn pivot ball	Tighten nut Replace packing Replace packing and ball
Loose faucet	Loose shank nut Damaged metal or rubber shank washer	Tighten nut Replace washer
Dripping spray hose	Hose head valve does not close; debris clog	Clean or replace head
Leak in supply line	Damaged slip-joint washer Loose nut	Replace washer Tighten nut
Hose flow cut severely	Aerator or nozzle plugged Hose kinked or blocked Defective diverter valve	Clean or replace Replace unit or hose Clean or replace
Misaligned twin-faucet knobs	Seals or seat worn Incorrect assembly	Close faucet, remove knobs, align or replace parts.

sleeve, so it fully engages the stem of the faucet and the handle that turns off the water. If you suspect this is the trouble, reseat the handle or lever, reassemble the faucet, and test it. (Not the problem? Read on.)

To remove the cartridge, pull out a little metal clip that holds the cartridge in the faucet stem. You may be able to slip the tip of the screwdriver into the slot in the clip. Pry out the clip, but keep it square to the assembly. If the screwdriver doesn't work, use pliers. You now can lift out—and replace—the cartridge.

Take the old cartridge to the store so you can match it with a replacement cartridge; not all are alike.

Repairing Rotating Ball Faucets

Turn the knurled cap assembly with your fingers, or pliers padded with adhesive bandages. With the cap assembly removed, you will see a valve seat in the center of the faucet housing.

Remove the valve seat to expose a spring and, probably, two rubber valve seats at the bottom of the faucet housing. Replace these parts; take the old parts to the store with you for matching purposes.

Re-assemble the faucet. When you get to the ball and cap assembly, check the ball for any corrosion. You may be able to remove the corrosion with steel wool. If not, replace the ball. The ball fits into the housing with a tiny metal pin that projects from the ball. This pin must be aligned with the slot in the housing.

The cam assembly, which fits over the ball, also has a metal pin that fits a slot in the faucet housing. Be sure this pin is aligned and seated.

At this point, set the adjusting ring with the tip of a screwdriver. Just move it clockwise. Turn on the water and check for leaks. If water comes up through the stem, try turning the adjusting ring just a little tighter.

If the leak persists, turn off the water and replace the rubber-like parts in the cam assembly. To complete the job, re-install the handle, which is held to the cam assembly with a set screw that is usually under the handle.

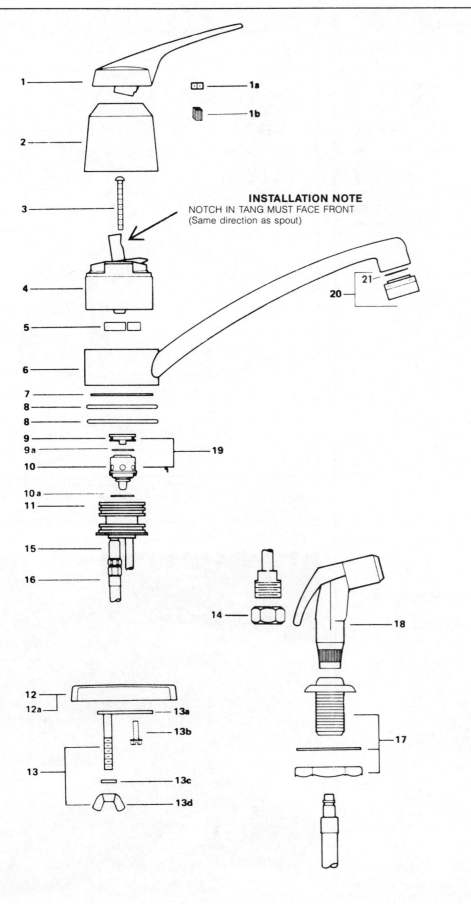

INSTALLATION NOTE
NOTCH IN TANG MUST FACE FRONT
(Same direction as spout)

NO.	PART
1	Handle
1a	Set Screw
1b	Insert
2	Escutcheon Cap
3	Cartridge Screw
4	+ ceramic Cartridge
	(Includes Key 5)
5	Cartridge Seal Set
6	Spout
7	Slip Ring
8	Spout O-Ring
9	Diverter Retainer (See 19)
9a	O-Ring (See 19)
10	Diverter (See 19)
10a	O-Ring (See 19)
11	Manifold S/A
12	Escutcheon
12a	Escutcheon
13	Mounting Bracket Kit
13a	Mounting Bracket
13b	Manifold Screw
13c	Retaining Bracket
13d	Wing Nut
14	Coupling Nut
15	Hose Connection
16	Hose Assembly
17	Spray Escutcheon Assembly
18	Spray Head Assembly
	(Includes Key 16)
19	Diverter & Retainer Set
20	Aerator (Includes Item 21)
21	Flow Restrictor

This American Standard faucet comes with a water saving device, and requires replacement of the complete cartridge for repair.

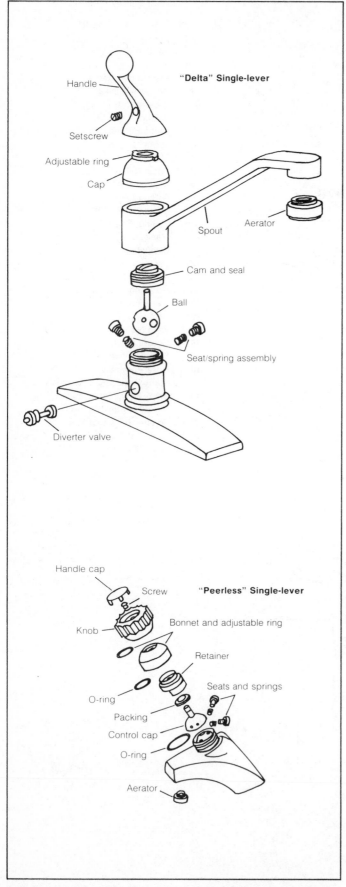

"Delta" Single-lever

Handle

Setscrew

Adjustable ring

Cap

Spout

Aerator

Cam and seal

Ball

Seat/spring assembly

Diverter valve

"Peerless" Single-lever

Handle cap

Screw

Knob

Bonnet and adjustable ring

Retainer

O-ring

Seats and springs

Packing

Control cap

O-ring

Aerator

A "ball-and-cap" type faucet can be operated by the lever, as shown in top kitchen faucet; or the handle can be rotated and rocked to control flow and mix of hot and cold as shown in lower faucet that is fitted on vanity basin.

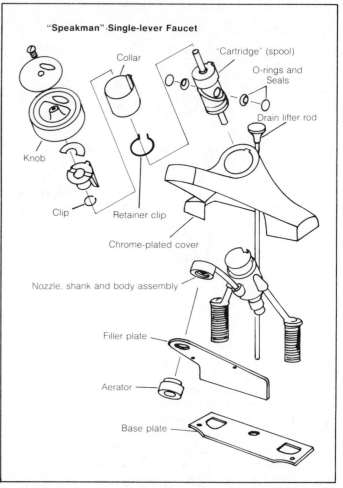

"Speakman" Single-lever Faucet

Collar

"Cartridge" (spool)

O-rings and Seals

Knob

Drain lifter rod

Clip

Retainer clip

Chrome-plated cover

Nozzle. shank and body assembly

Filler plate

Aerator

Base plate

Cartridge is replaced for repair of this one-lever faucet. The lock ring is removed to allow lifting cup-shape retainer that holds cartridge. This "pull-apart" drawing shows the relationship of the various components of the cartridge-type faucet.

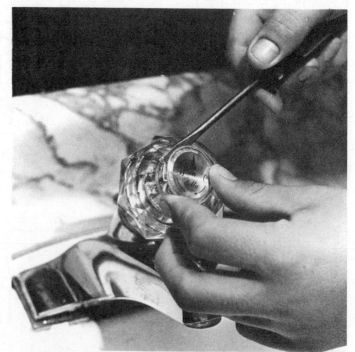

Ball faucets have a tipping turn-on/turn-off feature and work on a disc faucet principle. Pry off the decorative cap to expose the screw that holds the handle in place.

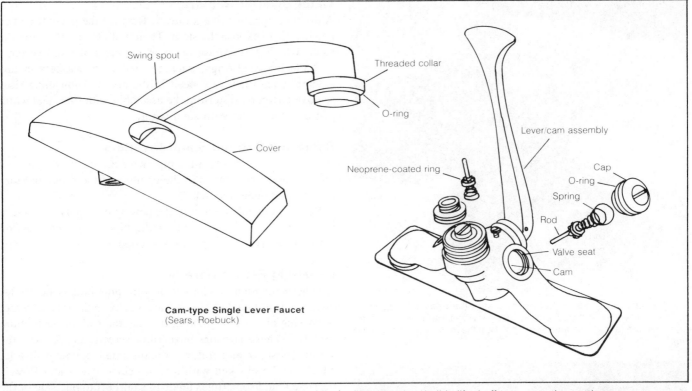

Cam-type Single Lever Faucet
(Sears, Roebuck)

Swing spout

Threaded collar

O-ring

Cover

Lever/cam assembly

Neoprene-coated ring

Cap

O-ring

Spring

Rod

Valve seat

Cam

To repair a faucet, the spout first is removed by unscrewing the holding collar, then the shell is lifted off to expose the casting.

With a Phillips head screwdriver, remove the handle screw, then pry up on the bottom of the handle to remove the handle. Pad when prying to avoid scratching the faucet.

Knurled retaining cap covers the "ball" of the faucet. Pad the jaws of the wrench to prevent marring the chrome cap, which turns counterclockwise.

The ball lifts out of the faucet housing after the retaining cap is removed. The water seals are located below the ball. Remove any corrosion from the faucet with fine steel wool. Buff the metal lightly; don't rub hard.

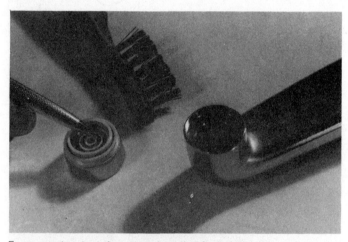

Frequent cleaning of aerators is called for at some times of the year, when there is a lot of sediment in the water. They also can become so encrusted with minerals that the complete unit must be replaced.

Aerator screen on faucets often becomes filled with sediment, causing the water to flow slowly. Unscrew the aerator and clean the screen with a brush and water.

Water Diverter Repairs

A diverter operates like a faucet. Remove the decorative cap and handle to expose the stem. Then, with pliers, back out the stem, which will expose the working parts of the diverter.

Replace any O-rings, packing, and worn washers in this assembly, and then replace it in the diverter housing. Also, remove any corrosion from the assembly with fine steel wool; just buff the metal with steel wool.

Replacing Bathtub Spout Diverters

Remove the old spout with a pipe wrench; one way is to stick the handle of the wrench in the opening of the spout and turn the spout counterclockwise.

Replace the old spout with the new spout, applying plumbing joint tape to the threads of the pipe to prevent leaking between the pipe and spout connection.

Repairing Faucet Aerators

Another item often overlooked in home plumbing is the aerator on the ends of faucets. This device breaks up the flow of water by mixing air with it, making it strike the sink or basin more "softly." These aerators have filter screens inside, and the various designs of aerators contain small openings inside, which can be blocked with bits of debris. The water flow is restricted, and sometimes tends to squirt off to one side or the other. We have seen some aerators that have not been removed for years.

They have to be removed with pliers, which usually damages them beyond repair. If not damaged, clean the screen and replace any worn gaskets or washers. If the aerator has been damaged, the solution is to replace them with new ones. Then make it a weekly maintenance chore to remove and clean each aerator. If you have difficulty screwing in (or on, depending whether the aerator has male or female threads) spray the new threads with WD-40 or similar. Turn in one or two threads, then back off a turn. Keep repeating this operation until the new aerator is fully seated. You can tell this when water no longer squirts from around the aerator. For which reason it is recommended you turn on the water very slowly to make the check.

Repairing Spray Hoses

A small retaining screw holds the spray assembly together in the nozzle of the hose, which is connected to a diverter valve under the faucet on the sink. If this screw is removed, the entire assembly will come apart. Replace any worn gaskets and washers you find, and re-assemble the nozzle.

If the nozzle or hose is damaged, replace the entire unit. You will have to disconnect the hose at the connection under the faucet. Use an adjustable or basin wrench for this. Then simply reconnect the new hose.

If the diverter valve is causing a no-water or little-water problem, turn off the water and remove the nozzle of the faucet. Under this, you will see a screw. Back out this screw, which will let you pull out the diverter valve. Around the valve will be a series of tiny holes. These holes might be plugged. If so, clean the holes with wire and replace the valve and nozzle. Do not use a matchstick or toothpick to clean the holes.

If the valve cannot be saved by cleaning, buy a new one. The cost is not high. Take the old valve to the store to match it.

Screens in shower nozzles can become clogged with sediment. Simply unscrew the nozzle to clean the screen. Check the nozzle washers, o-rings, and gaskets for wear at this time and make any replacements necessary.

TOILETS

This is probably the plumbing fixture that causes the most concern to the average homeowner. As mentioned in Chapter 6, most toilets bolt directly to the floor with the aid of "hanger bolts". The bolts have a wood screw thread on one end and a machine screw thread on the other. Generally, each toilet will have two bolts. The wood thread end is turned into the wooden floor, then a nut is turned onto the machine screw end to pull the toilet bowl down against the floor. This causes the bowl to press down on a ring of plumber's putty—or the modern counterpart, a ring of wax—which creates a waterproof seal between the bowl and the floor.

Leaks at the Floor Connection

A toilet that leaks at the floor line is usually one of the easiest problems to fix, with one exception that will be discussed later. If you note water around the bowl on the floor, it means that the seal should be replaced with a new one. In most cases you need not remove the tank from the bowl. But you do have to remove the tank and bowl from the floor or wall and then replace it again. You do have to be careful, and a helper is handy. First, remember to shut off the water, which is no problem if you have installed a shutoff valve in the supply line to the tank.

Next, flush the toilet so the tank is emptied. It will be necessary to hold open the ballcock to drain as much water as possible. There will still be some water in the tank, which will have to be cleaned out with a sponge. A sponge also will be required to mop up any water in the toilet bowl.

Now, remove the porcelain caps (if there are any) over the nuts on the hanger bolts. Remove the nuts, then gently rock the toilet to loosen the seal. With the help of a friend, lift the toilet up off the hanger bolts and place it on a stack of newspapers, or an old blanket or a rug. Remember that both the toilet bowl and tank are porcelain, a form of glass, and are fragile. The toilet can chip or crack if not handled gently.

Turn the bowl upside down and remove the old wax ring—or plumbers' putty—and install a new wax ring. The ring is available at any well-stocked hardware store, and should be used in preference to the plumbers' putty. Position the toilet

When removing or replacing the toilet bowl, rock it gently to free it from either the plumbers' putty or wax ring, or to seat it on the wax ring. This is for the toilet whose tank bolts directly to the bowl. The plumbing and bowl flange shown are plastic (photo courtesy of Genova).

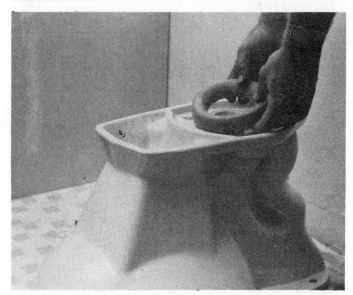

When installing a new toilet bowl, or after cleaning and unclogging the existing bowl, install a new wax ring around drain (photo courtesy of Genova).

back over the hanger bolts and gently press it down so it is about level. Replace the nuts on the hanger bolts and turn them gently but firmly, so the toilet bowl is pulled down flush with to the floor.

The previous description is for working with a toilet that sets on "conventional" cast iron pipe. If your home has plastic drain lines, the toilet will be fastened with bolts that fit into slots in the flange (see also Chapter 6) at the top of the drain.

The plastic flange is fastened to the floor (wooden) with wood screws. The square-head bolts fit in curved slots in the flange and thus are prevented from turning when you install or remove the nuts that hold down the bowl. The same wax ring is used for a toilet set on plastic pipe as for one on cast iron or copper pipe. The hold-down nuts are turned gently but firmly to pull the stool down flush with the floor; however, do not turn too strongly because you can crack the fragile porcelain of the bowl.

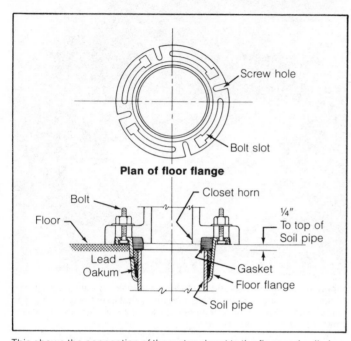

Plan of floor flange

This shows the connection of the water closet to the floor and soil pipe.

While you have the toilet/tank off the floor, check for water stains between the tank and toilet that would indicate a water leak. If there are such stains, unbolt the tank and replace the gaskets between the tank and toilet. It is much easier to do while the toilet is inverted, since the nuts that hold the tank to the toilet are under the back flange of the toilet. This means you will not have to stand on your head to remove and replace them. Again, use caution when tightening the nuts, as the tank and bowl are both fragile porcelain.

If your toilet tank connects to the wall rather than to the bowl, it will fasten to the wall and be connected to the bowl by a curved section of pipe. To take the bowl off the floor, you must first disconnect the curved section of pipe between the tank and bowl. If it is badly corroded, cut it free with a hacksaw and plan to replace it. Have a pan handy to catch any water left in the pipe. Buy a new section of pipe to replace the one you cut, then carefully remove the pipe sections from the tank and bowl. If you are replacing a toilet bowl and/or tank, simply discard the units and use a new curved section of pipe. You might also decide to install a new toilet with the tank fastened to the bowl. All gaskets and parts will be provided with the new unit.

Installing a New Toilet
The steps given above are also those for replacing an old toilet with a new one. The ony difference is that replacement calls for a complete collection of new parts.

The Exception
We mentioned that there is one exception to any easy solution for a toilet leaking at the floor line. While it is an unusual

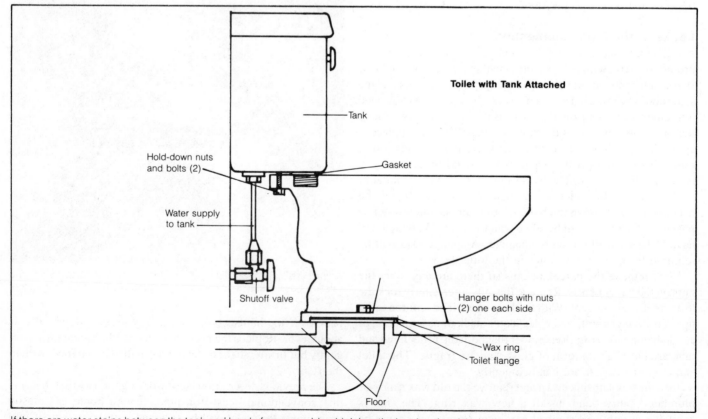

If there are water stains between the tank and bowl of an assembly which has the bowl and tank bolted together, take off the nuts and remove the tank from the bowl. Reassemble tank and bowl with new gaskets between them.

situation, it can happen that in an older home a toilet has leaked for years without its being noticed. One such situation came to our attention not long ago when a single gal told us of a toilet that leaked, even though a plumber had fitted in two wax rings. The toilet was fine for a few weeks, and then it started to leak again—down through the floor into the basement. Emptying a large pan every evening did not seem to be the answer. We suggested that possibly the hanger bolts no longer were holding firmly in the floor, because the wood had rotted where water had leaked and soaked the wood. What could she do? Either replace a section of the floor, or drill down through the floor and use bolts long enough to fit up through the floor and up through the flange of the toilet bowl. The young lady told us that on his next visit, the plumber did exactly that. The clue to the cause and solution of the problem was the need for two wax rings. There simply is not enough space under a toilet in normal circumstances for it to accept that much thickness. And at today's wage rates for plumbers, there was no reason why a "professional" should not have fixed the leak the first time, with the method he ended up using the second time around. This once again points up the savings in time, as well as money, available to a homeowner who handles his (or her) own plumbing problems.

Leaking Flush Valve

The other, and more common problem with toilets, is a leaking flush valve (ballcock). If you have to jiggle the handle to stop the water from trickling into the bowl, or if even that does not stop the water, then the ballcock assembly needs to be replaced. While you can get replacements for the old-fashioned float/ballcock assembly (and you might, if you are restoring an

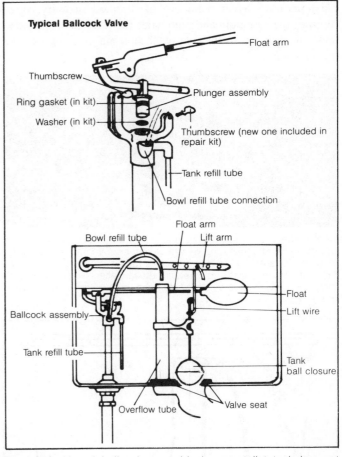

The old-fashioned ballcock assembly in your toilet tank has not changed much since the Englishman, Thomas Crapper, invented it in 1860.

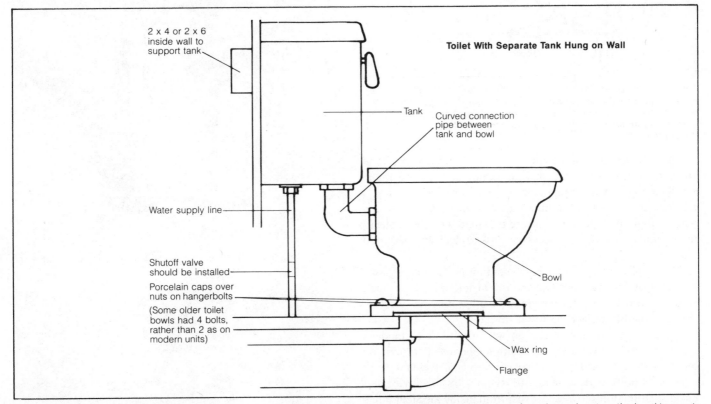

If the tank and toilet bowl are separate units, there will be a curved pipe joining them through which water from the tank enters the bowl to create flushing action. The curved pipe should be removed or, if badly corroded, cut with a hacksaw for easier removal later. Note that the water supply to tank is not connected to the toilet bowl.

old home) we recommend one of the modern units which replaces the assembly and eliminates the float that is prone to leak, or hang up on the tank wall or some other part of the mechanism.

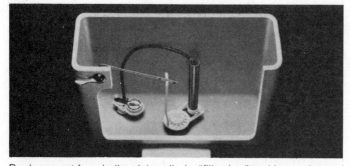

Replacement for a ballcock is called a "fill valve," and has an internal diaphragm that senses the weight of water above it to control water level in the tank. A screw on device is turned to adjust water level. Installation of the device does require shutting off the water and removing the supply line and existing ballcock (photo courtesy of JH Industries).

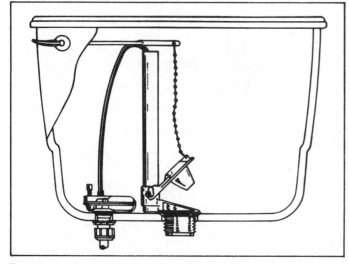

The fill valve has no float ball, shaft-mounted float, external levers, lift rods or tubes for the homeowner to worry about aligning. Instead, the compact unit actually measures water level from its position totally *underwater* at the bottom of a toilet tank (photo and line art courtesy of JH Industries).

The replacement is not difficult. You shut off the water, then flush the toilet to drain the tank. You can either sponge up the small amount of water remaining, or catch it in a pan when you unscrew the large locknut under the tank that connects to the water supply line. Instructions are provided with the replacement units, as well as necessary gaskets and any required adapters.

There are two types of replacement units. One type has a plastic float that is adjusted up or down to determine how much water is allowed to enter the tank; the other kind has a screw that is turned to adjust the water level.

There is very little that can go wrong with these modern replacements, but we offer one caution: one installation made by the author caused a very slow refilling of the tank, and eventually no flow of water at all! Removal of the device and close examination showed that rust from inside the steel pipes was loosened during some plumbing work, and had lodged in the small orifice in the flush valve and blocked it completely.

Cleaning the rust out of the orifice solved the problem. To prevent this happening to you, we suggest flushing the steel pipe at the nearest valve to remove any rust or sediment which might have come loose during work on the lines.

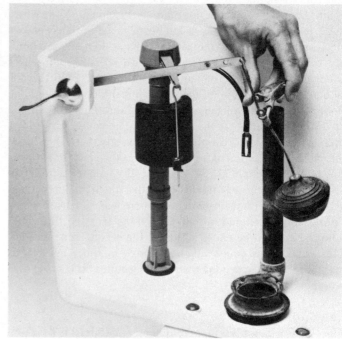

A corroded and misaligned flush valve assembly can be replaced with a noncorrosive valve. To install, drain water from the tank, remove the worn tank ball or flapper, lift the wires and the guide (photos courtesy of Fluidmaster).

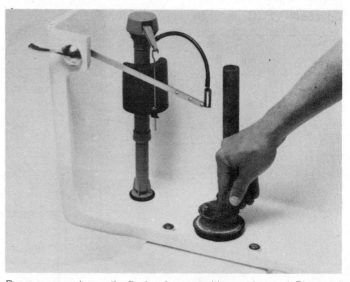

Remove corrosion on the flush valve seat with scouring pad. Rinse and dry the surface.

Cut in half the length of epoxy sealant included in the kit. You will only need half for most tank installations.

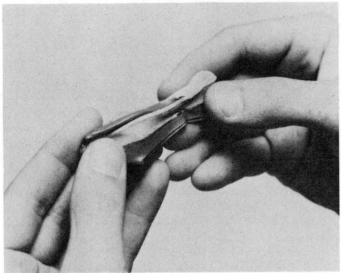

Knead the sealant's blue and yellow sections together until the color turns solid green.

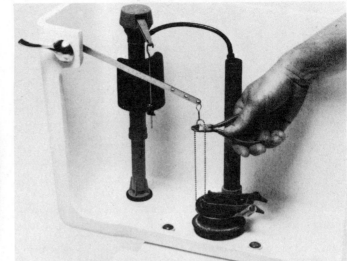

Connect stainless steel ball chain and clip to trip level. Trim any excess chain.

Roll the sealant into a rope and press into the stainless steel seat, overlapping the ends. Spread rope evenly, without gaps or lumps.

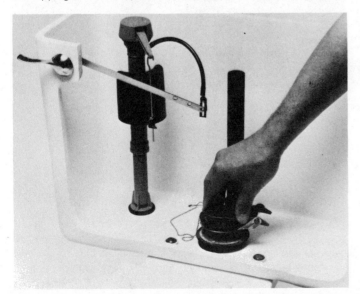

Place stainless steel seat directly on old drain seat and press down firmly.

This is the infamous leaking toilet, a prodigious water-waster which can consume as much as 78,000 gallons of excess water a year. Note the corroded and deteriorating metal ballcock and float ball. Leakage can occur in a variety of ways with a worn ballcock. In the foreground, the flush valve assembly is also corroded and misaligned, a source of "silent" leaking (photos courtesy of Fluidmaster).

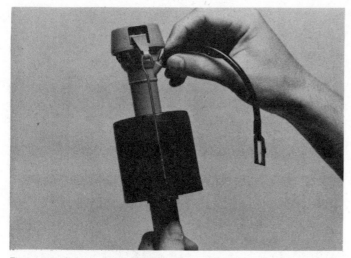

First, shut off the water supply to the tank. Flush the tank and sponge out remaining water. Loosen and remove nut and bolt on underside of tank. Lift out the old ballcock-and-float assembly. Attach the refill tube to the new valve.

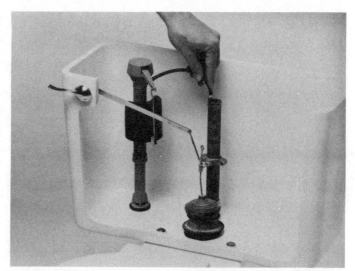

Attach clip at the end of the refill tube to overflow pipe. The end of the refill tube must always remain above the overflow pipe, or water leakage due to siphoning could occur.

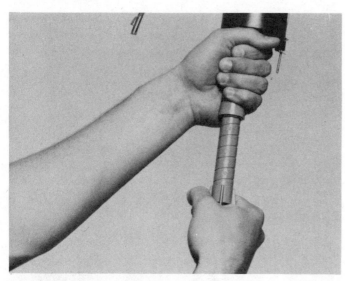

Adjust the new valve to fit your particular toilet tank by twisting to extend the shaft to the proper length. Once installed, the valve should reach just below, but not touching, the tank lid.

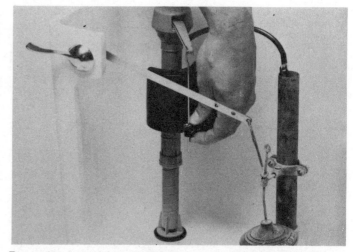

Turn on the water. Hold the float cup under water during the first fill cycle to fill the float with water used for ballast. Adjust water to desired level (a half-inch below the top of the overflow tube) by squeezing water level adjustment clip and moving the float cup. Be sure that the float clip does not touch the tank walls.

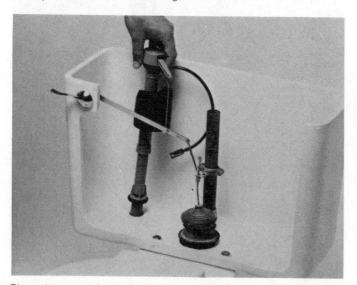

Place the new valve in the water-supply hole, slip end of the water supply tube into threaded shank of the unit and tighten connecting nuts on tank underside, ½ turn past handtight.

Once the new valve is installed, it is advisable to clear the water line of any debris before using the toilet. Turn off water and flush the tank. Rotate the FLC Valve cap ⅛ turn counterclockwise and remove.

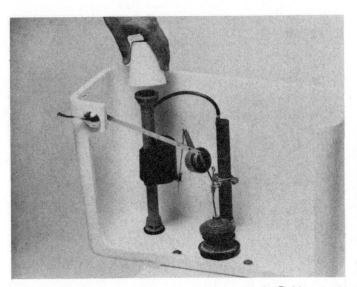

While clearing the water line, hold a container over the Fluidmaster to eliminate splashing. Turn water full on and off a few times. Replace cap and rotate ⅛ turn clockwise to stop. Turn on water, and tank will fill.

Replacing a Float Ball

Do not try to repair a leaky float ball. The repair will be only temporary and a new ball is inexpensive. First turn off the water and flush the tank. Just unscrew the old float ball on the float arm and screw on the new float ball.

Replacing a Tank Ball

After turning off the water, flush the tank. Unscrew the old tank ball from the lift wire that connects it to the flush handle. Then screw on the new tank ball. Check lift wires to make sure they are in good working order. If not, this is a good time to replace them.

Replacing a Guide Arm

As always, turn off the water and flush the tank. Remove the lift wires from the tank ball and unclip the bowl refill tube. Then unscrew the old guide arm, which is connected to the overflow tube.

Slip the old guide arm up and off the overflow tube. Insert the new arm down over the overflow tube and tighten the set screw after the lift wires have been relinked and aligned in the new guide arm. Attach the lift wire to the tank ball and then hook up the refill tube.

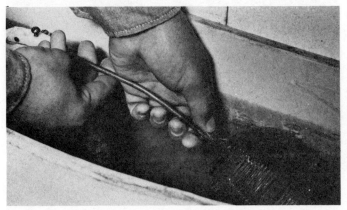

If the water in the flush tank is too high, gently bend the float arm downward. You may also be able to adjust the float with a screw located on top of the inlet valve.

Aligning a Guide Arm

This is a very simple repair. Turn off the water and flush the tank. Then loosen the set screw in the guide arm. Turn the guide arm so it is in alignment with the lift wires and tank ball. Finally retighten the set screw.

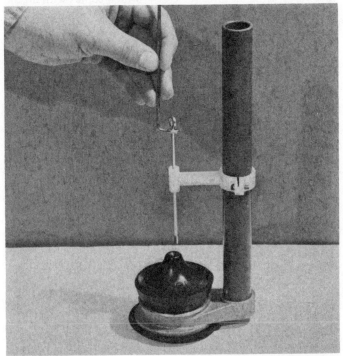

Lift wires should align with the valve seat, tank ball, and guide arm. Do not bend them for alignment; move the guide arm on the overflow pipe.

Repairing Flush Handle Assemblies

The collar connection between the outside flush handle and the inside trip lever often becomes corroded from the water in the flush tank which makes the handle difficult to work.

First, try loosening the nut that holds the handle in place. If this does not work, remove the nut and the handle assembly after you disconnect the lift wires.

Buff this assembly with steel wool and reconnect the assembly. If this does not solve the problem, you will have to replace the entire handle assembly. The parts are not very expensive.

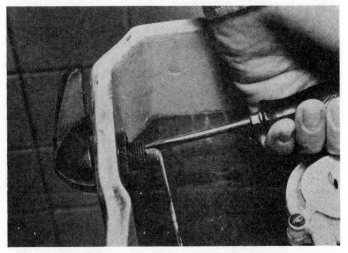

Corrosion can make the flush handle difficult to operate. Remove the assembly and buff it with steel wool, or try loosening the assembly slightly to free it.

How to Replace an Inlet Valve

First you must turn off the water and flush the tank. When the tank is empty, sponge out any remaining water. The tank must be dry or the water will leak onto the floor when the inlet valve is removed from the flush tank. You can choose to replace the inlet valve using an inlet valve kit—which comes with all the necessary parts—or you can replace the washers and seals, and hope that it will solve the problem.

With an adjustable wrench, loosen the cap nut under the tank. This nut connects the water supply pipe to the inlet valve. Then loosen the retaining nut that holds the inlet valve to the flush tank. Be very careful when you remove these parts. You do not want to crack the flush tank with the wrench. If the valve nuts are difficult to turn, try using two pipe wrenches. Hold the inlet valve inside the tank with one wrench while you loosen the retaining nut below the flush tank with the other pipe wrench—or with an adjustable wrench.

Once the inlet valve has been loosened, remove the float and float arm from the valve, along with the overflow tube. Now, unscrew the inlet valve and replace it in the same order with the new valve. The new kit should contain all the necessary washers and nut.

Reconnect the water supply pipe to the inlet valve and turn on the water. If the connections leak, turn off the water and turn the connections a little tighter. Do not overtighten the connections.

Replace the float arm and float and the overflow tube, turn on the water, and flush the toilet several times to make sure all the parts are properly aligned and seated.

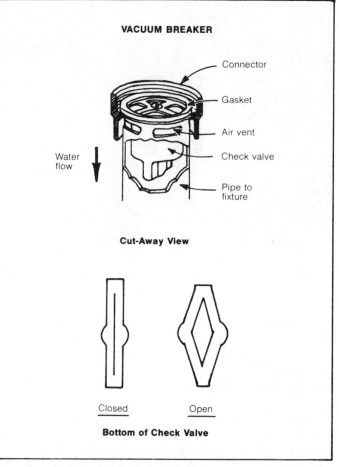

An anti-syphon device is also known as a vacuum breaker or a backflow preventer. It is necessary in water supply connections to all fixtures or appliances where an air gap does not exist between the water supply terminal and the fixture. It will prevent syphoning of water from the fixture if a sudden lowering of line pressure occurs, or while the supply line is open during repairs. The vacuum breaker shown is for use with flush toilets. As the water flows, the flexible rubber check valve opens. Any reversal of a vacuum in the water line causes the rubber valve to close. At the same time, air enters through the vent and prevents syphoning action that could draw water out of the fixture.

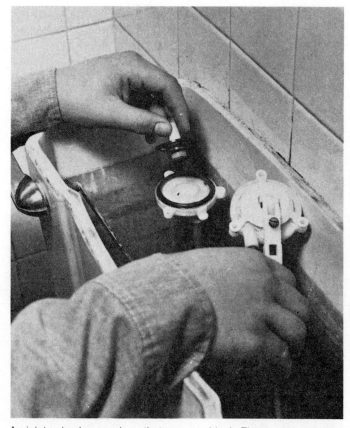

An inlet valve has washers that wear and leak. These washers—and O-rings—can be replaced. Remove the top of the valve with a screwdriver to expose the parts.

When water seals start leaking around the inlet valve and overflow tube, turn off the water, remove the retaining screws at the bottom of the flush tank, and replace the seals.

First, mark the water level on the inside of the tank, using a grease pencil or crayon.

Sweating Toilet Tanks

If you have a toilet tank that sweats, especially in the summer when warm, humid air causes condensation on the cool surfaces of the tank, there are two ways to eliminate the problem. One method, which we do not recommend, uses a special connection which allows warm water to flow into the tank to "temper" the water and raise the temperature. While this does eliminate the sweating, it also uses hot water that is heated by gas, oil or electricity, and is an expensive way to solve a problem.

A more economical solution to the problem is to line the inside of the tank with insulation. You can buy "kits" of material to install in the tank, but it is less expensive to use sheets of foam plastic or foam rubber and glue them inside the tank. First drain the tank (after shutting off the water) then mop the inside of the tank completely dry with a sponge. To adhere the liner, use one of the rubber-base exterior construction adhesives that is compatible with the rigid plastic or foam rubber. These calks are sold in cartridges to fit calking guns.

Toilets in Basements

Installing a toilet in a basement can be expensive and/or take a lot of hard work. It generally is necessary to break up the concrete floor to reach the existing drain, which then must be cut so you can insert a Tee. Then a line must be run up to the

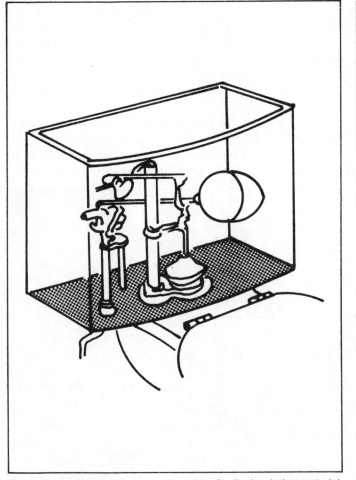

Create a newspaper pattern as a template for the insulating material. Cut out spaces that are taken up by the mechanism on the floor or near the sides of the tank. This will keep the insulating material from interfering with the various parts.

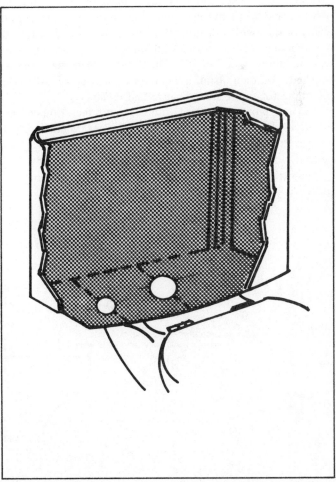

To fit rounder corners, cut rigid styrene foam into narrow strips and then glue them in place.

location of the toilet, and a flange installed flush with the floor. Last, the concrete must be replaced.

One way around this is to install a toilet that "flushes up". Such toilets are expensive, costing several hundred dollars, but their cost is more than offset by the expense of the alternative—tearing up the basement floor and installing the new drain line. These special toilets operate by utilizing water pressure from a supply line to create a sort of syphon action that pulls water and waste matter from the bowl and sends it to an overhead drain line. Minimum pressure is 40 pounds per square inch for a lift of 10 feet to the overhead drain line. A special valve in the toilet first injects water to break up solids, then the valve switches to the flushing action.

These toilets are not difficult to install and come with complete instructions—which should be followed explicitly. The toilet, incidently, is quite economical, as it uses only 2½ gallons for a flush, as opposed to a conventional toilet that requires 5 gallons or more.

TUB INSTALLATION

If you have an old bathroom, you can update it by installing a new tub with shower. In most cases you can utilize the existing hot and cold water supply lines and drain. The exception occurs where the plumbing is against an outside wall. Once you set a modern self-enclosed tub in place there is simply no way to reach the plumbing to make the connections. If there is a wall against which the plumbing end of the tub will fit, with the other end against another wall, an opening can be cut in the wall to allow work on the plumbing. When the work is finished, you then install a trap door to provide access to the plumbing for future maintenance and repairs.

The length of a "standard" tub is about 5 feet. You can get tubs that are shorter and some that are longer. Make sure you can get a tub in the space you have. If there is more space than needed, you can build in a ledge of plywood and cover it with ceramic tile or plastic laminate.

If there is more than enough length for the tub, an attractive method of installation is to fit one end snugly against a wall, then build a "stub" wall a foot or so higher than the tub at the plumbing end. It can be covered with ceramic tile or other material. A plywood access door can be covered with the same material so it is barely noticeable.

A new built-in tub will require 1 x 4 or 2 x 4 support rails on the three walls. When you order the tub, explain which side you want against the wall and which end is to have the plumbing. You can locate the faucets and shower head in the wall, completely separate from the tub, but the drain and overflow are part of the tub.

If the bathtub is porcelain coated steel, it will have to be screwed to the supports on the wall; a cast iron tub is heavy enough to set in place without being fastened. Once the tub is in place — and you'd better have a stout friend or two help you carry out the old tub and bring in and position the new one — wallcovering of some kind can be applied. First you must make all the plumbing connections, however, and check them for leaks, or you will damage your new wallcovering.

Calk around the joint between the tub and wall with the special flexible calking formulated for this area. The best method is to run about 4 inches of water into the tub, then do the calking. When the tub is drained it will adjust slightly upward due to the reduction of weight, and compress the calking. If you calk the tub when it is empty, it can lower as much as ⅛ inch or more when filled. The movement will stretch the calking, perhaps breaking the seal.

The faucets and shower head can be whatever height you want, but the "average" height for a shower head is about 5 feet and the water spout is about 22 inches above the bottom of the tub. Spout, faucets and shower head are centered above the tub.

Most shower receptors require a shower pan to catch water that may leak through a cracked or porous wall or joint. The pan will carry the water down to the drain. If a pan is not provided, the water can seep through to the ceiling below.

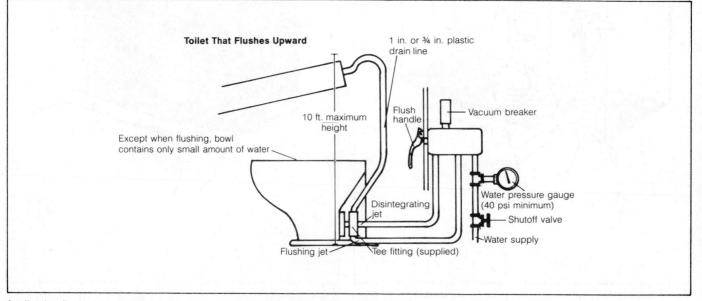

A toilet that flushes upward is the solution to installing a toilet in the basement, where the only other option is to tear up concrete floor and cut into the existing drain line buried deep under the floor. The toilet also uses less water than the conventional type, despite an unorthodox discharging overhead of water and waste.

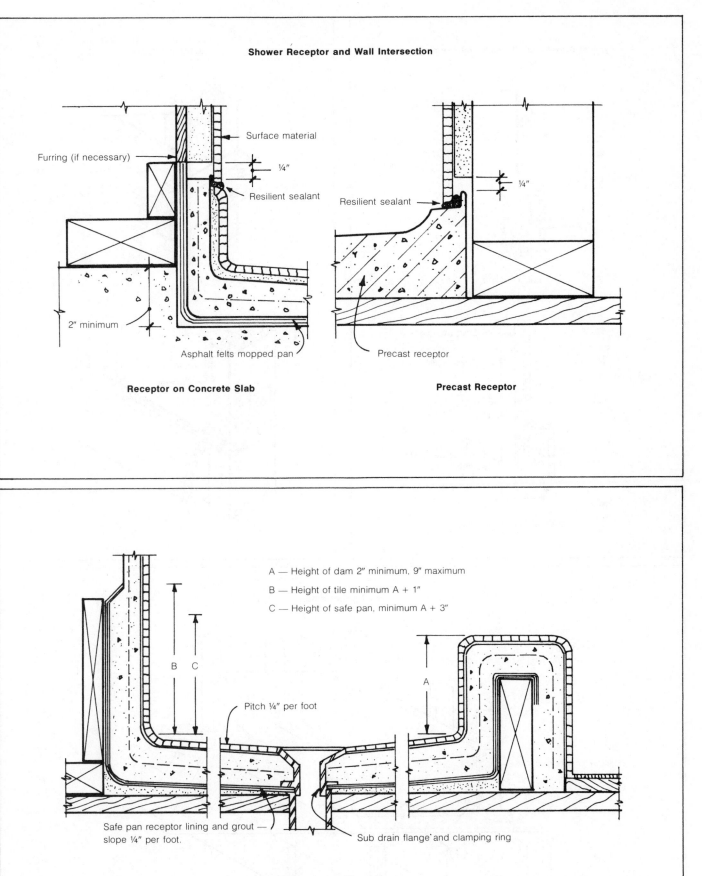

Shower Receptor and Wall Intersection

Surface material

Furring (if necessary)

¼"

Resilient sealant

Resilient sealant

¼"

2" minimum

Asphalt felts mopped pan

Precast receptor

Receptor on Concrete Slab

Precast Receptor

A — Height of dam 2" minimum, 9" maximum

B — Height of tile minimum A + 1"

C — Height of safe pan, minimum A + 3"

B C

A

Pitch ¼" per foot

Safe pan receptor lining and grout — slope ¼" per foot.

Sub drain flange and clamping ring

Receptor on Wood Floor

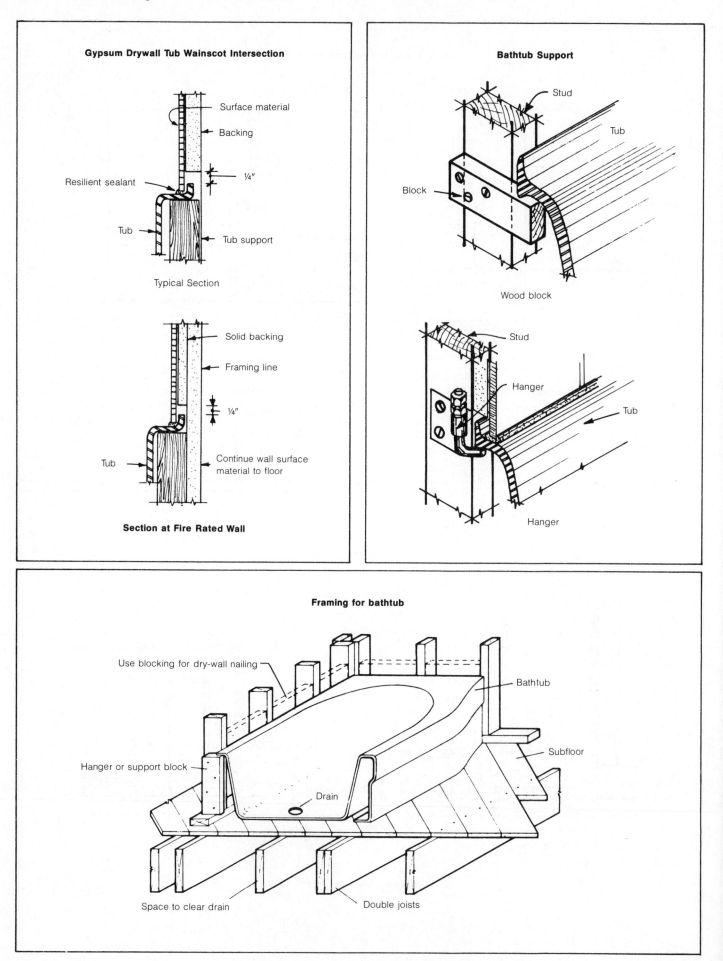

Gypsum Drywall Tub Wainscot Intersection

Surface material

Backing

Resilient sealant

¼″

Tub

Tub support

Typical Section

Solid backing

Framing line

¼″

Tub

Continue wall surface material to floor

Section at Fire Rated Wall

Bathtub Support

Stud

Tub

Block

Wood block

Stud

Hanger

Tub

Hanger

Framing for bathtub

Use blocking for dry-wall nailing

Bathtub

Hanger or support block

Subfloor

Drain

Space to clear drain

Double joists

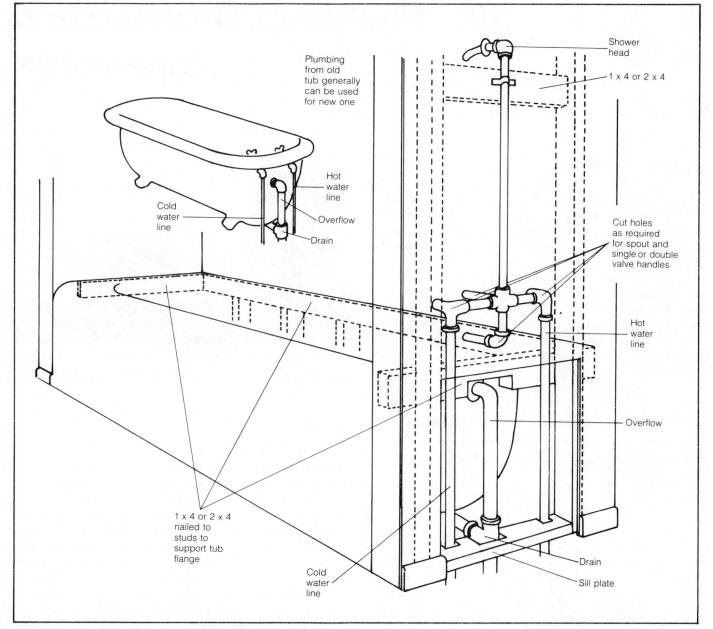

Plumbing from old tub generally can be used for new one

Hot water line

Cold water line

Overflow

Drain

Shower head

1 x 4 or 2 x 4

Cut holes as required for spout and single or double valve handles

Hot water line

Overflow

1 x 4 or 2 x 4 nailed to studs to support tub flange

Cold water line

Drain

Sill plate

Old fashioned footed tub can be replaced with modern enclosed unit, but some carpentry work may be required. The supply lines and drain generally can be utilized by extending them as necessary, but not if they are on the outside wall. An access door should be provided at the plumbing end for maintenance and repairs in the future. Not shown are the rod for shower curtain, or more attractive shower enclosure with sliding or folding doors.

CLOTHES WASHERS

One of the biggest users of hot water is an automatic clothes washer, although the actual amount will vary with the size of the machine and the kinds of "cycles" used. A setting used to wash synthetic fabrics, for example, will be cooler and less hot water will be used than for white items that require straight hot water.

A clothes washer needs both a hot and cold water line, and the minimum size should be ½ inch. Also required is a drain line, which must be at least 1½ inches. Because the water is pumped out of a washer so rapidly, a standpipe is required—especially if the washer is located in a basement. The drain cannot handle the sudden rush of water and it would back up if it were not for the standpipe.

When a washer is located on the first floor, a standpipe is installed, but it may be inside the wall. One common device used for washing machines is a metal inset in the wall. This

In first-floor laundry room where piping is in the wall, frequent installation is with a metal box open at the front (although it may have a cover) where any leaks from hot or cold lines will run down drain over sloping bottom of the box. The hook of the washer drain is fitted into the opening, through which 1½ inch drain line is turned. Because there is air space around the drain from the washer, it acts as an "anti-syphon" connection.

metal box with an open front provides for draining away any leakage from the hot or cold water connections, as well as a small amount of water backing up from the drain line.

Because the solenoid valves in a washer open and close quickly, water hammer can be a problem, so air chambers should be installed on both the hot and cold water lines. Some may argue that the flexible rubber hoses to the washer will absorb water hammer, and this may be true. But the constant hammering will wear out the hoses, and having one burst is rather unnerving, not to mention damaging to the surroundings. Install air chambers and be sure. Also, while most people never shut off the valves for the hot and cold water lines when not in use, they really should be closed. Otherwise the hoses are under constant pressure, as are the electric solenoid valves, and this is not good for them. The main problem seems to be that the shutoff valves are awkward to reach, usually being located behind the washer. There is obvious room for improvement in such installations.

Besides the electrically operated solenoid valves, there is a high-torque electric motor in an automatic washer that starts and stops frequently as the cycles change. A grounded circuit should be provided with a minimum capacity of 15 amperes. The fuse or circuit breaker for the circuit should be the delay type to allow for the surge of electric current required by the motor.

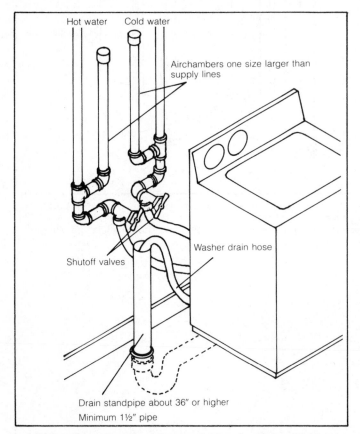

Hot water   Cold water

Airchambers one size larger than supply lines

Shutoff valves

Washer drain hose

Drain standpipe about 36" or higher
Minimum 1½" pipe

Installation of an automatic clothes washer requires hot and cold water supply lines at least ½ inch in size, along with a standpipe that should be a minimum of 1½ inches. Air chambers should be on both hot and cold water lines because solenoid valves in washer shut off water so quickly that water hammer is a problem. In a basement, piping will be exposed; in laundry room on first floor the piping may be inside the wall.

Leveling the Washer

Once the water supply lines, drain and electrical connections have been made, the washer should be leveled by means of the four bolts at the bottom corners. If you are installing a washer that has been moved from another location, or house, the adjustment is absolutely necessary because no two floors will be the same. You may find that at one corner the threads in the bottom of the washer have become stripped and adjustment is not possible. In this instance, raise the washer and remove the bolt. Turn on a nut, then replace the bolt. Turning the nut against the bottom of the washer will raise that corner and, conversely, lowering the nut on the bolt will allow that corner of the washer to drop down. Use an ordinary carpenter's level to level the washer from side to side, and front to back.

Hoses

It is a smart idea to check washer hoses every month or so to make sure that they are not cracked or leaking, especially around connections and where the hoses are bent to fit against a laundry room wall. Also, periodically turn off the water at the faucets, unscrew the hoses, and check the screens in the hoses for sediment.

Sediment from the water supply can cause all kinds of trouble—mostly blockage of supply lines. You can clean the screens with a stiff brush, replace the screens if they are broken, badly worn or bent.

If Your Washer Won't Fill with Water

The trouble can be one or a series of malfunctions. Follow the procedures below, in order.

(1) Open the water valves fully.

(2) Turn off the valves. Remove the hoses from the valves; you may need pliers to break the connections. Clean any sediment from the water supply screens with a brush. Or replace the screens with new screens.

(3) Remove the back from the washer. It is held by four, six, or more screws. Now check the inlet hoses to make sure they are not kinked.

(4) If the washer is getting water as far as the inlet hose connections, the problem probably is in the water valve or water valve solenoid. This is a job for a repair person.

Water Won't Discharge from Washer

Make sure the timer on the control panel is properly set and the timer has gone through the complete cycle.

Inspect the discharge hose for any blockage within the hose or kinks or severe bends in the hose.

Turn off the power and water. Remove the back panel of the washer. Check the wires leading to the impeller and the water pump motor. These wires could have vibrated loose from connections. Or, the wires could be burned out.

The trouble could also be a worn impeller, stuck wash-and-spin timers, or a malfunctioning motor—all problems for a professional service person to solve.

Water Leaks

First find the leak. It probably will be in a hose connection, around the tub seals, at the drain valve, pump assembly, or water supply valves.

With pliers, tighten all clamps to stop leaks. If a leaking gasket is the problem, try tightening the connection with a screwdriver or pliers to stop the leak. If this does not work, you will have to replace the gasket.

Tub seals may be replaced by removing a retaining ring held by screws. Or, the seals may be held with adhesive. Leaking parts, such as impellers, pumps, and drains, should be replaced, not repaired, as a general rule.

When an Agitator Doesn't Agitate

The problem here probably is a defective timer or water level pressure switch. The replacement is a job for a professional. But, before you make a phone call, check these points.

(1) Turn off the power and water.

(2) Remove the back from the washer.

(3) Check the drive belt from the motor to the agitator. The belt may be loose. Tighten it by loosening the mounting brackets on the motor, moving the motor backward until the belt is tight, and retightening the bolts in the brackets.

(4) If the drive belt is broken, replace it.

(5) Check the transmission. First, set the washer in the "Wash" mode on the control panel. Then remove the drive belt from the motor. By hand, turn the agitator pulley clockwise. If the agitator is not moved by this action, the transmission probably has to be replaced by a professional.

If Washer Drains Between Cycles

Reposition the drainage hose from the washer so that the hose is higher than the water level in the washer.

DISHWASHERS

Dishwashers are of two basic types: built-in and portable, although the latter may be designed to be built-in if the situation warrants it at a later date.

No plumbing is required for a portable, as the hot water supply is provided by snapping a flexible line onto a special fitting that replaces the aerator, and the drain is simply dropped into the sink. A built-in dishwasher requires a drain and a hot water supply line; no cold water is used. An electric connection also is required, which powers the motor that rotates the spray impellers, the water pump (if one is used) and the solenoid valves that open and close the drain and turn the hot water on and off. The circuit must be a grounded one, as we again are dealing with an appliance that uses water and presents a hazard if there were to be any kind of an electrical short circuit.

If a dishwasher does not seem to be washing properly, the first thing to do is to check for any clogged filters, such as the one around the drain. If there is a water leak around the door, this indicates the need for a new gasket. Get the model number of the machine and purchase a new one from a dealer who handles that brand, or from one of the supply houses that sell appliance parts to do-it-yourselfers.

If the machine will not run at all, check the fuse or circuit breaker. If you install a new fuse and it blows immediately, or the circuit breaker immediately kicks out, call a serviceman; you have a real problem.

Timer switches often cause a dishwasher to malfunction. This switch turns the water on and off for the various cycles, tells the impellers when to turn, and the drain when to open and close. If the dishwasher stays in one cycle, or goes through just a couple and then stops, it is probably the timer that is causing the problem. Replacement of this part is fairly easy. First check the make and model and buy a replacement. Next, remove the front panel and find the switch. Because the timer has a number

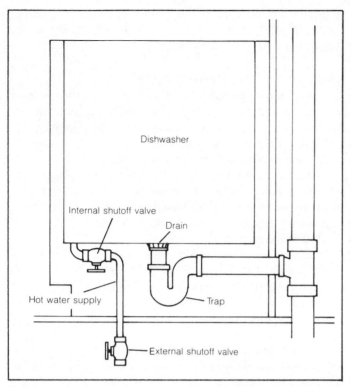

of wires connected to it, tag each one and make a sketch of the switch so you can be sure of making the proper connections on the new one.

If the timer switch does not solve the problem, or if there is more than one problem, it is best to call a serviceman. This is especially true if the water does not seem hot enough, or if the dishes will not dry properly. There is a heater in some dishwashers that heats the water to 160 degrees or so, and also

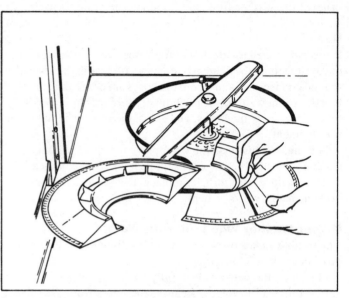

There are only two plumbing connections to a dishwasher. One is the hot water, the other is the drain. If the shutoff valve on the hot water line is inside the machine you may have to remove the lower front panel of the machine to reach it. There should be an external shutoff valve on the line; for example, in the basement ceiling under the machine so it can be reached quickly if the machine overflows and will not shut off.

Clogged strainers can be easily removed for cleaning. The units are usually plastic or metal; to clean, just run under the tap and rinse well.

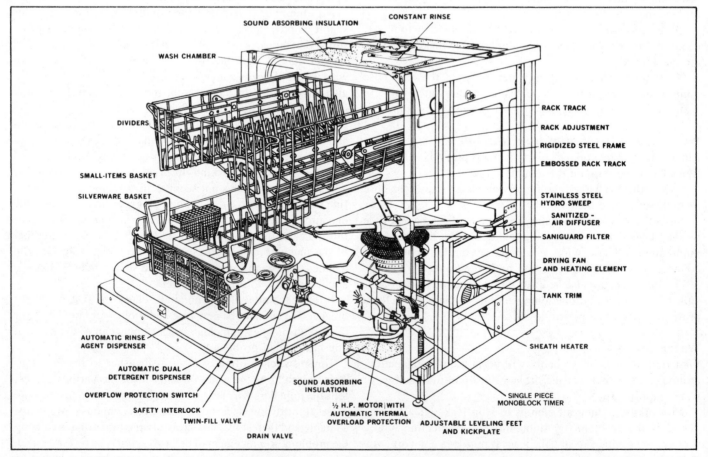

The components of a dishwasher vary in arrangement from manufacturer to manufacturer, but the basic functions remain the same (art courtesy of KitchenAid, Hobart Corporation).

DIAGNOSING DISHWASHING PROBLEMS

Trouble	Cause	Cure
Won't Start	Door not closed completely	Close door
	Faulty switch or timer	Replace
	Switch linkage	Adjust as needed
	Open line	Replace fuse or set circuit breaker
Dishes not clean	Cool water	Set up hot water tank thermostat or have service man check heater in washer
	Insufficient water	Clear water supply inlets
	Plugged strainer	Clean strainer
	Faulty timer switch	Replace
	Bad solenoid coil	Replace (usually requires serviceman)
	Measuring coil out of adjustment or malfunctioning	Replace or repair (job for serviceman)
Water drains out of tub	Drain valve leaking	Tighten valve flange
Does not fill	Supply valve does not open	Adjust linkage, or replace or repair valve
Noisy machine	Core of solenoid not centered	Realign core
	Misaligned motor	Realign (serviceman)
	Noticeable vibration	Shim up washer so it is level and solid on floor
	Impeller scraping screen	Adjust as required
Door won't close	Gasket binding	Loosen screws in gasket retainer, reset as required
Low water level	Low water pressure	Hot-weather heavy-water use; other times, check for blockage in inlet line
Drains slowly	Malfunctioning drain valve	Replace drain solenoid (serviceman)
Dishes not dry	Water not hot	Increase temperature of hot water tank or replace heater in washer (If washer set on "energy saver," heater may not turn on; dishes must drain and dry at room temperature)
	Inlet valve leaking	Repair or replace valve
	Faulty heating element	Turn timer to heating cycle. If heater works, then timer is bad. If timer okay, then heater should be replaced
Silverware tarnishes	Water contains chemicals	If reducing amount of detergent makes no difference, then water softener or filter may be required

provides heat for drying. A serviceman can quickly tell if this heater is not working. Replacing it requires a rather complete disassembly of the dishwasher, and is a project not recommended for the do-it-yourself homeowner.

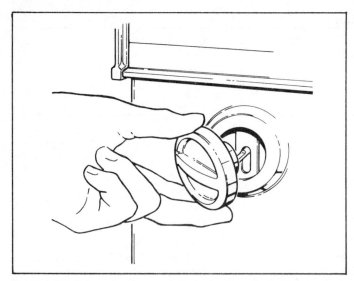

To reach the dishwasher timer switch, the front panel must be removed. The first step is to pull off the control knob. Make sure it does not have a setscrew that must be loosened.

On this dishwasher the door is opened and the screws are removed from upper edge to remove the front panel. There are also screws on the edges of the door that must be removed.

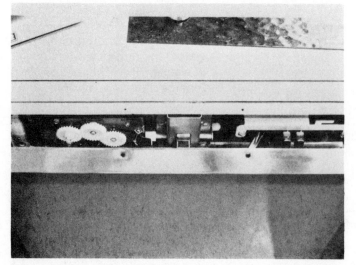

The panel is shown tipped back (but not removed) to reveal switches and components that can be removed and replaced.

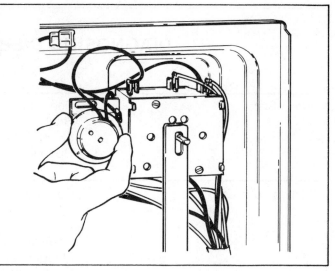

Before you touch the timer, unplug the dishwasher. Place the wires from the old switch, one by one, onto the new one to avoid making wrong connections.

GARBAGE DISPOSALS

At one time garbage disposals were a very popular kitchen plumbing item. In recent years they have somewhat fallen out of favor and, in some localities, are even forbidden by local plumbing codes or laws. The problem is that the disposals discharge garbage into the sewer system, overloading it if it happens to be marginal—and many are.

Disposals work on the principle that any garbage from the kitchen that can be pulverized by a whirling set of steel blades and mixed with water can be flushed down the drain. There have been disposals that claimed to be able to even grind bones. Perhaps they could, but the resulting heavy slurry certainly did not help the sewer system.

If your city or locality has an up-to-date sewer system, disposals are probably allowed. Installing one is not too difficult. Most disposals come with a special drain fitting to replace the existing one. The disposal is suspended from the fitting by bolts that hold it up under the sink against a shock-absorbing collar of some kind that minimizes the vibration and noise of the disposal.

Some types of disposal are fastened with a large rubber sleeve that provides the shock absorbing action. Stainless steel clamps on the sleeve hold the disposal at one end, the sink drain at the other.

Water should always be run into a disposal when it is being used. The water lubricates the blades that pulverize the garbage, flushes the garbage down the drain and cools the electric motor. The water should be allowed to run even after all the garbage has passed through the disposal, to assure that it will be flushed through the drains of the house and out into the street drain. A disposal should be fitted with a heavy cord and plug and fitted into a grounded receptacle. Any appliance that uses water should be grounded, because of the very real possibility of a short circuit.

Also, because the drain line from a disposal carries a heavy slurry of pulverized garbage, it is a good idea to have a separate drain from it to the main vertical drain, rather than running into the sink drain. Because the slurry of garbage tends to stick to the inside of the drain line and hold moisture, the drain from

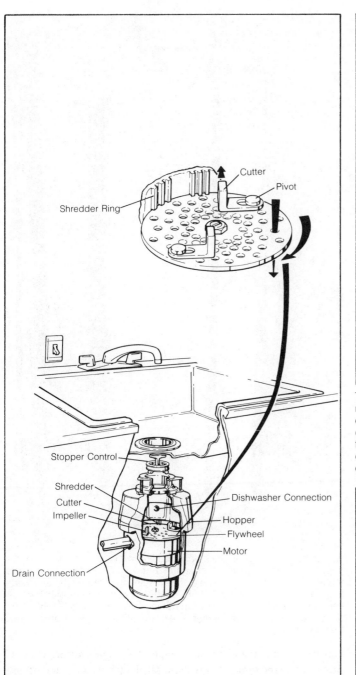

When the garbage disposal is turned on, the flywheel will spin at approximately 1725 rpm. The centrifugal force created by the disk forces the food against the walls of the disposal. The food waste then hits the shredder ring located at the rim of the disk, where it is ground up into a liquid mass.

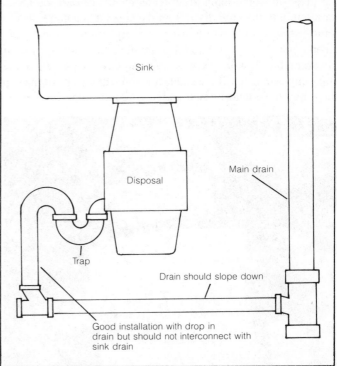

This installation has the drain interconnected with that of sink, which is not a good idea because of the possibility of the drain plugging up from excess of garbage, and thus also plugging the sink drain. A slope in drain is preferred over a more horizontal line because it assures freer flow of the water/garbage mixture. If the disposal is quite old and extensive repairs are required, it is quite possible that it would be less expensive for you to buy a new unit and install it yourself.

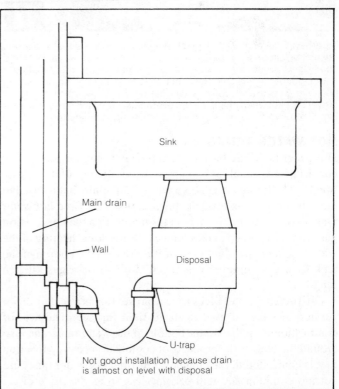

The disposal has its own connection to the main vertical drain in this installation. This is preferred over interconnecting it to the sink drain. Local plumbing codes may dictate how the drain must be connected. Electrical supply must be through grounded circuit. A cord with plug is preferred, if permitted by local code, since this simplifies removal of disposal for repair or replacement.

the disposal to the main drain tends to rust or corrode much more quickly than the drain from the sink. It is a good idea to remove the drain line of a disposal every couple of years and clean it out. It is a messy job, but it will assure a longer life for the drain line. It will be necessary to replace the gaskets in the slip joints when you disassemble the drain, and some of the slip nuts may have deteriorated and also require replacement.

A garbage disposal with a typical special drain bracket that suspends the unit on shock-absorbing mounting. The drain is shown at right and consists of a number of slip-joint fittings and a trap. Electrical cord enters bottom of this unit. Reset button is on bottom of motor housing near the wire. Reset controls thermal overload switch that acts as circuit breaker when motor jams or overheats. When the motor cools, or jam is removed, circuit is restored by pushing reset button.

HOT WATER TANKS

Hot water tanks are basically simple plumbing devices. They consist of a vertical tank, with the better quality units "glass-lined." The lining actually is a type of porcelain that is fused to the steel of the tank inside to prevent rust. Gas fired hot water tanks have a flue up the middle through which the combustion gases are discharged to the chimney. While some heating of the water occurs in the flue, most of it is done on the bottom of the tank by a gas burner that is much like that on a gas kitchen range.

Oil-fired hot water tanks have a blower that is a scaled-down version of the kind used in an oil-fired furnace. The heat of combustion is applied to the bottom of the water tank, and also around the tank as the products of combustion pass up to a flue that is connected to the chimney. Oil-fired hot water tanks are not too common and will become less so as the price of oil escalates.

Electric hot water tanks have no flue, as there is no combustion involved. Instead, there are two electric heating units inserted in the wall of the tank in threaded watertight connections. The "rate of recovery"; that is, how quickly the water

A hot water tank is simply a steel tank filled with water, to which heat is supplied on demand by a thermostat. Shown is a gas-fired tank with a metal shell around it, inside which is insulation. Note the union in gas line near thermostat/temperature control at bottom center of shell. A line from the safety valve (hidden behind gas line on top of tank) runs down side of tank at left. In this installation there is a floor drain a few feet away.

can be heated to the preset temperature again after water is drawn from the tank, is slowest with electricity. Gas and oil are quite rapid in response. For this reason, electrically heated tanks need to be larger than oil or gas-fired tanks to supply the same quantity of hot water.

All hot water tanks will have a pressure/temperature relief valve with a pipe from it leading down the side of the tank. In the event that the automatic controls malfunction and the water gets too hot, or pressure is built up inside the tank (one condition generally means that the other is present) the safety valve opens and relieves the pressure before it can damage the tank.

Cold-water supply lines and hot-water outlet lines also are common to all three types of hot water tank. Cold water is introduced near the bottom of the tank, where it is heated. It rises to be discharged through the hot water supply line. In some tanks the cold-water line enters near the top of the tank and passes down through the tank to discharge near the bottom. This arrangement preheats the cold water as it enters.

REPLACING A HOT WATER TANK

If you have to replace a hot water tank (generally because it is leaking), first shut off the hot and cold water lines. Then shut off the oil, gas or electric supply. Drain the tank through the valve provided for that purpose. This valve also should be used to drain 10 gallons or so of water about once a year to eliminate sediment that could slow the heating by gas or oil; the sediment causes an insulating effect. Electric tanks also should be drained of 10 gallons or so periodically to prevent the buildup of rust and sediment in the bottom of the tank.

Some new water tanks will be provided with a safety valve. If your new tank does not have one, remove the valve from the old tank and install it on the new one. Making sure, of course, that it works properly. Older types of safety valves had a "fuse" in them that melted under heat and pressure. Spare fuses were provided with the valve, since you had to disassemble the valve and install a new fuse whenever it "blew" because the tank overheated. More modern safety relief valves are spring-loaded and release the pressure only as long as it exists. When the pressure and temperature drop, then the valve closes again. If your old tank has the relief valve with the lead fuse, we suggest you discard it and install one of the spring-loaded types.

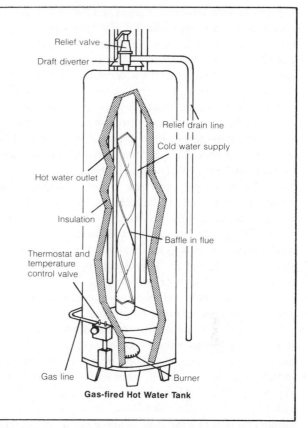

Gas-fired Hot Water Tank

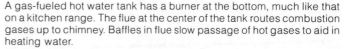

A gas-fueled hot water tank has a burner at the bottom, much like that on a kitchen range. The flue at the center of the tank routes combustion gases up to chimney. Baffles in flue slow passage of hot gases to aid in heating water.

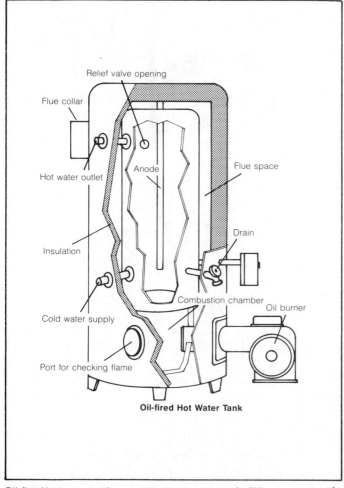

Oil-fired Hot Water Tank

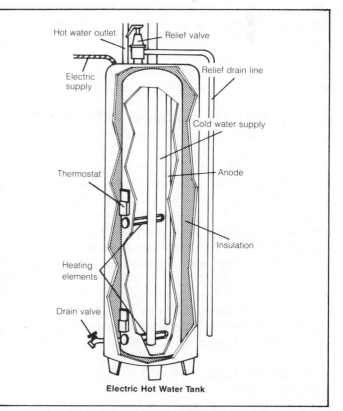

Electric Hot Water Tank

Oil-fired hot water tanks are not very common and will be even more of a rarity as heating oil becomes more expensive and difficult to obtain. In Northeast many users of fuel oil are converting to gas because of lack of availability of oil. The configuration of the tank inside the shell is somewhat different than gas or electric tanks due to the need for a combustion chamber for the oil burner.

Electric hot-water tanks used to be the most expensive to operate, but increased costs of other fuels make them somewhat more economical today. They also are a favorite with solar-assisted homes, where much of the hot water is supplied by the sun.

After the tank has been drained and the fuel or electric lines disconnected, uncouple the hot and cold water supply lines. There usually is a union at the connection to the tank, and a shutoff valve on each line. If there is not, now is the time to install one. As long as all the water in the house is already shut off, you might as well do the job right.

Hot water tanks are relatively heavy, so have a friend to help you slide the tank over, away from the connections, and tip it over to drain the final gallon or two of water from it. Carry it outdoors and hope that you don't have to wait too long for a "solid trash" pickup in your neighborhood.

Installation of the new tank is pretty much a reverse of removing the old one. If the tank is a bit higher or lower than the one it replaces, you will have to do some plumbing work.

For the electric tank, you will have to reset the circuit breaker after the wiring has been hooked up. A gas line may have to be "bled" of air. This usually is done by first connecting the line and turning on the gas. A connection then is "cracked" and the air allowed to escape. The moment gas is smelled, the connection is retightened.

Before any heating device is turned on, a hot water tank must be filled. This means opening both the cold water inlet and the hot water outlet. A faucet nearest to the tank is opened and when the tank has filled, water will be discharged from it to confirm the filling. Absolutely never turn on heat in a hot water tank before it is filled; the flame of a gas or oil unit could damage the steel of the tank, while electric units could overheat and be damaged themselves.

Modern hot water tanks have one other feature in common and that is an anode rod. This will be a rod of magnesium, which is an "active" metal. The magnesium is "sacrificed" to prevent damage from galvanic action in the plumbing system.

If you have a water tank that is 10 or 15 years old, it would be worthwhile checking to see if the anode needs replacing. Once the anode is gone, the steel and copper or brass in your plumbing system will begin to interact and cause leaks.

HOW TO INSULATE A (ROUND) WATER HEATER

To cut energy costs, Owens Corning Fiberglas offers a kit for an insulation jacket. For electric heaters, the kit can be trimmed to size and installed. You must, however, be careful to trim or remove insulation from areas which cover the heating element controls and the power connection. If you do not, it could cause control wires to overheat, and deteriorate their insulation. The result would be a dangerous electric shock. For gas heaters, you must take care that the jacket does not interfere with proper venting across the top. You must also watch that the jacket bottom does not restrict air flow into the burner area. Do not use this kit on a gas heater which is equipped with a flue damper. Improper installation on a gas unit could cause an explosion. Be sure to wash off any insulation after handling, and wear loose clothing. Wash work clothes separately.

Materials Included
1 48″ wide insulated jacket
3 3″ x 12″ white vinyl tape for side seam — horizontal
1 6″ x 48″ white vinyl tape for side seam — vertical
2 3″ x 36″ white vinyl tape for top of heater
    Tools required. Scissors or knife, pen, straightedge.

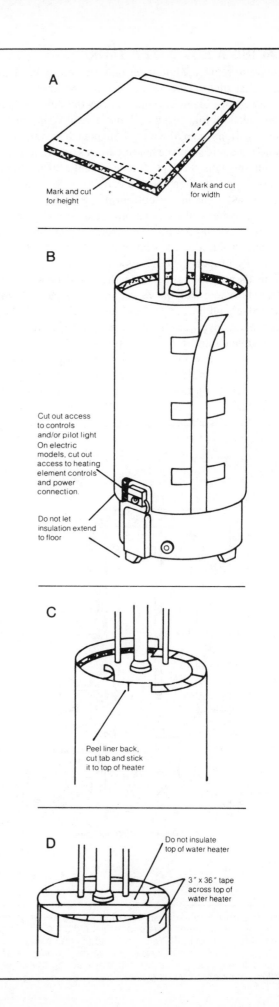

A Mark and cut for height   Mark and cut for width

B Cut out access to controls and/or pilot light On electric models, cut out access to heating element controls and power connection.
Do not let insulation extend to floor

C Peel liner back, cut tab and stick it to top of heater

D Do not insulate top of water heater
3″ x 36″ tape across top of water heater

Installation Instructions

Clean the top of the water heater using warm water and detergent. DO NOT USE SOLVENT BASE CLEANERS. Water heater top must be completely dry before installing jacket. Avoid contact with water piping and flue pipe as they may be hot.

Wrap the insulation jacket around the water heater with the vinyl side out and the 4″ collar at the top. Mark the vinyl jacket where the insulation begins to overlap itself. This mark will establish the final cut width of the jacket.

Lay the jacket on a flat surface vinyl face up and cut the jacket to the width established in step 2. If using a knife, draw along a straight edge while compressing insulation. See Figure A. Mark and cut the jacket height as follows:

For electric water heaters. For electric water heaters less than 50 inches high, wrap the jacket around the water heater as in step 2 with the **insulation** even with the water heater top. Mark and cut the bottom of the jacket at a level 2 inches above the floor. For electric water heaters greater than 50 inches high, no cutting is required.

For gas water heaters. For gas water heaters wrap the jacket around the water heater as in step 2 with the **insulation** even with the water heater top. Mark and cut bottom of the jacket 1 inch above the top of the burner access cover and provide cut out for burner controls. See Figure B.

Wrap the jacket around the water heater as in step 2 with the **insulation** even with the water heater top. Locate cut out over burner control on gas units or side seam over thermostats covers on electric units. Apply tape across the side seam at top, middle and bottom using the 3″ x 12″ vinyl tape provided. Now center and apply the 6″ x 48″ vinyl tape over the entire length of the side seam. See Figure B.

Note: Peel off release paper slowly while applying vinyl tapes.

Slowly peel off the release paper on the vinyl collar about 6 inches. Cut a notch in the collar 4 inches from the side seam, fold and secure to the water heater top. Continue this procedure around the entire collar. See Figure C.

Apply the two pieces of 3″ x 36″ vinyl tape across the top of the water heater as shown in Figure D. Extra insulation may be used to wrap hot water piping. Do not apply insulation on top of gas water heaters.

SUMP PUMPS

Sump pumps are familiar plumbing fixtures in some parts of the country—where wet basements are a way of life. In other regions homeowners find water in their basements only when there is an unexpected storm or some other temporary and unusual situation. In either circumstance, a good quality sump pump will prevent a flooded basement.

Automatic sump pumps evacuate water from a "pit" or "sump", which really is just a hole in the basement floor. Operation of a sump pump is automatic; a switch turns on the pump when the water level in the sump reaches a predetermined level. When the water drops below that level, the pump shuts off. A check valve in the discharge line from the pump prevents water from draining back into the sump when the pump stops.

There are two basic types of sump pumps: the pedestal and the submersible. Pedestal types have a conventional electric motor on a long column that drives a shaft that is connected to the pump at the bottom. Submersible pumps have the motor mounted directly on the pump inside a watertight housing, and the complete unit fits below floor level down in the sump.

A pedestal pump is turned on and off usually by a float that is connected to a long rod. When water lifts the float the rod actuates a microswitch that turns on the pump. A similar type of switch is used for a submersible pump except that it is watertight. In an alternative version, there will be an air bell on the pump that uses air pressure to operate a diaphragm in a sealed switch.

Sump pumps used in home installations generally are powered by a ⅓ horsepower electric motor, and ½ horsepower motors are available for extreme situations. When you buy a sump pump, make sure it has the Underwriter's Laboratory label and that it is certified by the Sump Pump Manufacturers

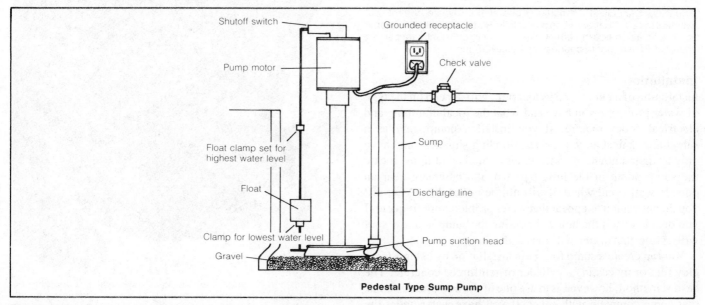

Shutoff switch

Grounded receptacle

Pump motor

Check valve

Float clamp set for highest water level

Sump

Float

Discharge line

Clamp for lowest water level

Gravel

Pump suction head

Pedestal Type Sump Pump

Pedestal pump has a motor at the top of the column to keep it above water. The long shaft inside the pedestal drives the pump. A check valve keeps water from running back into sump when pump stops.

Association. These two factors will assure that the pump is electrically safe and will handle the load of pumping water.

Electrical service to a sump pump should be a separate line to a single, grounded receptacle box. No other devices should be on the circuit, to assure that the pump always has power. Make sure the receptacle is high enough on the wall to be above the level of any expected water. Most wiring in a basement is up under the joists. However, wiring on a wall may be low, so check to be sure that all the wiring from the receptacle to the service box is above the highest possible water level.

There are a lot of complaints about the failure of sump pumps to operate when there is an emergency. Except for loss of power because of storm damage (and battery-powered pumps overcome this problem) the main reason that sump pumps fail to operate is lack of maintenance. It really is too much to expect a pump that has been sitting in a puddle of water for five years, corroding and rusting, to suddenly start working during an emergency.

"AquaNOT SAFEGUARD™ normally operates on house current, but switches to 12 volt battery when power fails. Pump capacity is the same on 12 volts as on house current. The battery is constantly recharged when not in use (photo courtesy of AquaNOT, Inc.).

Installation

Installation of a pump, and its location, will depend on the type of water problems you have and what the local plumbing and electrical codes require. If you install a pump only as a safeguard against an unexpected flooding situation, and have only a slight amount of water under normal conditions, locate the sump pump in the lowest part of the basement near an outside wall—and where it will not be noticeable. After all, you do not want it to appear that water problems are frequent if you decide to sell the house. Locating the sump in a low spot will assure that water will run to the sump.

You can create a sump for a new installation by using a large clay tile, or by casting a cylinder of reinforced concrete. The easiest method, however, is to use one of the new plastic sumps that come complete with cover. If you have water under the floor of the basement, drill holes in the bottom of the sump (the

plastic ones have a bottom), so that any water under the floor will drain up into the sump.

If you are installing a sump pump because you have a serious problem with a wet floor, or if the floor has cracked or buckled, you may need to run drain tile directly to the sump. It may even be necessary to break up the floor, or at least part of it, and install perforated plastic drain tile around the wall and lead it into the sump. The tile is covered on top when you pour the new floor, so the perforations on the sides and bottoms of the tiles will receive and channel the water.

In such a situation where flooding is an expected event, a submersible pump with watertight electrical connections will help assure that the pump operates satisfactorily.

Getting rid of the unwanted water from the pump is done most easily by piping it directly into an existing sewer line. But first make sure there are no blockages in the line that would prevent a full flow from the pump, and also that the sewer does not back up during a heavy rainstorm. Finally, make sure that local codes permit such a hookup. In areas where there are no storm drains, connections from sump pumps are forbidden.

Another means of getting rid of the water from the pump would be a line to a good-sized dry well, or simply a line out a basement window. Make sure the line extends far enough from the house so the water does not flow back into the basement. The discharge line from the pump should be as large as the outlet on the pump. A flexible connection enables easy maintenance of the pump because it is easy to remove if necessary.

Pump Maintenance Program

Every three months, and/or when leaving overnight or longer, as on a vacation, carry out these checks:
  (1) make sure the pump inlet screen is clean;
  (2) check the electric cord and make sure the pump is plugged in;
  (3) Operate the pump to be sure it runs.
Once a year:
  (1) take the pump out of the sump and clean it;

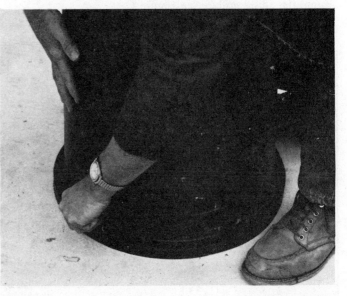

While sump can be large clay tile, or can be cast of concrete, the easiest method is to use plastic pump that comes complete with lid. Here the plastic sump is inverted on floor and a mark made around it to show the size hole required (photo courtesy of Genova).

(2) clean the sump;

(3) examine both pump and sump for wear or damage;

(4) oil or grease the pump as specified in the owner's manual;

(5) replace the pump and run it, and adjust the float level if necessary.

Here are some do's and don'ts that should also be followed:

1. Use the pump receptacle only for the pump. Don't plug power tools into it and then forget to replace the pump plug.

2. Always keep the cover on the sump; replace or repair it as necessary.

3. Never store material near the sump, and don't place furniture near the sump. Either of these things could cause the pump to malfunction when it is needed.

4. Never, under any circumstances, allow children to play near the sump.

A hole is chopped in the concrete floor for the sump; dirt is removed. Final sizing of hole may require use of hammer and chisel, but rented electric jack hammer speeds the job (photo courtesy of Genova).

The plastic sump is light and easily handled. It is dropped into a hole that should be deep enough so the rim of the sump is just below floor level (photo courtesy of Genova).

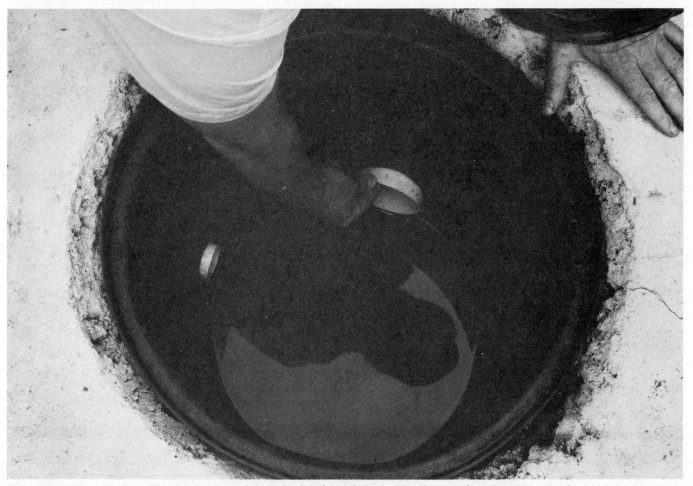

In situations where water is a real problem you may have to lead perforated plastic tile to the sump from the surrounding floor. Holes can easily be cut in the sides of the plastic sump (photo courtesy of Genova).

11 Outdoor Plumbing and Private Systems

SEWAGE DISPOSAL

Although most people in the United States live in urban or suburban areas, almost 30 percent of the homes still rely on septic tanks or cesspools. In some states, the figure is closer to 40 percent.

There is a difference between a septic tank and a cesspool system, and it is enough so that in most locations cesspools are completely illegal. A cesspool is quite literally a hole in the ground with a wall (or walls, as it need not be round) composed of a porous assembly of bricks, blocks or stones. Sewage is run into it through a pipe from the drainage system in the house, and the liquid portion then seeps through the wall, while solids

settle to the bottom. This is the way it operates in theory, but too often the cesspool overflows, or saturates the ground around it or both. Efficient operation of a cesspool depends upon a condition that seldom occurs; that is, a loose, sandy soil into which the liquid portion of the sewage is quickly absorbed. This condition might occur along a seashore or the shore of a lake, but even here the effluent is more likely to contaminate the lake or seashore than to dissipate harmlessly — as it is supposed to do.

The preferred private sewage system is a septic tank with a dispersal (disposal) field. The system consists of a watertight tank buried in the ground to which a line is run from the house

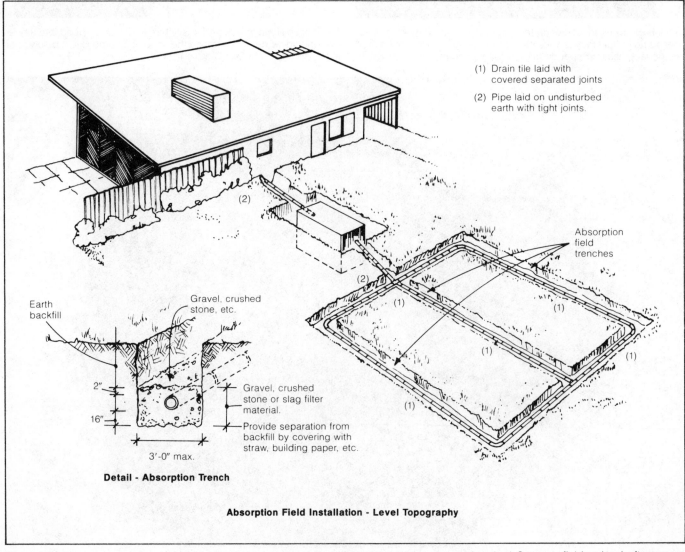

(1) Drain tile laid with covered separated joints

(2) Pipe laid on undisturbed earth with tight joints.

Absorption field trenches

Earth backfill

Gravel, crushed stone, etc.

2"
16"

Gravel, crushed stone or slag filter material.

Provide separation from backfill by covering with straw, building paper, etc.

3'-0" max.

Detail - Absorption Trench

Absorption Field Installation - Level Topography

Where private sewer systems are required, a septic tank system with a disposal field is the approved method. Separate field and tank often are run from the kitchen and laundry, so that the main field which handles human waste is not overloaded.

drain system. Joints in the pipe from the house to the tank are watertight, so no sewage leaves the system until it passes through the tank. From the tank, another watertight line might run to a distribution box, and from it the actual disposal field is run. There may be three or four outlets from the distribution box. Depending upon soil conditions the field may be fairly short, or may run a hundred feet or more in several directions.

The field is made of lengths of pipe that can be plastic, concrete, clay tiles or fiber pipe. The concrete and clay tiles come in 1-foot lengths, while the perforated plastic or fiber pipes will be 10 feet long. The short pipes or tiles are laid with short spaces between the ends, over which tar paper is placed. The sewage then seeps through the openings between the pipes. With perforated pipe, the liquid effluent disperses through the perforations. With either type of pipe, after it is covered with tar paper to prevent the backfill soil from entering the pipe, a foot or so of gravel is poured over the pipe, then the soil is replaced. Grass or moisture-loving plants are planted along the lines of pipe.

Installing a septic system is a big job, and unless you are crazy for backbreaking labor, we suggest you have a contractor handle it. He will bring in a backhoe that will dig the hole for the septic tank in an hour or so, and all the field trenches in a day. He also will know how to slope the field lines so they drain properly away from the distribution box and septic tank. In addition, he will know how to reach the inspector if one is required by law to check the system at each stage of installation.

Even before you start the installation, a good contractor will contribute. He should conduct a "percolation test" that will dictate how many square feet of absorption area will be required for your particular situation. For the percolation test, six or more holes (depending on local code) are dug to a depth of 18 to 36 inches and filled with water. The level of water in the holes is adjusted to about 6 inches deep 24 hours later, then a rule and a watch are used to determine how long it takes for the water level to drop one inch. Some codes will require that this be carried out more than once.

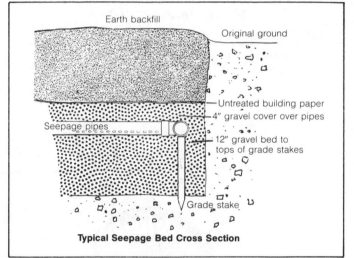

Typical Seepage Bed Cross Section

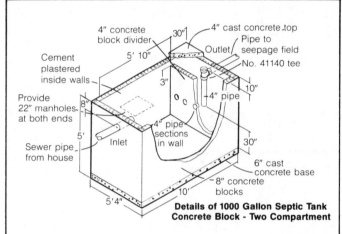

**Details of 1000 Gallon Septic Tank
Concrete Block - Two Compartment**

Locate the tank to meet minimum local distance requirements. It should be at least 5 feet from the house, ten feet from any lot line. Other parts of the system should be at least 8 feet from the house and 10 feet from lot lines (art courtesy of Genova Manufacturing Co.).

A two-compartment tank is more efficient than a one-compartment tank, and needs cleaning out less frequently. If you build the tank yourself, follow these general details, sizing for the required gallonage of your tank. There are approximately 7½ gallons in one cubic foot (art courtesy of Genova Manufacturing Co.).

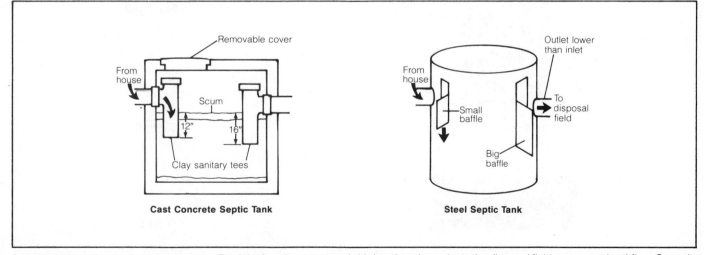

Cast Concrete Septic Tank

Steel Septic Tank

A septic tank can be steel or cast concrete. The inlet from house sewer is higher than the outlet to the disposal field, to prevent backflow. Capacity of the tank is determined by number of persons in household, usually described by the number of bedrooms. A steel tank will have asphalt coating to protect it against rust and corrosion. Baffles in the tank prevent splashing of liquid sewage. A concrete tank has T-fittings to prevent splashing and to keep scum from entering disposal field.

The area of the absorption field can be determined from the accompanying graph. It also is possible in some areas that a septic system cannot be installed because the soil is simply not absorbent enough. In such a situation you will have to use a chemical or composting toilet, plus some sort of settling tank for handling water from sinks and tubs. Water from toilets is called "black" water, as it contains toxic matter, while water from sinks, tubs and washing machines is called "gray" water. The latter contains only light soiling from people or clothes, plus biodegradeable soap or detergent.

Even with a septic system, it sometimes is recommended that you have a separate system for washing machines and tubs and sinks, because the waste water presents much less of a health hazard than does waste water from a toilet. The local

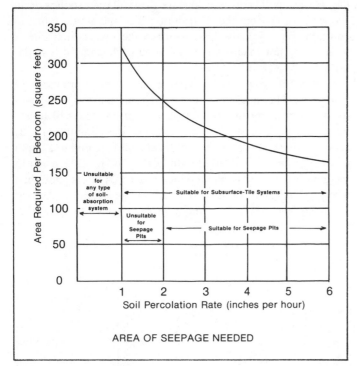

AREA OF SEEPAGE NEEDED

Soil percolation test determines the size of the septic field required for the type of soil involved. Note that it is possible that soil is not suitable for any type of seepage system.

REQUIRED SEPTIC TANK CAPACITY

Bedrooms	Minimum capacity
2 or fewer	750 gallons
3	900 gallons
4	1,000 gallons
5	1,250 gallons

SEPTIC TANK HEIGHT
FROM BOTTOM OF OUTLET TO TOP OF SLUDGE

Capacity of tank in gallons	Liquid depth in feet		
	3	4	5
500	11	16	21
750	6	10	13
900	4	7	10
1,000	4	6	8

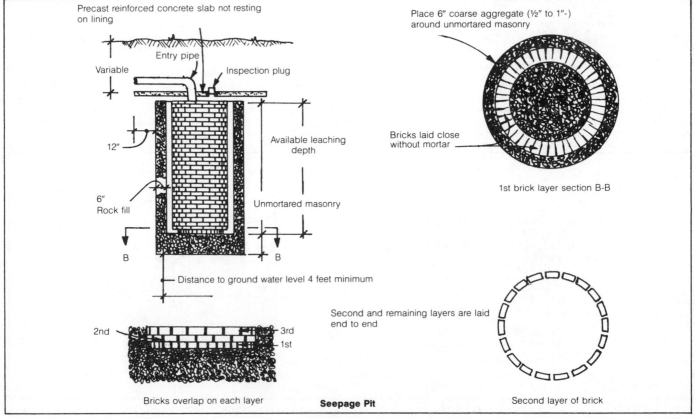

Seepage Pit

It is crucial that you take safety precautions when digging percolation holes or larger excavations to install septic tanks or seepage pits. One means of preventing sidewalls from collapsing is to brace semicircular sections of corrugated metal sheets; compression rods are bolted on the inside with expansion bolts. For any deep excavation, hire a professional.

plumbing code will tell you how far a septic field must be from a well or other source of drinking water and, even if there is no local code it makes sense from a health standpoint to follow the local guidelines.

Grease traps or septic tanks must be a minimum of 50 feet from a fresh water well, and the fields must be at least 100 feet from a well. You must also be careful not to locate a well downhill from a septic tank or field, as the aquifer or water table may carry toxic waste hundreds of feet beyond the septic field, down into the well.

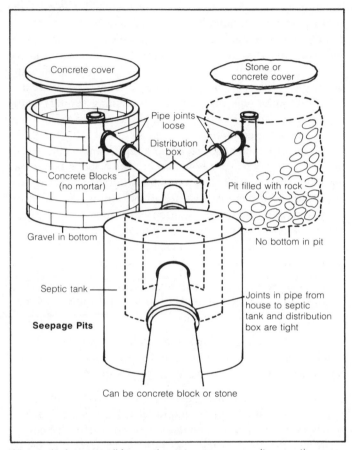

Seepage Pits

Where a lot is too small for septic system, seepage pits sometimes can be used if the soil is suitable. These pits are simply holes in the ground lined with rock or stone. Larger pits can be filled with loose stone, over which a cover of rock or cast concrete is installed.

Septic systems work on the principle that aerobic bacteria (requiring free oxygen) attack and break down the solid wastes in the septic tank, while anaerobic bacteria (those not requiring oxygen) attack the material in the disposal lines and in the soil around the lines into which the liquid matter leaches. This basic natural process can be disrupted or destroyed by a number of things, rendering the septic system inoperative.

Installing With Plastic Pipe
Installing a septic system is hard work, but doing the work yourself can save considerable money. The easiest material for the do-it-yourselfer is plastic pipe, which has now been approved for septic systems.

First, draw your septic system out on paper and, if necessary, have it approved by the proper authorities. Then dig the trenches for the disposal field, and for the septic tank itself. You will have to have the seller of the tank deliver it and drop it

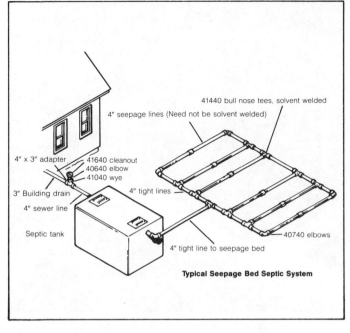

Typical Seepage Bed Septic System

into the hole with the aid of a hoist on his truck. It would be a good idea to know just how deep and big the hole must be; the seller of the tank can tell you.

Plastic pipe with solvent-welded joints is used from the house to the septic tank and (where one is used) to distribution boxes.

Perforated plastic pipe is used for the disposal field, and the joints can be left open or solvent welded. The Genova Company has a new system of drainage pipes for septic systems called "Liberty Bell." One end of each 10-feet section of pipe is enlarged as a "self coupler" and can be solvent-welded to the next length of pipe. As an alternative, a Genomeric™ flexible sealing ring can be used to make a watertight joint.

This company also suggests you might want to go from a 3-inch building drain to a 4-inch line for the septic system. They have adapters for this purpose. We believe that most houses will already have 4-inch drain systems, however.

Be sure the slope of the septic system is at least ¼ inch to the foot, and a few inches deeper than required. The additional depth is filled with pea gravel or earth fill that is free from rocks or frozen lumps. Be sure to dig a cross trench to accept the bells (hubs) on the ends of the pipes. You want the full length of each pipe to rest on the soil or gravel, not just the bells. You can assemble the line with solvent welding or seals, in the trench or on the ground. It is easier to assemble the lines on the ground, but then you must wait 12 hours for the solvent to harden completely. The joints then will resist the considerable forces applied to them when you lift the several lengths of pipe and lower them into the trenches.

Backfill around the pipe with gravel or earth. If the latter is used, tamp it lightly around the pipes. Be sure there are no rocks against any of the pipes.

The top of the septic tank should be at least 12 inches below the ground, and 24 to 36 in colder climates. Do not set the tank too deep, however, keeping in mind that you will have to dig down to the access hatch every couple of years to inspect the tank and to perhaps clean it.

Plastic pipe can be run right into the septic tank if it has no

Genova sewer-septic system pipe (left) is thinner walled than Schedule 40 DWV pipe (right). While it should not be used for indoor DWV purposes, sewer pipe is fine for underground use.

Genova 400 Series pipe comes two ways: perforated for seepage lines (top) and solid walled for sewer and other tight lines. A complete selection of fittings is also available.

Solvent welding of pipe joints may be done either in the trench or on top of the ground. Follow the usual procedure. Out-of-trench welds need 12 hours curing before lowering the pipes.

fittings and if the joints are sealed with mortar. If there are connections, they probably are clay tile, for which there are tile-to-plastic adapters available. Calk the adapters to the fittings.

Preventive Care

People who move to a home with a septic system from a city home, where anything and everything is poured into drains or flushed down the toilets, must learn different habits. For example, the bleach used in an automatic washer will kill the bacteria in both the septic tank and the fields. Part of the solution is to ocassionally renew the bacteria by mixing a powder with water and flushing it down the drain. The powder (or other material) contains bacteria that come to life in the presence of moisture, and immediately go to work breaking down the solid materials in the septic tank. The product is called a "septic tank renewer" (or something similar) and is available in hardware stores and home centers in areas where septic tanks are common.

The major maintenance steps for a septic tank include addition of "renewer" every few months, and a septic tank clean out every few years by a contractor who specializes in this work (and who has facilities for disposing of the material). However, day-to-day commonsense practices are the best means of preventing backup or plugging of the system. It might even be a good idea to make a list of the rules and post them in the bathroom and kitchen in a conspicuous place.

(1) Dispose of grease and coffee grounds in separate containers that will be picked up as solid trash. Never pour these materials down the drain.

(2) Paper, cigars, cigarettes, cloth products and feminine sanitary napkins should not be disposed of into a septic system. Treat these items as solid trash.

(3) Do not use caustic drain cleaners, or acid-based products in an attempt to unplug a septic system. They will corrode the pipes and reduce the porosity of the soil around the field. They also kill the bacteria that are absolutely essential for proper operation of a septic system.

With both pipe end and fitting socket coated with Novaweld™ cement, join them with a slight twist and hold 10 seconds. The pipe end is supported off the ground to keep it clean during the process.

(4) Occasionally run a snake through the solid-joint drain line between the house and the septic tank. Solid materials can settle in this line when the tank is full from heavy usage, or even a very heavy rain.

(5) Check with local residents who have had septic systems a long time. They can tell you what maintenance practices and problems to expect, and what products or services to employ to keep the system working properly.

One product that has had wide acceptance for maintaining septic and cesspool systems is called "Drainz," made by Jancyn Mfg. Corp. 4437 Park Drive, Norcross, GA 30093. This product cleans the lines and also aids in maintaining the porosity of the soil. Unfortunately, at the time of this writing, the State of Connecticut has banned the sale of Drainz, claiming it causes chemical pollution in the soil. Once the situation is resolved the product will again be on the market.

WELLS

Septic systems are used in some urban areas where there is a city water supply, but in suburban and rural areas the need for a septic system also indicates that water must be supplied by a well.

Gone are the days when you could dig a surface well 20 or so feet deep and be sure of clean, safe water. There are too many pollutants in the air and soil, and the water tables in many areas of the country have been dropping steadily as more and more water is drawn from the earth. It is necessary to *drill* a well in this day and age. The depth will be more than 100 feet, and may be several hundred feet. Drilling a well requires a professional contractor who has the necessary specialized equipment, and knows the character of the soil in your area. The cost of drilling a well is so much a foot, and it can run several hundred to several thousand dollars for the job. Which means you had better know the contractor and his reputation before you sign a contract — and read the fine print. You do not want to pay for several "dry" holes before you reach water.

Once the well has been drilled and capped (a steel liner is inserted as the well is drilled) you must pipe from the well to a pump. The pump can be in a recess in the ground, basically an insulated box — or it can be in the basement of the house. There are several types of pumps available, such as the "jet"

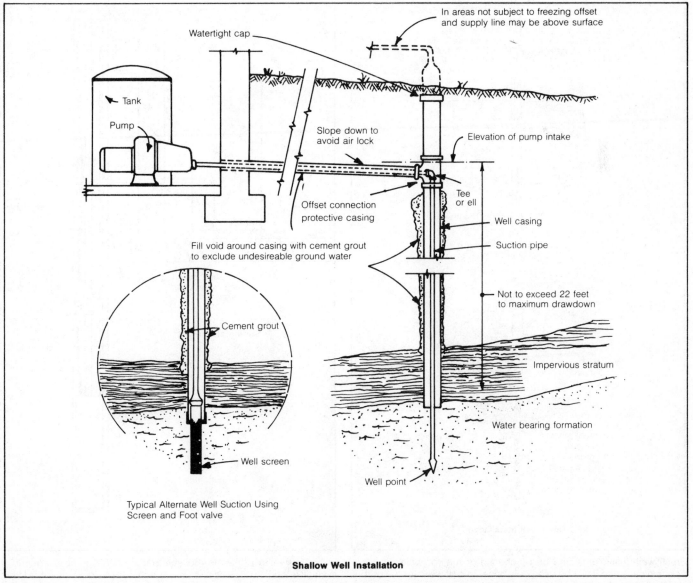

Shallow Well Installation

A well must be drilled as much as several hundred feet deep, and the hole lined with steel pipe to prevent contamination from the soil.

pump, which is a centrifugal type that can be designed to lift water from 20 feet to as much as 110 feet. Your contractor will know which type of pump is the best for your depth of well.

If your well is really deep, you may need a submersible pump that is slipped down inside the well casing and can pump water from depths to 480 feet. Regular maintenance is required for these submersible pumps. This involves pulling them up out of the casing and cleaning the "foot valve," a type of check valve that prevents water from draining out of the pipe line to the surface. This assures that when you turn on a water faucet you get water almost immediately. One symptom indicating that a foot valve is faulty or dirty is a delay of several moments after a faucet is opened. Another way to assure a constant water supply from a well is to have a storage tank in the house. When water is turned on and the tank starts to empty, an automatic device turns on the pump to refill the tank. The best pump and tank setup should be known by the contractor who drills the well, and he often will sell a complete system along with his drilling services.

For the do-it-yourself homeowner, replacement pumps, tanks and other parts are readily available from Sears, as well as from some local plumbing supply outlets.

COMPOSTING TOILETS

Plumbing codes are becoming more restrictive all the time, even in rural areas. In some regions it may not be possible to utilize a septic system because of soil conditions or other factors. The best solution is probably a "composting" or chemical toilet and system. Probably the best known of the composting toilets is the Clivus Multrum. This device composts with aerobic bacteria, and is designed to handle both toilet and kitchen wastes.

The main drawback to the system is the initial cost, which can run from a thousand to several thousand dollars. Once installed, however, the Clivus Multrum requires no energy and practically no maintenance. The device consists of a large container to which are attached tubes that come from the toilet and kitchen. The upper of three partitioned chambers receives

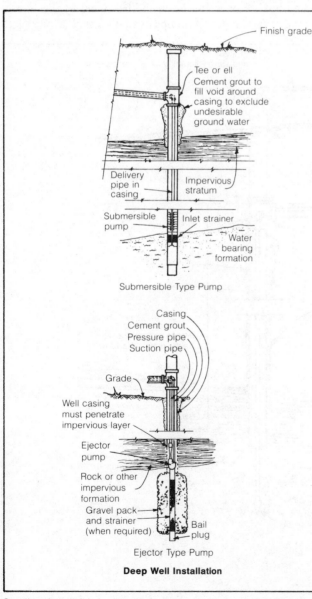

Deep Well Installation

Small well-drilling rigs can be purchased or rented (which is more economical since it will be used only once) to drill wells for water that will not be used for drinking, but only for lawns and gardens.

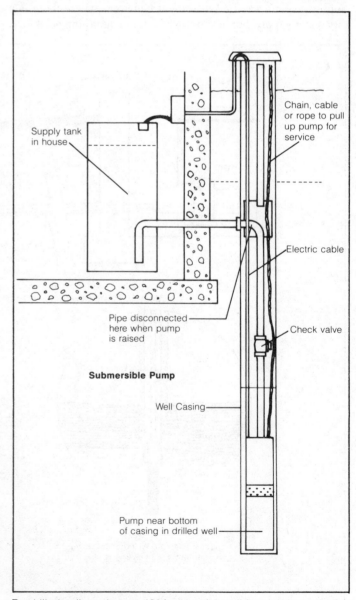

Submersible Pump

For drilled wells as deep as 480 feet, a submersible pump is required. It is small enough to fit down inside a 4-inch well casing. It has little lifting power, but enormous "head".

toilet wastes, and the middle one kitchen garbage. The combined wastes decompose at the same time and settle and slide to the lowest of the three compartments. By the time the waste matter reaches the bottom chamber it has become an organic compost. Two or three years are required for the first compost (humus) to reach the bottom — or storage — chamber. From then on, three to 10 gallons of soil may be removed per person per year, and the process is continuous.

The only other disadvantage of the Clivus Multrum is that a separate disposal system is required for water from the kitchen, laundry and bathrooms. Since this is "gray" water with no toxic matter in it, a simple settling tank or cesspool generally can be utilized.

Returning to the cost factor: considering that a septic tank and field are not required, the overall cost probably is comparable. Even if a septic tank and field are required for the "gray" water from bathroom, laundry and kitchen, the septic system can be much smaller than one required if toilets are included as part of the drainage setup. In an ideal system, water from the

Just introduced to the U.S. market, the "Humus" composting toilet requires no water, chemicals or septic system, and is completely self-contained. It does require electricity to power a fan in its system.

A composting toilet that has been around for several years is "Clivus Multrum" from Sweden. Units now are sold all over the U.S. and can be used wherever approved by local codes.

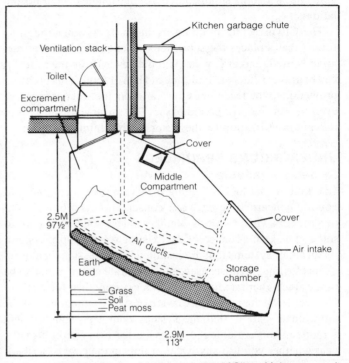

No power of any kind is required for operation of Clivus Multrum, once it is "charged" with peat moss as per instructions with it. The upper chamber receives material from toilets, and the center section is for kitchen refuse. The bottom chamber is where all materials finally are deposited as germ-free humus that can be used on your garden.

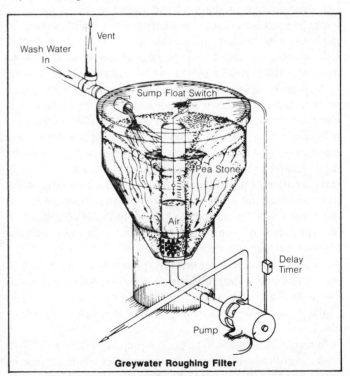

Greywater Roughing Filter

Where a composting toilet is installed, some provision must be made for "gray" water from sinks, vanities, washing machines, etc. This is a "Graywater Roughing Filter" sold by Clivus Multrum USA.

laundry would be run into a separate settling tank because of the laundry bleach that would kill the bacteria in the septic system. An alternative is to use products other than chlorine bleaches for whitening clothes. A number of products that contain borax will whiten clothes and are relatively safe for septic tanks. Almost all clothes washing detergents are biodegradable, with only small amounts of phosphate in their formulation.

The Clivus Multrum company has a "graywater roughing filter" that replaces the septic tank when the Clivus Multrum toilet is used, and gray water is routed away from the toilet. A bed of gravel filters out hair, lint and bits of food. This provides protection to the leach lines that can be in the soil outdoors, or even in an indoor greenhouse. The arrangement assures maximum utilization of the water, with minimum waste.

UNDERGROUND SPRINKLERS
Systems Available

One kind of outdoor plumbing that we do not recommend if you are concerned about water conservation is a built-in underground lawn sprinkler system — unless you install it yourself and make it a branch of the existing water supply system.

Sprinkler systems that are installed by professionals require a separate line, in most cases, and a separate meter. You may be billed at a higher rate for the sprinkler system than for water to the house. We are personally aware of such a situation, and the unfortunate part is that the system cannot be shut off and forgotten. You are charged a service fee every month of the year whether you use any water or not. In the case described, any time the water is turned on for part of the year, the monthly service minimum is double that for the time the water is shut off — regardless of whether or not any water is used.

A sprinkler system is convenient, no doubt, and can assure that every corner of the yard and garden receives plenty of water. If you connect it to the existing water supply system of the house you should be aware that when it is being used there will be a considerable drop in pressure in the house system, so never use the sprinkler system when it is meal or bath time.

A sprinkler system can have a simple manual control, with each section of the lawn or garden on a different line that is controlled by a gate or globe valve. Automatic controls get more expensive, but can be set to sprinkle the lawn for a few minutes at 3 or 4 o'clock in the morning when no water is being used, whether you are at home or not. These automatic controls are based on solid-state circuitry, but a lightning strike nearby burned out diodes and transistors in the control box in the house under discussion, and all the sprinkler circuits came on. The only way to stop the electronic monster was to pull the 1½ ampere fuse at the front of the box.

For automatic sprinkler systems, plastic boxes are buried in the ground and waterproof wiring and components are used. The shutoff and drain valves (used to drain the lines at the end of the season to prevent freeze-ups) are included in the boxes also.

Sprinkler heads should be the "pop-up" type that stay flush with the ground and clear of the lawnmower when not in use. Water pressure lifts the center of the valve a couple of inches above ground to assure the water is sprayed wherever it is needed. When a garden is raised, as shown in one of the

Sprinkler heads normally are flush with the lawn so that the mower does not contact them. Heads are solid brass to minimize corrosion and rust problems.

Center portion of sprinkler head raises when water pressure is turned on in the system, either by manual or automatic control. The heads can be lifted by hand to permit cleaning the orifices that can get filled with dirt. The small screw at center of head is used to increase or decrease the flow of water.

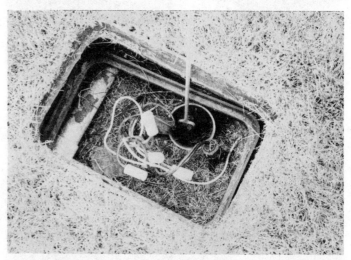

Plastic boxes recessed in the lawn contain plastic piping, waterproof electrical components and shutoff valve. Here a long-handle wrench is being used to turn on the valve. Other boxes in the lawn contain valves that permit draining the system for the winter.

When a vegetable garden was raised by building it up with railroad ties, a short brass nipple was installed to raise the sprinkler head so that it would spray part of the garden.

accompanying photos, you must screw on a pipe nipple to raise the sprinkler head the necessary added height.

The built-in sprinkler systems utilize plastic pipe because most of the system is underground. There is also a chance that water will settle in part of the system and freeze in the winter; plastic pipe resists damage from freezing much better than steel or copper lines.

Repairs

Grass, grass clippings, and dirt are the most common trouble-makers for spray heads in underground sprinkling systems. To repair your system, you will need a special sprinkler head core wrench (usually provided by the manufacturer of the system), screwdriver, pliers, adjustable wrench, and fine wire.

Turn off the water. Remove the sprinkler head core with the special core wrench or screwdriver or adjustable wrench. The threads turn counterclockwise.

With fine wire — not wood because it can break in the tiny water jets — clean the jets. Then replace the core and turn on the water. Sometimes you may be able to clean the jets without removing the core. Use fine wire for this job. If this treatment does not work, you will have to remove the core to clean it.

If the system does not have cores, unscrew the cap on the sprinkler head. Just loosen it; don't remove it. Then turn on the water full blast. The water pressure probably will flush out any dirt or grass debris. Retighten the cap.

If the piping has leaks, call in a professional to handle this trouble. Special equipment is needed; the equipment is probably too costly for you to buy.

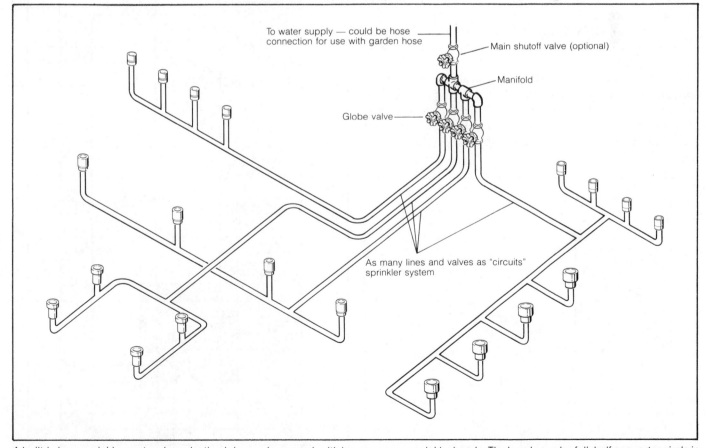

To water supply — could be hose connection for use with garden hose

Main shutoff valve (optional)

Manifold

Globe valve

As many lines and valves as "circuits" sprinkler system

A built-in lawn sprinkler system has plastic piping underground, with brass pop-up sprinkler heads. The heads can be full, half or quarter circle in distribution pattern.

Installation

If you want to put in a sprinkler system, check into the kits sold in hardware stores and home centers. They come complete with all fittings, pipe and step-by-step instructions. If your yard and garden are other than a simple square or rectangle, it would be better to buy individual components. You can then choose among the sprinkler heads that come in full circle, half circle and quarter circle patterns to cover your needs more exactly. Several manufacturers of this equipment, and their addresses, are listed in the appendix.

For this job you will need a tiling spade, a razor knife, pliers, hammer, chalkline, 1 x 3 stakes, the sprinkler kit, hose, special fittings, and a level.

Draw a plan of your lawn, showing the placement of the sprinkler system. The best way to do this is on graph paper, each square representing one foot or one yard. Each spray head will sprinkle a circle of grass from 20 to 50 feet in diameter. Choose the type of spray head most suitable for your needs and begin laying out the sprinkling pattern on graph paper. If you have a large lawn, you may need two or more systems to cover the area properly.

With the chalkline and stakes, lay out the lawn for the system, using the graph paper sketch as a guide. Assemble the system, using the various fittings.

Dig a V-shaped trench for the hose and sprinkler heads. The system should be in position and act as a guide for the trench. The trench should be about 6 in. deep. Just "fold" the sod over it, if you can. You don't need to remove the sod. Then bury the hose, fittings, and sprinkler heads in the trench. The sprinkler heads should be level in the ground. Now connect the system to an outside sillcock.

Since the sprinkler system is plastic, you don't have to drain it in the wintertime. However, you should disconnect the hose from the sillcock.

As the watering season passes by, check the level of the sprinkler heads from time to time. If they tip out of level, dig around the units and reposition them. If the spray jets become clogged with dirt or grass, you can quickly clean them with fine wire; do not use a wooden peg or toothpick in the tiny holes.

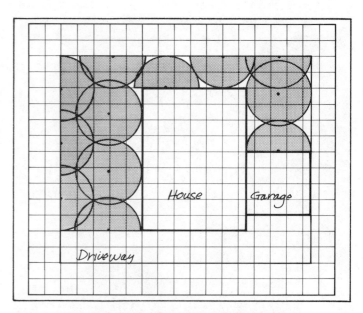

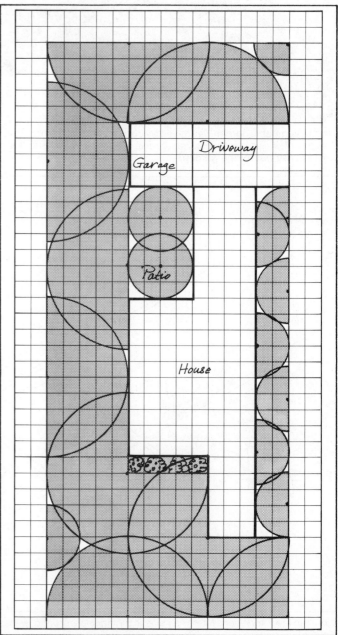

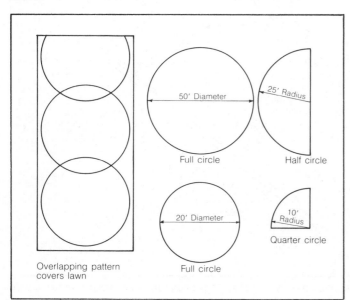

This underground sprinkler system kit contains plastic sprinkler heads, tee, elbow, and straight couplings. The connecting hose is a slip fit; the screw caps hold the hose tight without threads.

A slit with a tiling spade is usually all that's needed to bury the sprinkler parts. You may want to make a V-shaped trench, however, folding over the sod as you go.

After laying out and measuring the sprinkling system, cut the hose to fit the couplings. You can use a razor knife or hacksaw for this. Keep the cuts square.

Connect the sprinkler system to an outside sillcock. Or bore a hole through the siding, sheathing, and inside wall and then connect the hose to a water faucet.

SILLCOCKS

Very few houses have enough sillcocks (outside faucets), or they are not located for easy use. The simplest way to install a sillcock (in a frame house) is to bore a hole just above the masonry foundation, between the joists, or so it comes out through the blocking joist if the joists are parallel to the wall.

To avoid drilling through the wall and into the end of a joist, go down the basement and drill a small hole between the joists or through the end joist. If you do not have an extension bit (and many of us do not) start the hole with a regular bit about ¼ inch in diameter, then chuck a length of ¼-inch steel or brass rod in your drill motor. First grind a point on the rod. This improvised drill bit will be slow, but does save the cost of buying a bit that would be used only once.

After drilling from inside, go outside and drill a hole just a bit larger than the outside diameter of the pipe, or freezeproof faucet, through the house wall. You want the hole a little larger so you are able adjust to align with the pipe inside when you install the faucet.

If your foundation is quite low, you still will be able to connect a hose to it, but probably will not be able to fit a bucket or sprinkling can under it. If you want a higher faucet, locate the sillcock in the outside wall of an attached garage. Make it adjacent to the house wall of the garage, so you then can drill a hole through the wall to permit running a pipe into the basement. You make your hookup in the basement, then run the pipe up into the garage—and through the garage wall to the outside for the sillcock.

We recently installed such a faucet, but since the adjacent wall was for a room on a concrete slab, it was necessary to run plastic pipe the full length of the garage to a wall that did permit us to drill through to reach the basement. With this kind

The quickest way to cut in for a sillcock is to use a plastic Tee with compression fittings. Plastic valve also can be used, and with adapters can be joined to copper tubing or threaded steel pipe.

of a setup you can locate the sillcock as high as you want. The sillcock by the garage is used mostly for washing cars, and the convenient height does minimize the need for bending over.

In the basement you will have to cut a cold water supply line somewhere and install a T-fitting and a shutoff valve. In cold climates you want to shut off the water in the winter and drain the line to prevent freeze-ups. A plastic Tee and valve are the quickest way, but you can use threaded fittings or sweat-soldered fittings in the appropriate plumbing if you wish.

Freezeproof faucets generally are used for sillcocks where the inside of the wall is in a heated area such as a basement. The freezeproof unit is simply a long faucet that has the valve seat inside the house, where a freeze-up is not likely to occur.

Freezeproof faucets have a flange with notches to permit attaching them to the wall with wood screws, as do regular sillcocks. Just before pressing the flange against the wall, squirt calking into the space around the pipe or faucet. When you fasten the faucet with screws, excess calking will ooze out to assure a complete weathertight seal.

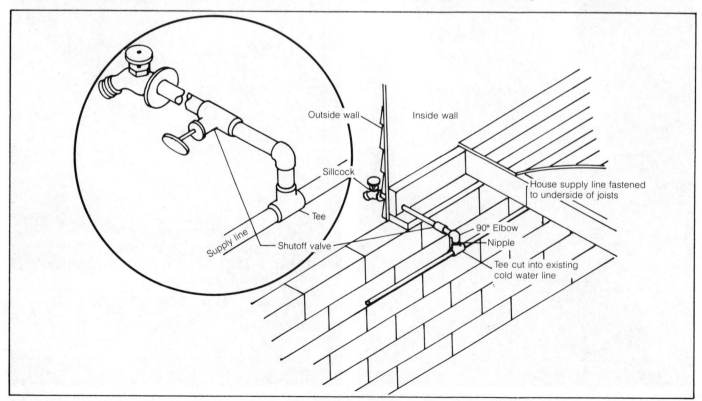

In basements and crawl spaces the piping is fastened up under the floor joists in most cases. Since you will run the piping from the sillcock above the bottoms of the joists, it will be necessary to use a 90-degree elbow and nipple to connect to Tee in the supply line.

12 How to Build Your Own Solar Collector

Despite reports to the contrary by prestigious engineering and research firms, solar energy is not only practical but has been in use since the 1930's for heating water in homes. In Florida and California solar units were in widespread use for many years. When cheap natural gas, and in some cases, oil came along with thermostatic control that eliminated any need for manual controls, solar units lost favor.

With each rise in price for gas and oil, solar heating units have become more competitive in overall cost — and certainly in "life-cycle" cost. That is, once a solar heating system has been paid for there is no cost for the free sunshine, only a minor cost of maintenance for the life of the system. But with gas, oil or electricity, you pay a monthly bill for the duration of your home ownership.

RETURN ON YOUR INVESTMENT

Flat-plate solar collectors, either air or water-cooled, are a "mature" technology with more than 50 years of experience.

Of the two types, water-cooled collectors (liquid-cooled, to be more precise) are the most efficient. Air-cooled collectors require sheet metal work, take up much more space, and entail construction of a heat-storage chamber.

A solar heating system with liquid-cooled flat-plate collectors is a form of plumbing. A skilled do-it-yourself home-owner-plumber can not only install the piping from the collectors to the space or water heating devices in the home, he can even build his own flat-plate collectors.

We owe thanks to Thomas Scott Dean, Professor of Architecture at the University of Kansas in Lawrence, Kansas for the design of the flat-plate collectors shown and described in this chapter. The collector is quite conventional and efficient, and it requires no special skills or tools to build. For the average family, four of the collectors will supply most of the hot water required for daily requirements to a minimum of 80 gallons. Considering that the collectors can be made for approximately half the cost of quality manufactured units, this

The home of Professor Thomas Scott Dean is just outside Lawrence, KS. Liquid-cooled collectors on roof are commercial units, and provide both space heating and domestic water heating through a solar water tank.

means that their cost can be recovered in less than six years. This takes into account the anticipated yearly increases in the cost of all forms of energy, oil, gas and electricity. At the moment we are not considering the price of coal, which at the present time seems slated to be used mainly for producing electrical energy.

CONSTRUCTION METHODS AND OPTIONS

Please read this entire chapter before rushing out to buy the parts to build the collectors. Alternative construction methods are offered, one of which should suit your own requirements and skills.

Building the Grid

A liquid (water or water-antifreeze) flows through the grid of tubing, as shown in the drawing. This grid consists of risers and manifolds, the small vertical risers being ⅜-inch I.D. (inside diameter) Type M copper tubing. No appreciable loss of efficiency will occur, however, if ¼ or ½-inch tubing is used instead. Each riser is cut exactly 73-⅛ inch long, and since Type M tubing comes in 20-foot lengths, two lengths are needed for each collector panel.

At each end the risers are connected to manifolds made of ¾-inch copper tubing. To equalize line friction, the inlets and outlets are at the opposite ends of the manifolds. Each manifold is cut to exactly 30 inches long, and drilled with the spacing as detailed in the drawing. Do not use a drill bit to make the holes, as they will be oval in shape rather than round. Instead, use a hole saw which will make round openings. Note that the hole saw contacts only part of the curved surface of the tubing as it first starts making the opening.

A simple U-shape jig made from two strips of wood nailed to a flat board will hold the manifolds, with the aid of a C-clamp, to keep them from turning as the hole saw cuts through them. A drill press should be used, even if you must borrow or rent it to assure that the holes are aligned and exactly at right angles to the axis of each manifold.

The holes in the manifolds should be the same size as the inside diameter of the risers. Cut the risers with a tubing cutter,

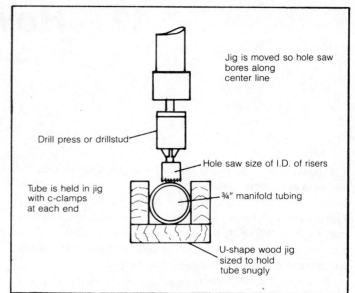

A simple U-shape jig holds manifold to the tubing while holes are cut in the tubing with a hole saw. Use a drill press, or drill stand, to assure that all holes are in line and are vertical to the manifold.

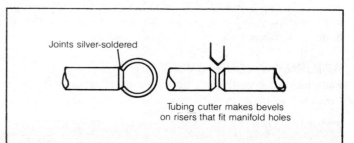

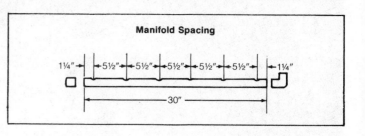

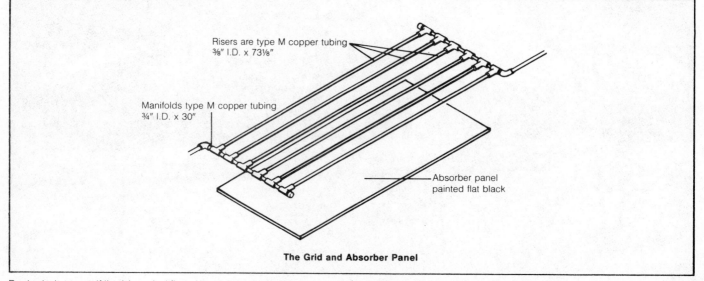

The Grid and Absorber Panel

Basic do-it-yourself liquid-cooled flat-plate solar collector consists of risers and manifolds cut from rigid copper tubing. Soldering is the only skill needed, since the absorber plate is steel or copper, and only a bit of sheet metal bending is required for using an aluminum absorber plate.

and the ends will be beveled as indicated for a perfect match with the holes in the manifolds. These connections, and the caps and elbows, are made with silver solder. More correctly called "hard" solder, as opposed to tin-lead "soft" solder, it does require more heat. If you do not have an oxy-acetylene torch, you can use a "MAPP" gas torch. This is similar to the familiar propane torch in most homeowner's workshop, but it creates a flame that is 500 degrees F. hotter. A special flux also is required; it comes in the form of a white paste. The metal at the joint first is cleaned with emery cloth or steel wool, then the flux is applied with a brush. The torch is played on the joint until the flux turns clear, then the stick of solder is applied to the tubing. The clearing of the flux indicates that the metal is hot enough to melt the hard solder. Do not play the flame on the solder (as also is the case with soft solder) because it will burn up. The base metal — the tubing in this case — must be hot enough to melt the stick of solder when it contacts the metal.

The Absorber Panel

Cut the absorber panel exactly 32 x 73 inches. (There is a reason for all these precise sizes and lengths.) The panel can be cut from 7-ounce sheet copper (per square foot), or 22-gauge plain or galvanized steel. The grid of copper tubing can be soldered to either steel or copper. Use 50-50 solder in ⅛-inch wire with an oxy-acetylene or propane torch. It would be a good idea to practice soldering some scraps of tubing to a piece of the metal used for the absorber plate in order to determine the best way to do the job while using the least amount of solder. The solder can be expensive, and you will use a considerable amount no matter

how well you apply it.

Position the absorber plate on a flat, smooth surface of heat-resistant material, locate the grid on it carefully and hold it in place with clamps or weights. Start soldering at the center of the panel and work toward the manifolds at the ends. It is almost impossible to prevent the metal of the absorber panel from warping slightly as you solder. It will not affect the efficiency very much, but will make it necessary that you use more solder.

Alternative Material

You can use aluminum for the absorber plate, but the grid of tubing is then fastened with aluminum cleats and heat-transfer cement. We suggest full-length cleats (the length of the risers) shaped from strips of aluminum 2½ inches wide. Use a length of tubing to shape the cleats, making sure the center of the tubing is in the center of the aluminum strip. The grid and cleats are positioned on the absorber plate and holes are drilled at 6-inch spacing to accept blind rivets from a rivet gun.

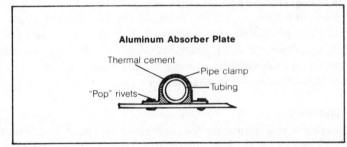

Aluminum Absorber Plate

Heat-transfer cement ("Thermon" is one good brand) is run in a bead along the center line of each riser on the absorber plate, and a bead is run along the top of each risers. Locate the grid on the absorber plate, fit the cleats over the risers and rivet them to the plate.

Painting the Grid/Absorber Panel

Any top-quality flat-black paint can be used to paint the grid/absorber panel, but for best efficiency we would recommend ''Black Velvet Nextel'' from the 3M Company. Be sure to clean

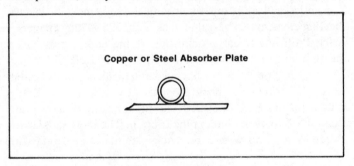

Copper or Steel Absorber Plate

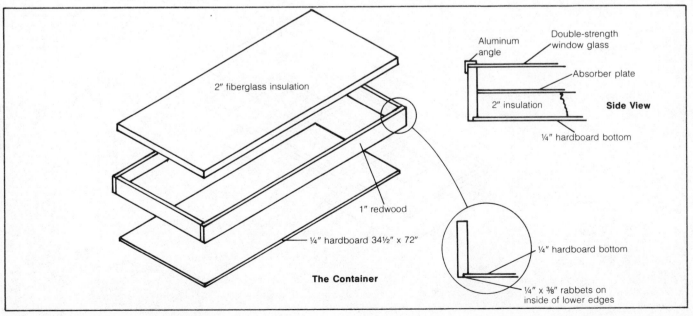

The Container

and prime, or etch the metal according to the instructions on the paint container. Failure to properly apply the paint could make it fail quickly and you would have to disassemble the collector, clean it and repaint it.

Building the Container

Once the absorber has been painted, put it/them aside and build the container. Use 1 x 6 redwood, and be sure it is top grade heartwood redwood. The container must last a long time and be watertight. Cut down the 1 x 6's (¾ x 5½ inches actual size) to 4½ inches wide. Save the 1-inch strips you cut off so you can use them with plastic material for the cover. Rabbet the bottom edges of the pieces as indicated, and assemble the four sides and bottom with waterproof glue and rustproof screws of either aluminum or brass.

A minimum of 2 inches of fiberglass insulation is fitted in to the bottom of the container under the absorber panel. If you can get high temperature insulation, that is best, but regular insulation can be used (with no paper facing) if it first is heated in an ordinary oven for a few minutes at 400 degrees. This will drive off the binder, which otherwise will fog up the inside of the cover glass or plastic the first time the collector is heated by the sun. The resulting fogging considerably reduces the clearness (transmissiveness) of the glass and thus cuts down the amount of solar energy that passes through it.

The Cover

If glass is your choice for the cover, tempered glass should be used. A 34 x 76 inch patio door glass (a standard size) is readily available, and it is placed on a bed of silicone sealer that first is run around the top edges of the container. Apply another bead of the silicone to the edges of the glass on top and clamp it to the container by using lengths of ¾ x ¾ inch do-it-yourself aluminum. Note that there is a ¼ inch gap between the four edges of the glass and the aluminum angle. This allows for the expansion of the glass when it is heated by the sun.

Higher water temperatures can be created in the collector by using a double cover plate. This utilizes two pieces of Type 546 plastic made by the Filon Corporation, and the cost would be about the same as a single thickness of tempered glass.

It is necessary to use a supporting framework when the plastic is used. Use the 1-inch strips ripped from the 1 x 6's, plus two more for intermediate supports, as detailed in the drawing. The plastic is attached to both faces of the framework, with a bead of silicone sealer under the plastic. Brass or aluminum wood screws are driven every 6 inches to hold the plastic to the frame. Be careful not to locate screws opposite each other, or so they run into each other. The screws can be ⅝ or ¾ inches long.

Make the frame/plastic assembly on a warm, sunny day with low humidity. This will minimize the water vapor that is trapped between the plastic sheets; it could cause fogging.

The frame/plastic assembly is attached to the upper edges of the container by first applying a bead of silicone, then drilling holes through the frame and driving screws into the upper edges of the container. Be sure the silicone sealer oozes out at every point around the container. This assures that there is an airtight, watertight seal.

The flat plate, liquid-cooled collector you have now assembled has an area of about 17 square feet. Most of the water-heating needs of an average family will be supplied by four of these units.

INSTALLATION

Your plumbing skills will be required to connect the collectors through piping to valves, a solar hot water tank, expansion tank, pump and controller. The solar tanks are available in a variety of capacities and most are fitted with a supplementary electric heating element. An 82-gallon tank without a heating element is what Professor Dean recommends. If the tank comes with a heating unit, he recommends that it be turned off.

The tank operates by having solar heated fluid circulate through a coil that is inside the tank, or which surrounds it. A pump for this kind of system can be quite small, as the only load it has to overcome to pipe friction. The most satisfactory setup is a pump with a bronze or stainless steel body and

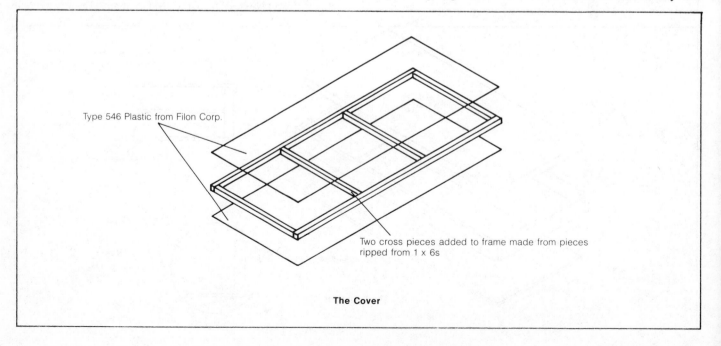

Type 546 Plastic from Filon Corp.

Two cross pieces added to frame made from pieces ripped from 1 x 6s

The Cover

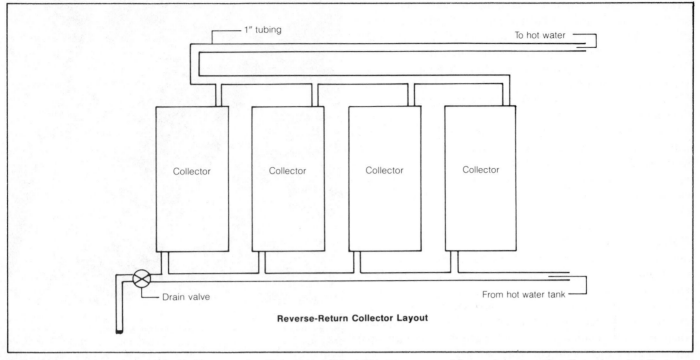

Reverse-Return Collector Layout

Collectors you make are assembled in "reverse return" layout as detailed. This assures equal flow and pressure drop through each collector, so each collector provides maximum of heated water. Be sure the inlet and outlet of each collector are at opposite corners, as detailed in construction drawing.

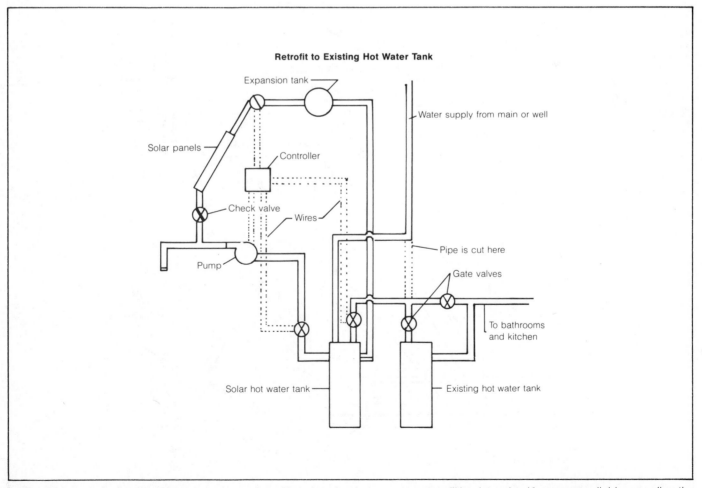

Retrofit to Existing Hot Water Tank

In "retrofit" system, the layout should be as shown. Actual location of various components will be determined by space available, as well as the present location of hot water tank. The differential controller has various wires labeled so you know which ones open the valve at collector and which turns on pump. Also identified: the valve that lets solar heated water enter the heat exchanger, and the valve that lets potable water enter the existing hot water tank.

permanent capacitor motor. The expansion tank may be as small as 3-gallon capacity, but a larger one can be used with no adverse effects. There is a pressure-relief valve on the tank, and the tank handles condensation of any liquid that might boil off the system due to a power failure or malfunction of a pump.

The collectors are assembled in a "reverse return" layout that assures equal pressure drop and flow through each of the collectors.

If you utilize an existing hot water tank in a "retrofit" installation, the drawing shows a typical piping layout. The actual installation, of course, will vary depending on the location of the hot water tank (in attic, first floor, basement, etc.) and the space available for the piping, wiring, controller and so on.

Piping

Use 1-inch Type M copper tubing, making all joints with 50-50 solder. Professor Dean says that at the present time there is no plastic piping that will stand up to the high temperatures that can occur under some conditions in a solar collector. These can be upwards of 200 degrees at "stagnation." That is, the period when the sun is shining on a collector and the pump (pumps) have not yet turned on to circulate the fluid.

All piping to and from solar collectors should be heavily insulated. This particular insulation bends around corners and elbows without cutting or splicing, making it very efficient (photo courtesy of Qest Products Corp.).

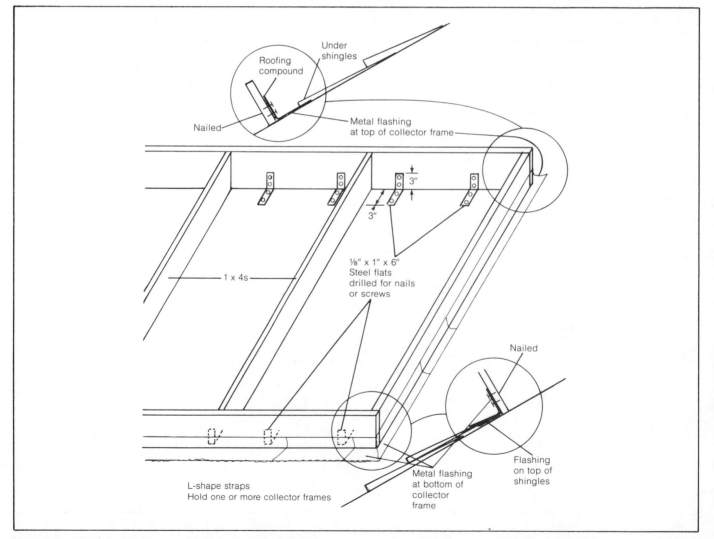

Your homemade solar collectors can be roof-mounted, or just staked in their container on the ground near your home. If roof-mounted, drill the steel flats to take nails or screws that hold down the L-shaped straps, which will hold the frames in place.

MOUNTING THE COLLECTORS

The solar collectors can be mounted on a south-facing roof, or against a fence, or simply installed as free-standing units in their own frame. The piping to and from the collectors should be heavily insulated. For maximum efficiency all year, the collectors should be positioned at the same angle to horizontal as your latitude. A few degrees variation will not seriously affect operation. Professor Dean installed his collectors at a 45-degree tilt angle, although his latitude is 40 degrees north. The collectors should face south, but a 10-degree variation will not measurably reduce the efficiency. If there is a choice, angle the collectors a bit to the West, where they will catch the hot afternoon sun.

CONTROLLERS

There are several excellent controllers for solar systems on the market. Temperature sensors attached to the collector outlet and storage outlet signal the controller to start or stop the pump. There is a high-limit sensor on the hot water outlet of the storage tank to prevent too-high storage temperature. Pump speed is varied by some controllers to assure optimum collection of solar heat.

About 50 percent of the energy used by a hot water tank is to maintain the temperature of the water at some predetermined temperature, for example about 140 degrees F. Water this hot is required only by an automatic dishwasher; for any other use the water is tempered with cold water, thus simply wasting the energy. Water at 120 degrees in the hot water tank is perfectly satisfactory for most uses, as few people use water hotter than about 105 degrees.

Professor Dean's home has a full array of commercial solar panels on the roof, only a few of which are used for hot water. The rest are for space heating, but only in the winter. He finds that water storage temperature is around 155 degrees during the course of a sunny day. After the dishwasher has been used in the evening the temperature will drop to about 130 degrees. After he and his wife have showered in the evening, the temperature will drop to about 100 degrees. Water at 140 degrees for the dishwasher will not be needed for another 24 hours, but sometimes the heating element in the tank is energized and it turns on and heats the water.

His solution to the problem was to put gate valves in the pipes leading to the tank; the heating mechanism could therefore be bypassed and water was heated only by the solar panels. At any rate, Professor Dean says, the electric element in the tank is shut off by pulling the circuit breaker in the service panel for at least half the year, and is turned on only occasionally during the most severe winter months, and during cloudy weather.

Flash Heater Alternative

One way to minimize the problem of "overheating" and guarantee a backup system on cloudy days (and this is also suitable as a replacement for your hot water tank even with a conventional heating system) is to use two or more small "flash" heaters. These units are small enough to fit under a kitchen or vanity cabinet; they have small storage capacity but heat water very quickly. Two 6-gallon heaters with 4500-watt, 240-volt heating elements would be suitable for most homes.

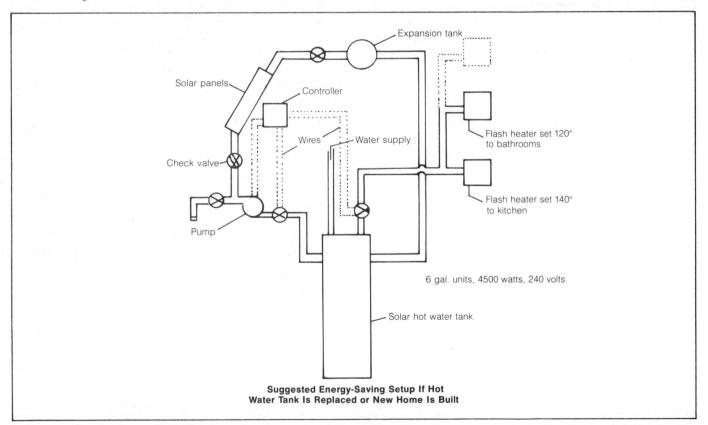

**Suggested Energy-Saving Setup If Hot
Water Tank Is Replaced or New Home Is Built**

Here is a suggested layout by Professor Tom Dean for a system that minimizes standby heat losses in the hot water tank. Preheated water from solar hot water tank is piped to flash heaters that quickly raise temperature required amount, for either kitchen or bathroom. If you are replacing an old hot water tank, or building a new house that will have solar assisted heating, this layout is ideal. (More information on these "flash" heaters is found in Chapter 7.)

Three of these flash heaters would cost about the same as one conventional electric hot water tank. Check local plumbing suppliers or contractors for current prices.

Both of the systems shown were designed by Professor Dean, who is a licensed mechanical engineer and architect; they operate with no attention even in the coldest weather because the solar circuit — collectors, piping, heat exchanger coil — is filled with antifreeze.

USING COMMERCIAL COMPONENTS
Building it Into the Roof

Professor Dean's house has commercial water-cooled units on the roof, to provide both space heating and hot water heating. The installed units actually constitute part of the roof; the 2 x 6 framework that contains the collectors is toe-nailed directly to the roof decking, and is flashed all around the outside. This arrangement permits all the piping to be kept inside the collector containers, and the pipes run directly through the roof decking down into the house.

This kind of arrangement is only possible with new construction, since the location of the pipes from the collectors must be planned to be inside walls in the house. Added touches of such a layout would be pipes under the bathtub to keep it warm, and a pipe as a towel rack to not only dry towels but to add warmth to the bathroom. There also must be provision to shut off the flow of the hot liquid during the summer when the extra heat is not wanted.

Air-Cooled Collectors

While we have said that liquid-cooled collectors appear to be more efficient and take less space than air-cooled units, there have been some interesting developments where air-cooled collectors have been used in combination with heat exchangers to provide hot water.

The advantages of air-cooled collectors are that there is no concern about the liquid freezing, and you need not worry

Air-cooled solar panels on modest home can supply both space heating and hot water heating. They may look a bit strange on the roof, but just consider them very efficient skylights (photo courtesy Research Products Corp.).

about water leaking through the roof, or from pipes. However, any reasonable craftsman will pressure-test the collectors and piping before they are installed, or during the installation.

One of the air-cooled collector systems is made by Solar Shelter Engineering, Kutztown, PA. Their setup is a system of components that are cost-effective against any electric hot water heater, and can supply between 50 and 80 percent of the hot water needs for an average family. The system can be added to either a new or existing hot water system. Note that as shown in the drawing, an auxiliary hot-water heater with a conventional heating element must be provided in addition to the solar

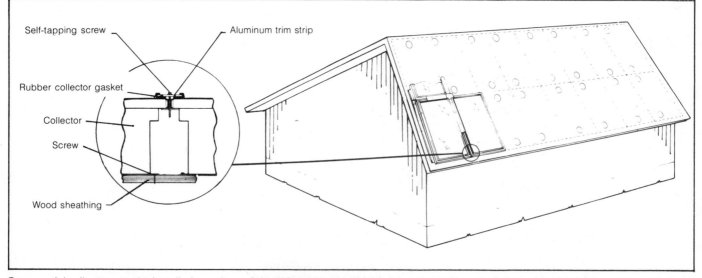

Commercial collectors can be installed onto the roof sheathing as well as installed between rafters. If rafters are 16" or 24" on center, the collectors are mounted onto the roof sheathing. Wooden starter strips are mounted along the bottom and left-hand border of the collector array. Eight-inch holes are cut into the sheathing to accommodate supply and return for each collector. Then the collectors are lifted into position. Starting at the lower left-hand corner and alternating from bottom to top row, the collectors are nailed into place. Once in position, wood framing is added along the top and right side; the entire border is then insulated to minimize heat loss. Flashing is applied to the perimeter of the array and metal trim strips supplied by Research Products Corporation are inserted between the rubber gaskets of each collector to ensure a watertight fit.

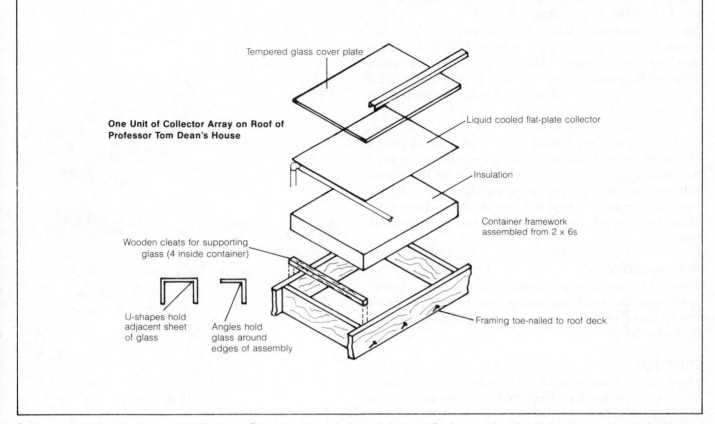

Tempered glass cover plate

One Unit of Collector Array on Roof of Professor Tom Dean's House

Liquid cooled flat-plate collector

Insulation

Container framework assembled from 2 x 6s

Wooden cleats for supporting glass (4 inside container)

U-shapes hold adjacent sheet of glass

Angles hold glass around edges of assembly

Framing toe-nailed to roof deck

Commercial units installed on the roof of Professor Dean's home are similar to do-it-yourself collectors, described in this chapter. Heavier 2 x 6 lumber is used as framing for containers because these collectors are bigger, and lumber also stiffens the roof of the house. The outside of framing is flashed, so the collector takes the place of any roof covering such as shingles.

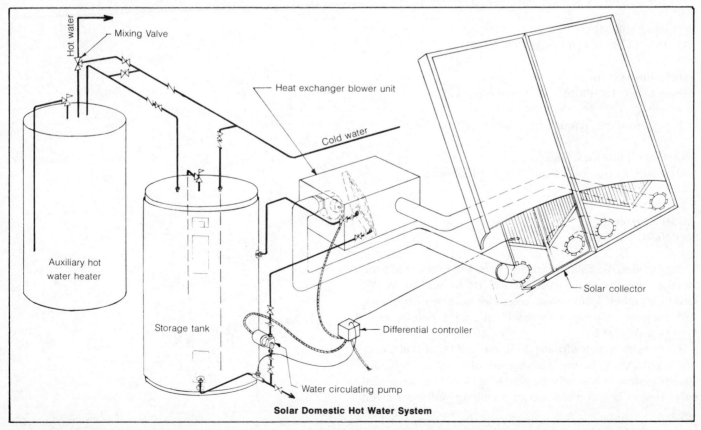

Hot water

Mixing Valve

Heat exchanger blower unit

Cold water

Auxiliary hot water heater

Storage tank

Solar collector

Differential controller

Water circulating pump

Solar Domestic Hot Water System

A system by Solar Shelter Engineering has air cooled collector panels that blow air down through a heat exchanger that heats water, which circulates through storage tank. This preheated water can be increased in temperature by a tank with a conventional heating element when the sun does not provide enough heat (drawing courtesy Solar Shelter Engineering).

system. A differential controller is required with the air system, as with the liquid system.

Another commercial solar system that has an optional water heating package is made by Research Products Corporation, 1015 East Washington Ave., Madison, WI 53701. Their claim is that the air system will provide up to 55 percent of heating needs for a home and 80 percent of hot-water requirements on an annual basis.

One installation of the Research Products unit is on a turn-of-the-century building in Madison, WI. The company figures a saving of 15 to 20 percent on heating fuel, but the owner of the building considers this conservative, since the system maintained a comfortable temperature all day, with an outside temperature of only 20 degrees F. The building contains 4200 square feet, and no output from the furnace is required on sunny days.

TAX INCENTIVES

If you decide that solar-assisted water heating is for you, be sure to investigate the federal and state tax incentives and credits for solar systems. They can reduce the actual cost of the installation by as much as one third.

SOURCES

Solar components can be purchased from the following sources: (solar water heaters priced from $200 to $300 are sold by local plumbing suppliers).

American Appliance Mfg. Co.
2341 Michigan Ave., Santa Monica, CA 90404;

W. L. Jackson Mfg. Co.
P.O. Box 11168, Chattanooga, TN 37401;

State Industries, Inc.
Ashland City TN 37015.

For Controllers, ranging from $45 to $75:

Hawthorne Industries, Inc.
1501 South Dixie, West Palm Beach, FL 33401;

Rho Sigma
15150 Raymer St.
Van Nuys, CA 91405.

Several brands of pumps costing from $40 to about $75 are suitable. Two excellent units are Teel 1P761 sold by W. W. Grainger (check local yellow pages for nearest distributor), and one from Grundfos Pumps Corp., 2555 Clovis Ave., Clovis, CA 93612.

There is no reason why any do-it-yourself homeowner cannot install either a liquid- or air-cooled solar system. A liquid-cooled system is basically all plumbing, while an air-cooled solar system is a combination of plumbing and sheet metal work.

13 Plumbing for a New Bathroom

Addition of a bathroom requires a building permit and a plumbing inspection. The inspection is for the health and safety of the homeowner and his family and should be considered in that light.

SPACE REQUIREMENTS

Bathrooms can be located nearly anywhere in a home, and very little space is required — much less than you might think. This is even truer if you are considering adding a "powder room" that has just a vanity and toilet. In this case, a space as small as 4x4 feet would be adequate.

The simplest way to add a bath is to build it on the opposite side of the wall from an existing bathroom. This might be in a closet, or in a bedroom that is large enough to spare the necessary floor space.

Space for Insulation: Preventing Frozen Pipes

When planning the space requirements for a bathroom addition, allow enough room to permit addition of pipe insulation. Plumbing might require extra insulation to prevent freezing in cold weather, or you might want to build a foundation with insulation inside the walls and on the floor to prevent freezing. As an alternative, and in combination with insulation, cut two openings in the existing foundation wall (3 to 4 inches in diameter) so warm air is circulated from the basement to warm up the space.

Planning the Pipe Route

Although it is possible to run hot and cold water supply lines almost anywhere in the house, the same is not true of the soil pipe drain. This will be a cast iron or copper line that is three, four or more inches in diameter. It really is not practical in most instances to reroute this pipe very far.

Whenever you add new pipe — or reroute pipe for a more efficient path to the area where you plan to put in new fixtures — draw up a plan before you begin disassembling or installing

A large and dramatic bathroom such as this can be created as part of a master suite. The plumbing changes required for this room are more extensive than those for an ordinary bathroom addition.

When adding a bath to an attic area, skylight or clerestory units will offer as much light as a dormer, but more privacy. They also cost less to add than a dormer.

the pipe. Draw the plan to scale, with ¼ inch or ½ inch equal to one foot, on graph paper. Mark in the existing cold and hot water lines and then make several copies of this drawing. Now you can draw in alternative routings, rearrangements, and branchings. This type of preplanning means that you will not get halfway into the project and then find that your measurements did not take into account the existing pipe, or that you did not leave enough room for air chambers. For new hot and cold water supply lines, keep the pipes at least 6 inches apart.

The main drain runs directly to the bathroom wall and up through the roof, while a Tee runs just under the floor to connect the toilet to the drain. The vanity and tub drains connect to the main drain, and revents run to the main drain at a point several feet above the fixtures. Adding a toilet fixture will require a main drain of 3 or 4 inches in diameter. If moving the toilet location, the old main drain will have to be connected up to the new fixture. Drains from the bathtub and vanity basin can be connected to the main drain below the toilet, rather than running them back to the main house drain.

EXTENDING THE EXISTING PIPES
Exposing the Old Pipes

Tools needed. Steel tape measure, spirit level, keyhole saw or heavy utility knife.

Likely locations. Look on the roof for a projecting vent and then check at the base of the vent for an exposed cleanout. This pinpoints the location of the vertical drain-vent stack, which is the largest pipe in your house. It will be 4 inches or larger, and usually of cast iron. Runs nearly straight; you can use its location as a starting point to find other pipes and fixtures.

Although you can figure that the hot and cold supply lines will run near the drain stack, keep in mind that often they jog in surprising directions. You may have to drill test holes to exactly determine the locations of the pipes. Then you can plan the

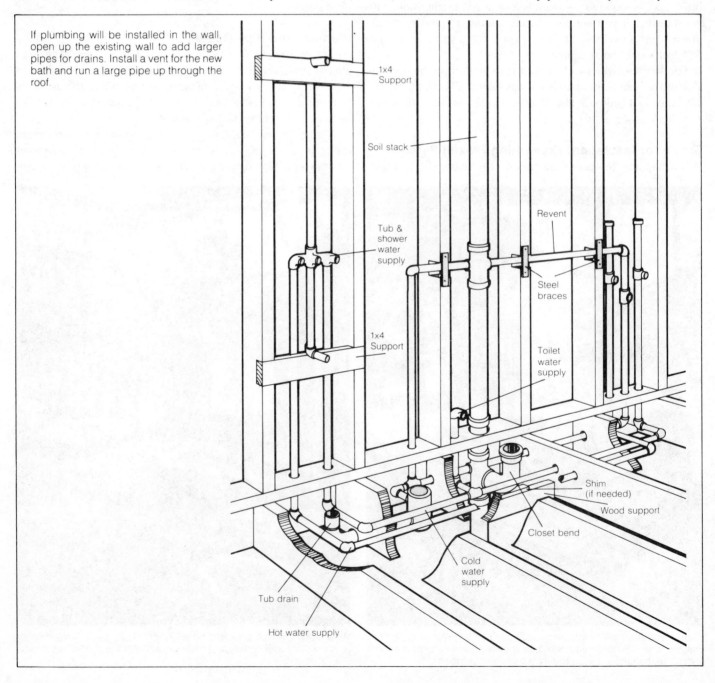

If plumbing will be installed in the wall, open up the existing wall to add larger pipes for drains. Install a vent for the new bath and run a large pipe up through the roof.

1x4 Support

Soil stack

Tub & shower water supply

1x4 Support

Revent

Steel braces

Toilet water supply

Shim (if needed)

Wood support

Closet bend

Cold water supply

Tub drain

Hot water supply

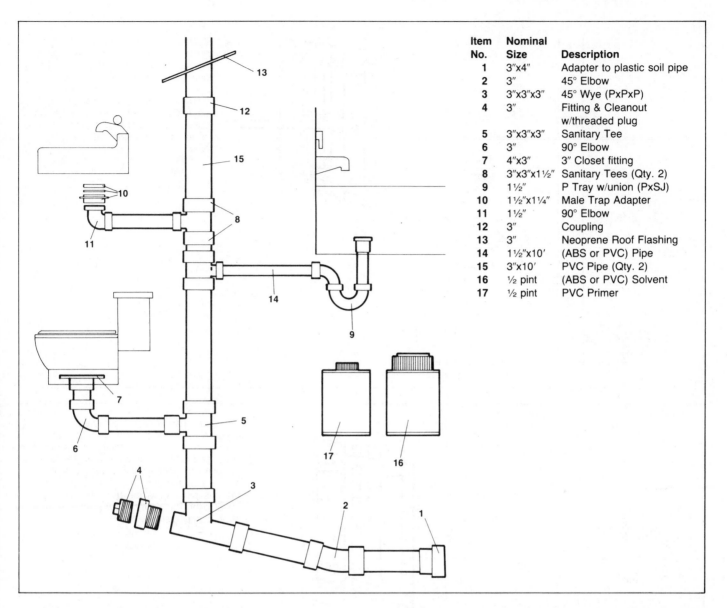

Item No.	Nominal Size	Description
1	3"x4"	Adapter to plastic soil pipe
2	3"	45° Elbow
3	3"x3"x3"	45° Wye (PxPxP)
4	3"	Fitting & Cleanout w/threaded plug
5	3"x3"x3"	Sanitary Tee
6	3"	90° Elbow
7	4"x3"	3" Closet fitting
8	3"x3"x1½"	Sanitary Tees (Qty. 2)
9	1½"	P Tray w/union (PxSJ)
10	1½"x1¼"	Male Trap Adapter
11	1½"	90° Elbow
12	3"	Coupling
13	3"	Neoprene Roof Flashing
14	1½"x10'	(ABS or PVC) Pipe
15	3"x10'	PVC Pipe (Qty. 2)
16	½ pint	(ABS or PVC) Solvent
17	½ pint	PVC Primer

opening, which should always be between the studs flanking the pipes.

Cutting the opening. Tap on the wall to locate the 2x4 studs flanking the pipes. Carefully knock a hole in the plaster or plasterboard to expose the plumbing, which will be between studs. Reach a steel tape measure into the hole on each side of the pipework to contact the studs. Note the measurement on the rule. Mark on the wall the locations of the flanking studs. Hold

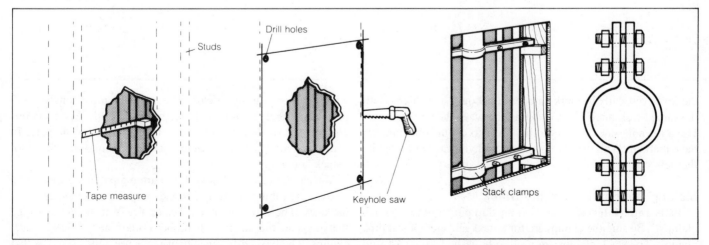

Open the wall to gain access to hot- and cold-water supply lines and main drain. Measure in each direction to locate wall studs. Mark their positions. Bore holes at corners of the work area; insert a keyhole saw, or use a heavy utility knife. Spike blocks to studs to support stack clamps above and below drain line to be removed. Stack clamp for supporting the main drain (vent) is shaped from heavy steel bar.

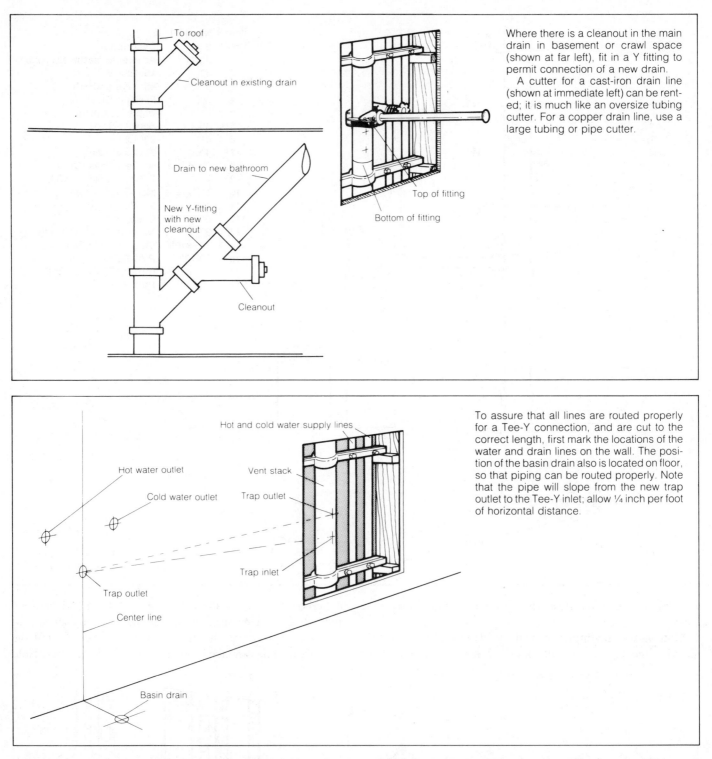

Where there is a cleanout in the main drain in basement or crawl space (shown at far left), fit in a Y fitting to permit connection of a new drain.

A cutter for a cast-iron drain line (shown at immediate left) can be rented; it is much like an oversize tubing cutter. For a copper drain line, use a large tubing or pipe cutter.

To assure that all lines are routed properly for a Tee-Y connection, and are cut to the correct length, first mark the locations of the water and drain lines on the wall. The position of the basin drain also is located on floor, so that piping can be routed properly. Note that the pipe will slope from the new trap outlet to the Tee-Y inlet; allow ¼ inch per foot of horizontal distance.

the level vertically to mark an opening about 3 feet high. With the same level, mark horizontal lines between the vertical ones. Use a keyhole saw or heavy utility knife to cut the opening you have marked. With the plumbing exposed you can start to make the new connections.

Making Connections to the Stack

Tools and Materials. You will need to purchase two "stack clamps." Be sure the clamps are for a stack and are not just pipe clamps. The stack clamps are used to hold the heavy cast iron (or copper) main drain line in position. If you do not use these clamps the stack can settle and loosen the flashing on the roof,

which will result in a leak. The stack clamps consist of 2 perforated steel straps bolted together at the ends. Stack clamps require 2x2 or 2x4 blocks nailed to the studs for support. In addition, you will need rubber sleeves and 4 regular (not "stack") clamps.

You can rent a cutter for cast iron drain pipe; this is much like an oversize tubing cutter. For copper or plastic stack pipes, use a hacksaw. The fitting will be a Tee or Tee-Y of the hubless type that joins to the stack with rubber collars and stainless steel clamps. The basic difference between a Tee and a Tee-Y is that the Tee has a right angle projection, while the Tee-Y has the projection at an angle to assure a smoother flow of the liquid in

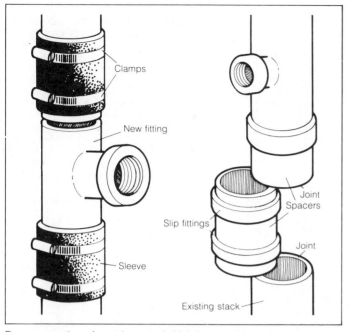

Remove section of cast-iron stack (right); use rubber sleeves to cover joints at old pipe and new fittings. In copper or plastic stack, use 2 spacers. Slide slip fittings from lower spacer over joints.

the line. In some cases you might want to use a cross, so you can install fixtures back-to-back.

Installing the fitting. Nail the cleats in, making sure they are level. Measure the height of the fitting. Mark this onto the stack. Nail the stack clamps to the cleats so that one is above and the other is below the cutting lines.

Turn off the water supply before you make any cuts. Cut along the marked cutting lines, using a pipe cutter. Slip the rubber sleeves over the cut ends, positioning them just above and below the pipe opening. Insert the Tee or Tee-Y fitting. Then slide the lower rubber sleeve upward and the upper rubber sleeve downward, so that both joints are covered by the sleeves. Place two metal clamps over each sleeve and tighten the clamps.

For addition of a cross where there was a Tee-Y, first disconnect the old fitting from the drain pipe. Then make the cuts 3 inches above and 3 inches below the old location of the Tee-Y. Immediately slide the sleeve collars and clamps for the connection onto the cut ends. Insert the fitting and clamp in place. You can leave the support clamps in place. The fitting should be angled at about 45 degrees to the wall so that the new pipe, which will extend from the fitting, is close to the wall.

Cutting the copper or plastic pipes. For a copper or plastic

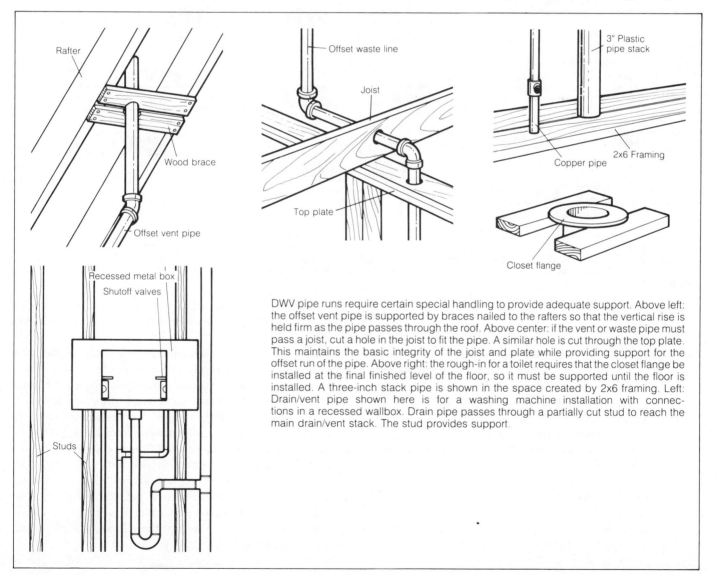

DWV pipe runs require certain special handling to provide adequate support. Above left: the offset vent pipe is supported by braces nailed to the rafters so that the vertical rise is held firm as the pipe passes through the roof. Above center: if the vent or waste pipe must pass a joist, cut a hole in the joist to fit the pipe. A similar hole is cut through the top plate. This maintains the basic integrity of the joist and plate while providing support for the offset run of the pipe. Above right: the rough-in for a toilet requires that the closet flange be installed at the final finished level of the floor, so it must be supported until the floor is installed. A three-inch stack pipe is shown in the space created by 2x6 framing. Left: Drain/vent pipe shown here is for a washing machine installation with connections in a recessed wallbox. Drain pipe passes through a partially cut stud to reach the main drain/vent stack. The stud provides support.

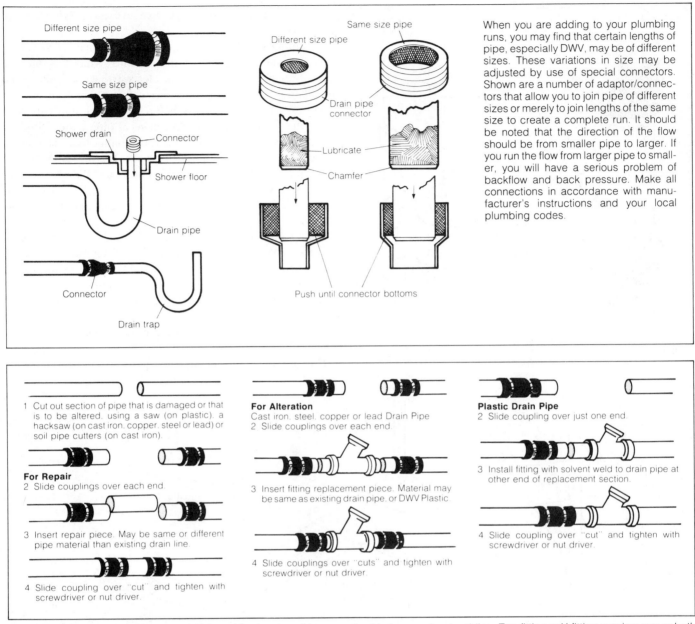

When you are adding to your plumbing runs, you may find that certain lengths of pipe, especially DWV, may be of different sizes. These variations in size may be adjusted by use of special connectors. Shown are a number of adaptor/connectors that allow you to join pipe of different sizes or merely to join lengths of the same size to create a complete run. It should be noted that the direction of the flow should be from smaller pipe to larger. If you run the flow from larger pipe to smaller, you will have a serious problem of backflow and back pressure. Make all connections in accordance with manufacturer's instructions and your local plumbing codes.

1 Cut out section of pipe that is damaged or that is to be altered, using a saw (on plastic), a hacksaw (on cast iron, copper, steel or lead) or soil pipe cutters (on cast iron).

For Repair
2 Slide couplings over each end.

3 Insert repair piece. May be same or different pipe material than existing drain line.

4 Slide coupling over "cut" and tighten with screwdriver or nut driver.

For Alteration
Cast iron, steel, copper or lead Drain Pipe
2 Slide couplings over each end.

3 Insert fitting replacement piece. Material may be same as existing drain pipe, or DWV Plastic.

4 Slide couplings over "cuts" and tighten with screwdriver or nut driver.

Plastic Drain Pipe
2 Slide coupling over just one end.

3 Install fitting with solvent weld to drain pipe at other end of replacement section.

4 Slide coupling over "cut" and tighten with screwdriver or nut driver.

Use clamp-on fittings to eliminate on-site joints of lead and caulking, sweat-soldering or solvent welding. Tee-fitting or Y-fitting requires one or both ends fitted with short pipe for cast iron and copper fittings. A plastic drain line can have a fitting solvent-welded to it on one end, with clamp-on connector and short pipe piece at the other end.

stack, the lower cut usually should be 8 inches below the pipe's inlet center.

Venting and reventing. The main drain for a new toilet will have to be vented out through the roof. Drains from the tub and vanity require "reventing." Venting and reventing allow atmospheric pressure to enter the drain and prevent a partial vacuum that could cause slow drainage, or even a backup of one drain into another. The need for vents and revents is clearly detailed in any building code, and is required for sanitary reasons. Do not under any circumstances make a drain installation without proper venting and reventing.

Connections to Hot and Cold Water Pipes

The first step is to find the nearest hot and cold water lines and to cut into them with a Tee pipe connector. As an alternative to cutting pipe, you may be able to disassemble plastic or steel pipe back to the nearest connection and install a Tee there. The

water must be shut off before you start the job. If you cut the pipes, whether with a pipe cutter or hacksaw, drain water from the cut.

Adding Tee fittings. The connections for hot and cold water pipe are made with Tee fittings. First, turn off the water supply. If the lines are copper, you can sweat-solder the Tees into the lines by cutting out an 8-inch section and springing the lines to one side while you insert the fittings. Another quicker and more practical method is to use polybutylene fittings that have compression nuts at each end. Seal the fitting onto the upper riser first. As described earlier, the fittings will seal on copper, plastic or steel pipe. The compression nuts at each end of the fitting are snugged up with a wrench, but don't overtighten the nuts. Leave the wall open for a couple days, with the pressure in the supply lines so you can see any minor leaks. A slight, gentle snugging up on the nuts each day will stop any leaks.

You can use various adapters from the compression Tees to

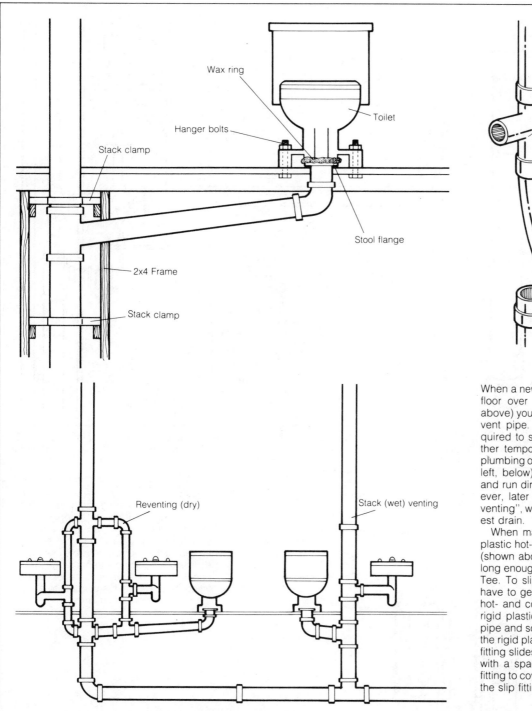

When a new bathroom will be on the first floor over a basement (shown at left, above) you can run the drain to a nearby vent pipe. A frame of 2x4s will be required to support the stack clamps, either temporarily or permanently. When plumbing originally is installed, (shown at left, below) the vents usually are "wet" and run directly to the main stack. However, later plumbing work requires "reventing", with a new vent above the highest drain.

When making connections in flexible plastic hot- and cold-water supply pipes (shown above) remove a section that is long enough to allow replacement with a Tee. To slip this new fitting in, you will have to gently bend the old tubing. For hot- and cold-water pipes of copper or rigid plastic, remove about 8 inches of pipe and solder the Tee or cement it (for the rigid plastic) to the riser above. A slip fitting slides onto the lower riser. Then fill with a spacer, and raise the lower slip fitting to cover the joint. Cement or solder the slip fitting.

return to rigid copper tubing, which is more practical than flexible polybutylene pipe. You also can go to rigid PVC or CPVC rigid pipe where the connections are solvent-welded.

Existing steel or brass hot and cold water pipes. Turn off the water supply and cut into the riser using a pipe cutter or hacksaw. Take out all of the pipe section between the two connection fittings. Since the pipe section can be quite long, this may involve more than one wall opening. Use two wrenches when unscrewing the fittings at the joints.

Add adapters to each steel coupling. Install plastic or copper pipe on the upper adapter. Then cement or solder in the new Tee. Add another length of pipe to the lower adapter, but cut it so that it reaches 3 inches below the bottom of the Tee. Last, cut

a spacer to fit into the 3-inch gap. Install it with slip fittings. The Tee should be placed at a 45 degree angle to the wall.

Back-to-back fixtures. For copper or plastic pipe, you can install new Tees on the risers either above or below any existing Tees. For brass or steel, place the new Tees at right angles from the wall, either above or below the old Tees.

Closing the Wall

To close up the wall after you have made your connections to the basin, nail cleats on either side of the opening you have made, against the studs. Nail the plasterboard to the cleats. It will be necessary to cut slots in the board to fit around the pipes. The slots then are closed with strips of plasterboard and taped to

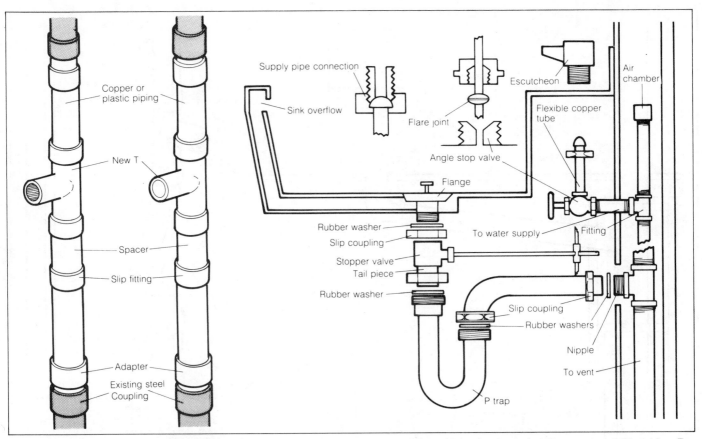

For steel pipe (at left, above), use hacksaw or pipe cutter. Take out all pipe between fittings. Use adapters to install copper or plastic tubing. Tee attaches to copper or plastic pipe placed below steel couplings. Another piece, 3 inches less than space between lower adapter and tee bottom, goes in lower adapter. Spacer fills gap, with a slip fitting. Sink installation (right) requires many small, essential components.

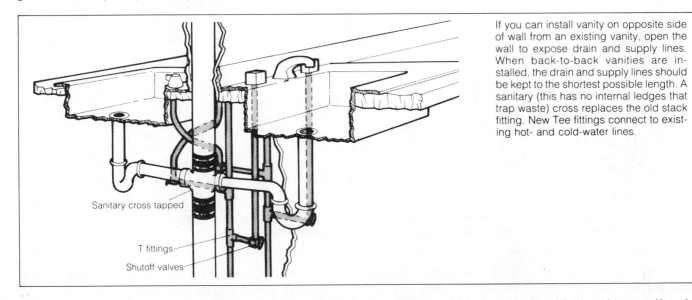

If you can install vanity on opposite side of wall from an existing vanity, open the wall to expose drain and supply lines. When back-to-back vanities are installed, the drain and supply lines should be kept to the shortest possible length. A sanitary (this has no internal ledges that trap waste) cross replaces the old stack fitting. New Tee fittings connect to existing hot- and cold-water lines.

smooth the wall. For a neater application, install the plaster-board before you make your connections to the basin. In this case you need only cut round openings for the pipes. Just as for soil pipes, leave the wall open a couple of days (to make sure there are no leaks) before you close up the wall. You can seal off the short lines to pressure-test them by using valves with compression nuts.

When you are sure there are no leaks, remove the valves (after you shut off the water), apply the wallboard, and finish the rest of the piping work. Once the wall has been closed, cut off the pipe extensions to the proper length so that a 90 or 45

degree elbow can be attached. It will direct the water line close to, and parallel to, the wall.

Projections through a wall. In most cases it will be necessary to run a short length of pipe from the Tees in the supply lines to reach through the wall surface. The plasterboard is fitted around the projecting pipes. Mark the replacement plasterboard and drill ¾ to 1 inch holes for ½ inch pipe or tubing. Use a wood bit or hole saw. Patch with plaster or taping compound. Install a chrome-plated escutcheon to hide ragged hole edges. Slide it on before making the connections or, if you forget to make the connections first, use a clamp-on escutcheon.

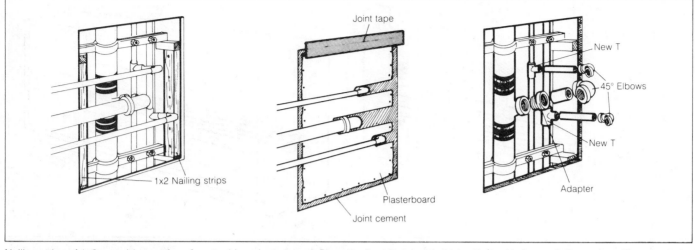

Nailing strips of 1x2s provide a surface for attaching plasterboard. Place the front faces of the strips flush with the stud's front edge. Then patch the opening with plasterboard. Short lengths of pipe will run to the wall's outside surface. Here, 90-degree or 45-degree elbows route the pipes along wall. Adapters on original fittings allow use of steel, copper or plastic pipe.

Pipework for the Toilet

If the new bathroom is to be on the first floor, with a basement under it, you also can install a toilet. The soil pipe can be plastic (if code allows) and run to the main vent in the basement. It would be necessary to build a temporary support for the two required stack clamps. If the fitting provides complete support to the soil pipe, the temporary support can be removed after the Tee or Tee-Y has been installed. If there is any doubt, the support should be made permanent. You may wish to have a professional plumber cut the vent and install this fitting for you. (See also "Hiding Exposed Pipes," below.)

Adding A Second Vanity Basin

Rather than a completely new bathroom, you might be thinking in terms of improving your existing bathroom. If what you want is a double facility in the bathroom, one easy solution is addition of a second vanity basin.

Extension within an existing bathroom. For this project you don't even have to open the wall. You make all connections outside the wall.

Cut the existing supply lines under the present vanity and install Tee fittings to provide water to the new vanity. Do the same for the drain line. Remove the existing trap with slip joint fittings and replace it with a Tee fitting to which the drain from

the new vanity will be attached. The drain for the second vanity must start higher than the existing one, so there is a definite downward slope from the new vanity basin to the existing one. If there is no slope to the drain you will have later problems with a clogged drain. Without the angled drain, the traps of both basins will keep the long drain line from the new basin filled with water; sediment and soap scum will plug the line.

Extension to an adjacent room. If you want a new vanity basin on the wall opposite an existing bathroom but not aligned with it, the work involved requires opening the wall and extending the supply and drain lines along the wall. However, the exposed pipes are not attractive to most people. Some homeowners paint them bright colors and consider them a sort of "graphic." For those homeowners who would rather hide the pipes there are several options, as discussed below.

Hiding exposed pipes for an extended pipe installation. An extended vanity cabinet can be built to conceal the

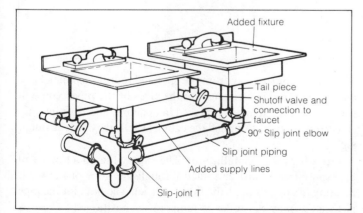

To install a second vanity in a bathroom, tie into the existing supply and drain lines. For proper drainage, the drain from the new vanity must slope down to the drain of the existing vanity.

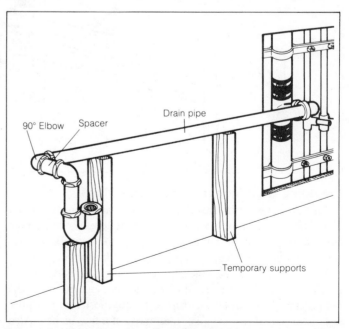

To run a drain pipe along the wall, mark the wall. Use a 90-degree elbow and finish off with a spacer. Place the trap over the spot marked on the floor. To prop, use pieces of lumber or bricks.

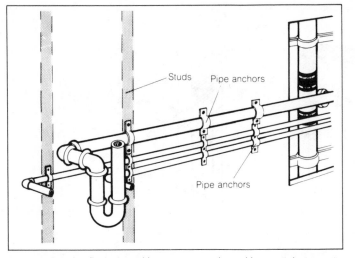

After testing for fit and position, connect pipes. Use metal straps to anchor the pipes. Install and connect the fixture to the trap. Before patching the wall, check for leaks and correct function.

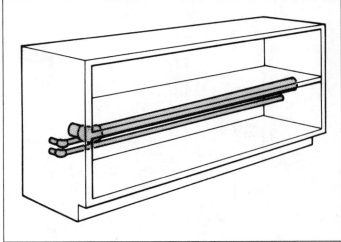

To hide exposed pipes, try boxing them in with shelves that also add needed storage. Cover pipes at corners with plasterboard that is first nailed to a frame.

pipes and to give more counter space and storage beneath. Or, storage shelves can be assembled over the pipes and the items on the shelves will pretty much keep the pipes hidden. Another option is to build out the wall to a point just above the highest pipe and to close it in. There will be a shelf several inches wide that can provide some storage and display space and the pipes will be out of sight. To be practical, the covering of the built-out wall should be hardboard or plywood attached with screws. This enables removal for access to the pipes if repairs are necessary. Hardboard or plywood can be painted to match the walls or can even be covered with ceramic tile.

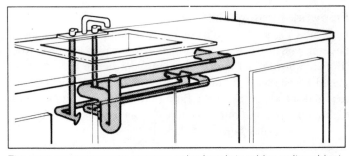

The most common way to cover up ugly pipes is to add a vanity cabinet, which can be built to fit.

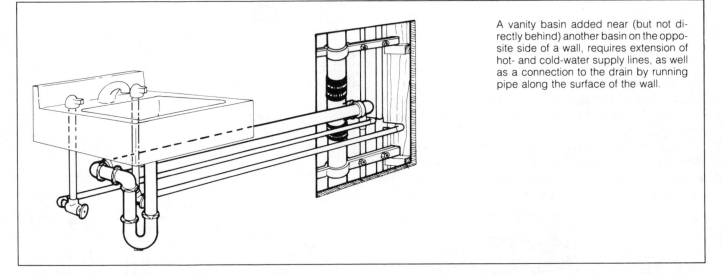

A vanity basin added near (but not directly behind) another basin on the opposite side of a wall, requires extension of hot- and cold-water supply lines, as well as a connection to the drain by running pipe along the surface of the wall.

Providing Openings in Fixtures for Pipes

Pipes for the vanity installation. For a new vanity cabinet, place the cabinet in position and drill pilot holes down through the bottom shelf of the cabinet and through the floor. Bore holes for the hot and cold water supply lines and for the drain line.

Before enlarging the holes, go down into the basement or crawl space; make sure the pilot holes are not located where the path of the pipe will be interrupted by any obstacle. If a pilot hole is on top of a floor joist, then move it a few inches. Also relocate the hole or holes in the bottom shelf of the vanity cabinet as needed. Then drill them a size to accept the pipes.

Move the cabinet away from the spot and redrill the holes large enough to provide clearance for the sizes of the pipes you will use. When the cabinet is replaced in position, and the pipes are run up through the floor and the cabinet shelf, they will be out of sight.

Pipes for toilet installation. The supply line to a toilet will be exposed and must be routed through the floor or the wall. Routing the line through the floor is easier. The hole for the pipe is located once the toilet is temporarily positioned. There is always a chance that the tank connection and the hole in the floor will be a bit out of line, but copper or plastic piping can be

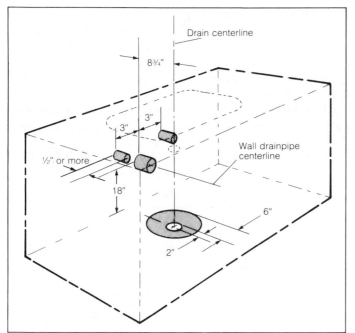

The drainline of a lavatory usually connects with the stack in the wall. The connection may be as much as 3 inches to either side of the drain. In a few cases, a connection will be to a floor drain.

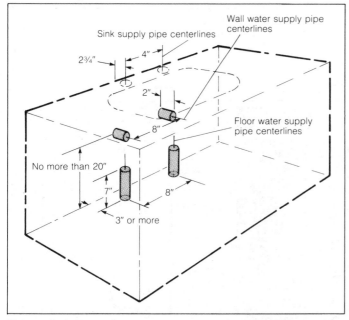

Sink supply lines usually come throught the wall at about 20 inches from the floor and are then connected to the faucets. You may find lines run up through the floor to supply water to the sink.

bent to accommodate any misalignment. Steep pipes will present problems, and the usual solution is to drill an oversize hole in the floor to allow movement of the pipe, and then to plug or caulk around the pipe after it is in place. Fit an escutcheon plate around the pipe at the floor juncture, to make the connection neat.

ADDING A BATHROOM IN THE BASEMENT

Of all the areas of the house, the basement is the easiest place to install another bathroom. You have several choices of the kind of bathroom: a basin for washing up after working in the shop or garden so you don't make a mess in an upstairs bathroom; a

When using a plastic stool flange, do not remove the center seal until work is done, to prevent debris from falling into the drain. Then knock out the seal.

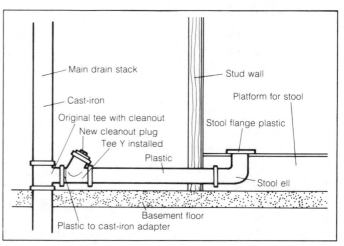

When a cleanout Tee or Tee-Y is used for connecting the toilet to the drain, a second Tee or Tee-Y should be installed first so that a cleanout plug will be available for the fixture.

toilet and shower for the youngsters after they come in from muddy play; a luxurious bathroom to go with a downstairs bedroom.

Because the supply water pipes and drain lines are readily accessible, a basement bathroom might be a good way to "practice" building an upstairs bathroom. Most operations are the same, and if you can solve the plumbing problems in the basement, they'll be a lot easier to solve upstairs.

An Example Project

In the example shown it was decided to build a complete bathroom, with a shower, adjacent to a bedroom that had been built in the basement. There was a soil pipe just outside the room, providing a drain for a half bath in the master bedroom upstairs. Cold and hot water lines also ran to the powder room, and were handy to the proposed bathroom.

Connecting the drain line. The usual way to connect a drain line in the basement is to tear up the concrete floor and install a Tee or Tee-Y in the drain that runs under the floor. This is both expensive and messy, so the homeowner opted for connection of a cleanout Tee down close to the floor. Another alternative to this would be to install a Tee or Cross near the floor by supporting the cast iron pipe, cutting out a section and installing the necessary fitting with rubber sleeves and stainless steel clamps, as has been described above.

The immediate problem then becomes: how do you connect a toilet to an above-the-floor connection? The answer is: you set the toilet on a low platform. This does require that the basement have at least 7 feet of headroom (or that you have only short people use the bathroom).

This view of the new bathroom is from the future shower location. Note the raised platform (disguised with carpeting). At left, a shop-built cabinet turns an old-fashioned basin into a vanity.

Installing a plastic adapter. The homeowner had researched modern plumbing supplies and had decided to use all plastic. The first task was to install an adapter in the cast iron Tee to accept ABS plastic drain line. For the installation shown, "lead wool" was compacted over oakum to replace the usual melted lead, which would damage the plastic. Even easier, there is a plastic product you can buy that is applied like a mortar to the joint; it seals the connection between the cast iron and plastic.

Laying out the location of the toilet. To find the desired

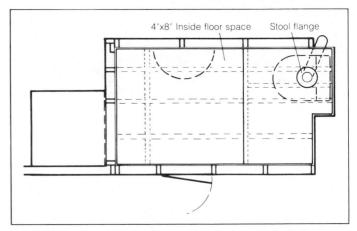

The original end wall framing is shown in this plan, with an indication as to where the shower stall installation will be added later. Also note the doorway entrances and wall corners.

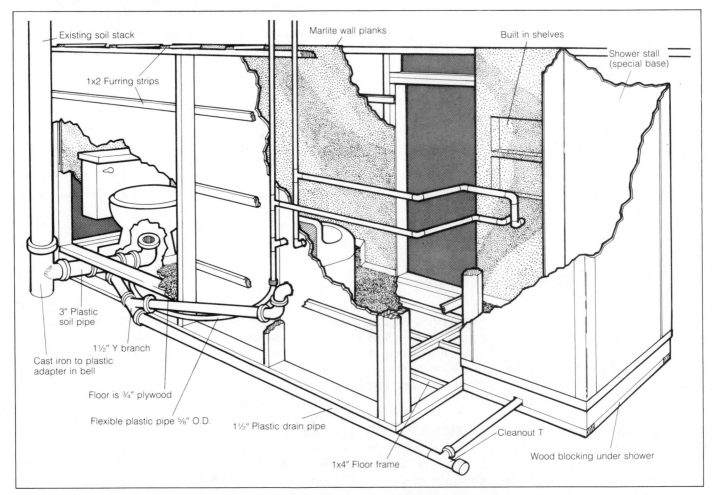

Wall framing was built with 2x4 studs, spaced every 24 inches, because horizontal furring strips were used to apply the wall paneling.

The stool was placed on a low platform to provide the rise necessary for installation of the drain line to main vent. After a trial placement to find position, the stool was set aside.

To use ABS plastic drain line, an adapter was selected. The joint between the cast iron Tee and the adapter was packed with oakum. Then cold lead wool was hammered into the joint to make it watertight.

The bathroom framing now is complete, with a removable wall placed and held with screws so it can be rebuilt later when the shower is added.

location of the toilet, a short length of plastic drain line was placed on the floor and the end slipped into the adapter in the soil pipe. It had previously been determined that the room would be 4 feet wide and 8 feet long. Because the Tee in the soil pipe could not be moved to change the angle, a compromise was made as to the location of the stool; it was not centered in the room. Extending the drain to center the stool would have wasted too much space behind it. If you install a new Tee in an existing drain line you can position it to suit, which was not possible in the installation shown.

Wall framing and pipe assembly. With the location of the stool determined, the walls of the room were framed, as was the platform for the stool. The plastic soil pipe, elbow and toilet flange were assembled and glued. Note in one of the accompanying photos how the 2x4s in the platform frame are spaced to provide support for the toilet flange. As a note of caution, do not try to just dry-fit the plastic soil pipe before assembly. The pipe will slip into the fittings only about halfway to the inside shoulder. When the adhesive is applied the pipe bottoms farther in, and your assembly will be short by about 1½ inches for each fitting. Measure to the inside shoulder to accurately determine the proper length of the pipe.

Floor height adjustments. Once the ceiling and walls were in place it was determined that the stool platform was a little high for a comfortable step up, so the floor was raised. This was done by assembling a grid of 1x2 lumber and covering it with exterior grade plywood. Interior grade plywood could have been used for the flooring, but the small additional cost for the exterior grade material was considered worthwhile, since it offers insurance against water damage — which is not uncommon in a bathroom.

The platform and flooring. The platform for the toilet was floored with ½ inch exterior grade plywood. To permit easy assembly around the stool flange, and later easy removal for access to the soil pipe, the flooring pieces were attached with

The drain line was positioned, and then the platform for the stool was built above it. The framing was positioned so that it would support the stool flange, while hiding the pipe and its support.

A plastic stool flange was cemented to the soil pipe and screwed to the platform. The platform floor was in 4 pieces, held by screws so it could be removed if repair work on the drain were necessary.

screws rather than nails. A trial fit of the toilet stool to the flange was made; its outline was drawn on to the plywood and the stool then was set aside while the room was finished.

Final stool placement. Once the carpeting was installed, it was cut to fit around the outline of the toilet stool that had been marked onto the plywood floor. Two bolts were slipped into the notched grooves in the plastic stool flange. Then a wax ring was placed over the flange. The stool was lowered gently while the two bolts were guided into the holes in the base of the stool.

The stool was pressed firmly downward to compress the wax ring, then nuts were turned on the projecting bolts and gently snugged up to both hold the stool in place and to further compress the wax ring for a watertight seal between the stool and the flange.

Variation: cast iron or copper stool flange. If a cast iron or copper stool flange had been used, the wax ring would have been installed in a similar manner, but "hanger bolts" would have been screwed into the floor. The hanger bolts come with a wood screw thread that turns into the wooden floor. The other end of the bolt has machine screw threads on which a nut is turned to clamp the stool to the floor and compress the wax ring seal. Usually, porcelain caps fit over the nuts to hide them.

Creating the ceiling and paneling the walls. Furring strips were nailed to the underside of the floor joists for the ceiling of the bathroom. Melamine-coated 16-inch square tiles were attached to the furring with small metal clips that came packaged with the tiles. The melamine coating waterproofs the tiles and permits cleaning. The wall panel used also was chosen with a melamine coating for easy maintenance. It was fastened with metal clips. Other types of ceiling material and paneling could be used, as well as water-resistant plasterboard. Panel adhesive and nails then would be used for attachment.

Installing the door. The entrance to the new bathroom was from the existing bedroom, which had a wall paneled with redwood. Rather than buy a door (keeping economy in mind, as we all must), the pieces of horizontal paneling were cut for an opening and carefully numbered, so they could be replaced in the same order. A frame of 1x2 lumber then was nailed just above floor level and was glued to the access opening to create the door. The redwood paneling was nailed and glued to the door on the bedroom side.

Because the resulting door was too thick to be handled by a standard lockset, a recess was cut in the paneling on the bathroom side and a piece of 1-inch stock was glued and screwed in it. The bathroom side of the door then was covered with melamine-coated paneling to match the walls. An opening was bored for the lockset and it was installed.

Adding the built-in shelves. Built-in shelves for the bathroom were created by cutting a hole through the paneling, between the studs. The opening was framed and then lined with paneling. For the "vanity," an old washbasin was used, for which a cabinet was built. The top and bottom of the cabinet were built of plywood cut to the shape of the basin. Strips of wall paneling covered the plywood sides of the cabinet.

To avoid damage to the plumbing out in the open on the outside of the bathroom wall, the wall studs later were shimmed out with strips of wood between the various plumbing lines. Wall paneling was attached with screws. This permitted easy removal for later access to the plumbing.

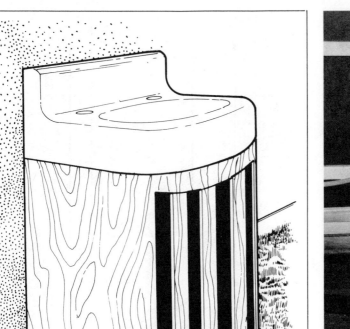

An old-fashioned wash basin was updated with a plywood cabinet that was covered with thin strips of paneling. The construction of the curved front of the cabinet under the basin was a "cut and try" project, so no real plans can be given for it.

Plastic ABS pipe (black) was used for drains, capped to allow later shower stall installation. Plastic Tees route water from stool to vanity and shower. A vertical line runs to future shower location.

Hot and cold water supply. The homeowner used flexible polybutylene (PB), joined with compression fittings, for the hot and cold water lines. Because the plumbing was readily accessible, less expensive PVC or CPVC pipe and fittings could have been used and assembled with solvent adhesive. The reason for using the PB plumbing was that the homeowner wanted some experience with it so he could use it in an upstairs bathroom he planned to build. (In some areas, this is the only type of plastic code will accept for certain types of projects.)

Providing a Shower Stall

To allow for later installation of a shower stall when the money was available, the homeowner attached the wall opposite the stool with long wood screws rather than nailing the panels. When he was ready to install the shower, the wall was removed.

The shower stall chosen was fiberglass, with a plastic pan. The pan comes with a drain that goes straight down, as for an upstairs bathroom, or one that goes out at right angles to the drain. The latter type was selected for the basement installation, which required cutting a notch in the side of the shower pan. To assure adequate drainage from the shower, the pan was placed on strips of lumber to raise it above the basement floor. This gave a slight drop in the drain line from the shower pan to the drain line that ran to the soil pipe. The shower and basin both drain into a reducing Tee fitting in the line between the 1½-inch pipe and the 3-inch main drain.

When the shower was installed, the wall that had been removed for it was taken apart and rebuilt to fit against it. The edges of the shower stall were caulked where they met the wall paneling.

Although not shown in the photos, the drain lines later were replumbed to provide venting. As stated previously, venting is one area where the amateur plumber runs into trouble, and requires the services of a professional unless the homeowner has had considerable plumbing background and experience.

Steel pipe was used in the house, so a section was removed and a Tee, nipple and union were combined to permit valve installation. An adapter from the valve joins the plastic pipe to a shutoff valve.

When the shower stall was installed later, the wall that had been removed for the construction was rebuilt to fit around the new stall. The resulting joint between the wall and the stall was caulked.

When time and money were available (later) for shower stall, the wall was removed. Shown here, the stall is in position. The shower pan has a right-angle drain that runs out through a notch cut into the side of the pan. Once shower stall was in position, the wall framing was rebuilt to fit around the stall.

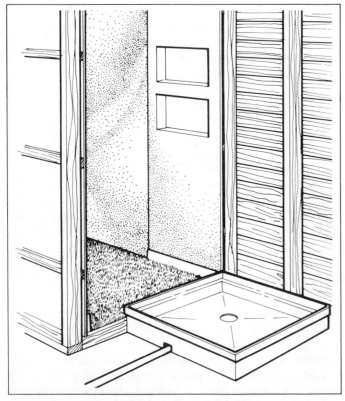

The end wall was built with screws for easy disassembly later, at which time a shower stall was added. The pan is shown here in relation to the placement of the old end wall.

Shown is a view of the shower drain which was blocked up on the floor. Because it was left unprotected, the system is vulnerable to damage.

The solution to the problem of the exposed pipe was to build a small platform that provided storage and also protected the exposed drain line.

Appendices

A   **Glossary**   143

B   **Where to Write for Appliance Parts**   146

C   **Metric Conversion Charts**   150

D   **Helpful Government Publications**   153

E   **Manufacturers' Addresses**   155

Glossary

Absorber panel   Part of solar collector, a flat panel set to catch the maximum daily rays of the sun.

ACR   Copper pipe (tubing) specifically for air conditioning or refrigeration work.

Adjustable wrench   Wrench with one stationary jaw, and another that moves up or down on a worm screw.

Aerator   Diverter/screen unit screwed onto the end of a faucet to control splashing.

Air bleeds   release air from inside the ballcock or flapper valve, so that the valve closes more quickly. Air bleeds require the flush lever to be held down to clear solid waste.

Air chamber   A vertical, air-filled pipe or spring coil set in above water line to absorb pressure when water is shut off at the faucet.

Air gap   In a drainage system, often used in a dishwasher's discharge in which the appliance discharges through air into a receptacle. Used to meet codes that prohibit pressurized discharge into a DWV system.

Air gap   In a water supply system, the distance between the faucet outlet and the flood rim of the basin it discharges into. Used to prevent contamination of the water supply by back-syphonage.

Allen wrench   Six-sided rod which fits inside of "Allen Nut" to turn the nut.

Anti-syphon   Term applied to valves or other devices that eliminate back-syphonage.

Aquifer   A stratum of water bearing, permeable soil, rock or gravel.

Backflow   Reverse flow of water or other liquids into water supply pipes carrying potable water. Back-syphonage is a type of backflow.

Backflow-preventer   A device or means to prevent backflow.

Back-syphonage   Backflow of contaminated water by negative pressure in the potable water system.

Backwater valve   A one-way valve installed in the house drain or sewer that prevents flooding of low-level fixtures by backing up of the sewer.

Ballcock   Toilet tank water supply valve, which is controlled by a float ball. Usually of the anti-syphon type.

Bidet   A bathroom fixture used for bathing immediately after using the toilet.

Branch   Any part of a pipe system other than a riser, main or stack.

Branch   (See revent)

Building drain   The lowest house piping that receives discharge from stack, waste and other drainage pipes and carries it to the building sewer outside the house.

Building sewer   Normally begins five feet outside the foundation of the house. Carries house sewage underground to the sewer or private disposal system.

Building trap   Device installed in the building drain to prevent gases from the sewer from circulating inside the house DWV system.

Bushing   (In plumbing) a device that permits reduction of one pipe size to another and/or male to female connections.

Cartridge   (faucet) Replaceable unit which controls flow of water. Should be replaced when faucet begins to leak.

Cast iron pipe   Heavy, strong, large pipe used for drain, waste and vent lines as well as sewer laterals (from house to street).

Cesspool   Lined or covered excavation in the ground that receives domestic wastes from the drainage system. Retains organic matter and solids; lets liquids seep into the ground through its porous bottom and sides.

Channel lock pliers   Pliers with adjustable, parallel jaws.

Check valve   A special valve which allows water to flow in only one direction.

Cleanout   Accessible opening in the drainage system used for removing obstructions.

Closet bend   A curved section of cast iron (drain) pipe which fits onto the base of the toilet.

Copper pipe   Drawn temper rigid form (hard) pipe. Sold in lengths.
  Type M — Thin wall
  Type L — Medium wall
  Type K — Thick wall
  DWV — Large size (Drain, waste, vent)

Copper tubing   Annealed (soft) tubing sold in rolls of same lengths as pipe and in same type specifications.

Crocus cloth   Grit on cloth backing — finer than sandpaper.

Cross connection   Physical connection between potable water supply and any non-potable water source.

Dams   Flexible panels pressed into place in the toilet tank. They block off a portion of the lower part of a tank, thus reducing the amount of water released into the bowl. But dams allow the tank to fill completely, maximizing water velocity. They can save somewhat more water than other devices.

Distribution box   Concrete or other receptable in the ground with one inlet located higher than two or more outlets. Used to equally divide the quantity of septic tank effluent among various branches of a seepage system.

Drain   Any pipe that carries waste water (water-borne wastes) in a building drainage system.

Drainage system   All the piping that carries sewage, rainwater or other liquid wastes to the point of disposal or sewer.

Dry well   Underground excavation used for leaching of other than sewage into the ground.

Dual flush units   The flush lever is moved in one direction to flush liquid waste (using very little water) and in the other direction to clear solid waste.

Effluent   The liquid discharge from a septic tank.

Fixture supply   Water supply pipe that connects a fixture to a branch water supply pipe or directly to a main water supply pipe.

Fixture unit, drainage (dfu)   A measure of the probable discharge into the drainage system by various plumbing fixtures. In general, on small systems, one dfu approximates one cubic foot of water per minute.

Fixture unit, water supply (sfu)   A measure of the probable water demand by various plumbing fixtures.

Flange   A rim which allows object to be attached firmly to another object or surface.

Closet flange   Rim on closet bend by which pipe is attached to floor.

Float ball   Hollow ball on the end of a rod in the toilet tank. It floats upward as the tank fills after flushing and eventually closes inlet valve.

Flush valve   A device at the bottom of a toilet tank for flushing it.

Flush valve stop   Works somewhat like a valve weight, causing the valve to shut down and stop the water flow as soon as the flush lever is released.

Flux   Material used to aid fusing of metals.

GFI   (Ground fault interrupter) Electronic device for shutting off current in any circuit when a short circuit occurs. National Electric Code (NEC) require a GFI in newly constructed homes for all outside circuits and for circuits in kitchens and bathrooms where there is high humidity.

Galvanic action   An electrical process by which metallic elements are leached from one substance and attracted to another.

Gasket   Device used to seal joint against leaks.

Gate Valve   A unit designed to interrupt flow of water through line. The shutoff must be all the way open or all the way closed for this valve to work.

Gland nut   Hollow nut which compresses flexible material around a valve stem to assure water tight connection.

Globe valve   Designed to interrupt flow of water through line, this unit has a flat headed rod which fits into a valve seat. The water passes through this unit (when open) by making two 90° turns.

Grade   The fall or slope of a line of pipes in reference to the horizontal. It is usually expressed as fall in fractions of an inch per foot of pipe length.

Ground   A line frequently attached to plumbing pipes which assures safe functioning of electrical system in the home. This line normally carries no current. (If there is a short circuit, there will be current.)

Guide arm   (In toilet tank) A rod which lifts tank ball or flapper valve when tank handle is turned.

Hydronic   Hot water heating.

Inlet valve   (In toilet tank) A valve which controls water flow into the toilet tank.

Joint runner   A special collarlike device used to keep molten lead in place while sealing a joint in a horizontal run of cast iron pipe.

Lavatory   Sink.

Lead   Heavy metal with relatively low melting point used to seal cast iron (drain) pipe.

Leaching pit   (See seepage pit.)

Liquid waste   Discharge from any fixture, appliance, etc., that does not contain fecal matter.

Main   Principal pipe to which branches are connected.

Main vent (or stack)   Principal vent to which branch vents may be connected.

Manifold   A pipe fitting with more than one lateral outlet to connect with other pipes.

Nonpotable water   Water that is not safe for drinking.

Oakum   A ropelike material used in sealing joints in cast iron pipe.

O-ring   A ring of rubber used as a gasket (with a circular cross section).

Overflow tube   In toilet tank — tube into which water flows if float arm fails to activate the shutoff when tank is filled.

P-trap   A curved piece of pipe (drain) inserted below sink to catch and hold water. Necessary to prevent sewer gas from entering the house through drain lines.

Phillips head   A screwdriver with a star-shaped, pointed head.

Pipe   Copper
Galvanized (Steel)
PVC — Polyvinyl chloride
ABS — Acrylonitrile buradine styrene
Cast iron

Pipe joint compound   Material used to seal threaded pipe joint against leak.

Pitch   (See grade)

Plumbing system   Includes water supply and distribution pipes; plumbing fixtures and traps; drain, waste and vent pipes; and building drains including their respective connections, devices and appurtenances within a building or structure to a point no more than five feet beyond the foundation walls.

Plumbing tree   A prefabricated set of drain, waste, vent and supply lines.

Potable water   Water free from impurities in amounts sufficient to cause disease or harmful psychological effects. Conforms to the requirements of the U.S. Public Health Service Drinking Water Standards or regulations of the public health authority having jurisdiction.

Replacement tanks   Much more difficult to install than most other water saving devices.

Revent   A pipe installed specifically to vent a fixture trap. Connects with the vent system above the fixture served.

Riser   Short, vertical pipe in the water supply system leading from the main.

Riser tube   Short, flexible tube that connects fixture to the water supply system.

Rough-in   The installation of parts of the plumbing system that can be done before installation of the fixtures. Includes drainage, water supply and vent piping and the necessary fixture supports.

Sanitary sewer   A sewer that carries sewage but not storm, surface or ground water.

Seepage field   Arrangement of perforated or open-joint piping underground that permits septic tank effluent to leach into the surrounding porous soil.

Seepage well or pit   Same purpose as seepage field but confined to a hole in the ground.

Septic tank   A water-tight receptacle that receives raw sewage from the house sewer, digests organic matter retained in it and allows liquid effluent to discharge to a seepage field or pit.

Shutoff valve   a device set into water line to interrupt flow of water to a fixture. Turns like a faucet handle.

Snake   A length of coiled, flexible wire which can be fed into plugged drain to clear debris from the line.

Solar collector   Device designed to absorb the heat generated by the sun and transfer it to air or liquid for the purpose of heating water or air inside the home.

Stop valve   Plastic or metal globe valve located under a fixture to shut off water to that fixture.

Tank ball   A rubber, metal, or plastic ball which fits into flush valve to seal tank outlet. Now more usually replaced by a "flapper" valve.

Union   A three piece pipe fitting with convex and concave faces held together by a large nut.

Valve seat   Opening into which valve fits (tightly) to shut off flow of water.

Water closet   Toilet

Water hammer   A knocking in water pipes caused by sudden change in pressure after a faucet is shut off.

Wax ring   A wax seal which replaces plumber's putty used to seal the base of a toilet so it won't leak.

Weights   Cause the flush valve to close sooner than it normally would. With some, either the amount of weight added or the weight's position on the valve can be varied. An adjustable weight allows the toilet to be flushed normally to remove liquid waste, but the flush lever must be held down to clear solid waste.

Appliance Parts Sources

ALABAMA

**Washer and Refrigeration
Supply Company, Inc.**
R. E. Smith
716 Second Avenue, North
Birmingham, Alabama 35201
Phone: (205) 322-8693

ARIZONA

**Appliance Dealer Supply
Company, Inc.**
Paul Zeller
P.O. Box 2017 (740 West Grant)
Phoenix, Arizona 85007
Phone: (602) 252-7506

**Appliance Parts Company
(Branch-Appl. Parts-Van Nuys)**
2215 East University Drive
Phoenix, Arizona 85034

**Akrit Appliance Supply Co.
(Branch-Akrit Appl.-Albuquerque)**
1132 North Richey Boulevard
Tucson, Arizona 85716

ARKANSAS

Mid-South Appliance Parts Company
Leonard Kremers
1020 West 14th St., P.O. Box 2722
Little Rock, Arkansas 72201
Phone: (501) 376-8351

   720 North 11th Street
   Fort Smith, Arkansas 72901

CALIFORNIA

**Appliance Parts Company
Division of Washing Machine Parts Co.**
Howard F. Parker, Sr.
15040 Oxnard Street
P. O. Box 2787
Van Nuys, California 91401
Phone: (213) 787-9220

   1575 Mable Street
   Anaheim, California 92802

   372 North Mt. Vernon
   Colton, California 92324

   14410 Hindry Avenue
   Lawndale, California 90260

   9870 Baldwin Place
   El Monte, California 91731

Cal Sales Corporation
Gene M. Sharpe
641 Monterey Pass Road
Monterey Park, California 91754
Phone: (213) 283-7741

   2945 West 5th Street
   Oxnard, California 93030

Coast Appliance Parts Company
Leonard A. Ellison
5915 North Kester Avenue
Van Nuys, California 91401
Phone: (213) 782-5770

   269 South Arrowhead Avenue
   San Bernardino, California 92408

   764 14th Street
   San Diego, California 92101

   8222 Lankershim Boulevard
   North Hollywood, Cal. 91605

   9817 Inglewood Avenue
   Inglewood, California 90301

Electrical Appliance Service Co.
Sabert L. Summers
J. Tribulato
290 Townsend Street
San Francisco, California 94107
Phone: (415) 777-1900

   145 Van Ness Street
   Fresno, California 93721

   4238 Broadway
   Oakland, California 94611

   1116 "F" Street
   Sacramento, California 95814

   1140 Lincoln Avenue
   San Jose, California 95125

Western Appliance Parts Company
Howard Parker, Jr.
1844 India Street
San Diego, California 92101
Phone: (714) 232-7871

COLORADO

Ray Jones Appliance Parts Company
Aud L. Hanna
376 South Broadway
Denver, Colorado 80209
Phone: (303) 744-6263

   1436 North Hancock
   Colorado Springs, Col. 80903

   1813 East Mulberry Street
   Fort Collins, Colorado 80521

**Niles-Noel Incorporated
(Branch-Ray Jones Appl. Parts Co.)**
562 South Broadway
Denver, Colorado 80209

**Akrit Appliance Supply Co.
(Branch-Akrit Appl.-Albuquerque)**
402 Arrawanna Street
Colorado Springs, Col. 80909

CONNECTICUT

Arcand Distributors, Inc.
Richard Arcand
845 Windsor Street
Hartford, Connecticut 06120
Phone: (203) 522-2214

   61 Erna Avenue
   Milford, Connecticut 06460

American Appliance Parts, Inc.
2516 Whitney Avenue
Hamden, Connecticut 06518
John T. Malatesta

   1196 Farmington Avenue
   Kensington, Connecticut

   10 Boston Avenue
   Stratford, Connecticut

Electric Appliance Parts Company
Anthony J. Ciarlo, Jr.
175 Freight Street
Waterbury, Connecticut 06780
Phone: (203) 753-1763

**Westchester Appliance Parts, Inc.
(Branch-All Appliance Parts)**
194 Richmond Avenue
Stamford, Connecticut 06902

DISTRICT OF COLUMBIA

Trible's Incorporated
John R. Trible
2240 25th Place
Washington, D.C. 20018
Phone: (202) 832-9300

FLORIDA

**Marcone Appliance Parts Center
(Branch-Marcone Appl.-St. Louis)**
777 N.W. 79th Street
Miami, Florida 33150

   1515 Cypress Street
   Tampa, Florida 33606

   2108 West Central Boulevard
   Orlando, Florida 32805

   1019 Rosselle Street
   Jacksonville, Florida 32204

GEORGIA

**D & L Appliance Parts Company
(Branch-D & L Appl. Parts-Charlotte)**
5799 New Peachtree Road
Atlanta, Georgia 30340
Phone: (404) 458-8191

**Harris Appliance Parts Company
(Branch-Harris Appl. Pts.-Anderson)**
5129 Montgomery Street
Savannah, Georgia 31405

   227 West Dougherty Street
   Athens, Georgia 30601

HAWAII

Appliance Parts Company, Inc.
Dave Dumas
P.O. Box 17976
1550 Kalani Street
Honolulu, Hawaii 96817
Phone: (808) 847-3217

   731 Kamehameha Highway
   Pearl City, Hawaii 96782

   3057 Waialae Avenue
   Honolulu, Hawaii 96816

   118 Hekili Street
   Kailua, Hawaii 96734

IDAHO

**IASCO Distributing Company
(Intermountain Appl. Supply Corp.)
(Branch-IASCO Dist. Co.-Utah)**
2895 North Holmes Avenue
Idaho Falls, Idaho 84501

**W. L. May Company, Inc.
(Branch-W. L. May Co.-
Portland, Oregon)**
202 East 33rd Street
Boise, Idaho 83704

ILLINOIS

Automatic Appliance Parts Corp.
Roger Flinn
4441 West Diversey
Chicago, Illinois 60639
Phone: (312) 278-8668

   1506 East Algonquin Road
   Arlington Heights, Illinois 60005

Midwest Appliance Parts Company
Morey Misles
2600 West Diversey
Chicago, Illinois 60647
Phone: (312) 278-1300

C. E. Sundberg Company
Truman Smith
615 West 79th Street
Chicago, Illinois 60620
Phone: (312) 723-2700

INDIANA

Appliance Parts, Inc.
John K. David
P.O. Box 22350
1734 West 15th Street
Indianapolis, Indiana 46222
Phone: (317) 635-3657

Appliance Parts Supply Company
(Branch-Appl. Parts-Toledo)
1241 Wells Street
Fort Wayne, Indiana 46808

Bell Parts Supply
Jule L. Bell
2819 45th Street
Highland, Indiana 46322

Evansville Appliance Parts
Orville N. Joergens
920 West Pennsylvania Street
Evansville, Indiana 47708
Phone: (812) 423-8867

IOWA

The Ricketts Company, Inc.
Mrs. B. L. (Bernice) Ricketts
801 S.E. 14th Street
Des Moines, Iowa 50317
Phone: (515) 244-7236

KENTUCKY

The Collins Company, Inc.
Daniel A. Smith
Appliance Parts Division
819 South Floyd Street
Louisville, Kentucky 40203
Phone: (502) 583-1723

   3071 Breckenridge Lane
   Louisville, Kentucky 40220

   150 Indiana Avenue
   Box 24
   Lexington, Kentucky 40508

LOUISIANA

Bruce's Distributing Company
Bruce J. Sterbenz
509 East 70th Street
Shreveport, Louisiana 71106
Phone: (318) 861-7662

Sunseri's, Inc.
Diego Joseph Sunseri
2254-60 St. Claude Avenue
New Orleans, Louisiana 70117
Phone: (504) WH-4-6762

MAINE

Appliance Parts Company
(Branch-Appl. Parts-Boston)
255 Danforth Street
Portland, Maine 04102

MARYLAND

Trible's Incorporated
(Branch-Tribles, Inc.-Wash., D.C.)
140 Halpine Road
Rockville, Maryland 20852

   2210 North Howard Street
   Baltimore, Maryland 21218

   3533 Fort Meade Road
   Laurel, Maryland 20810

MASSACHUSETTS

Appliance Parts Company, Inc.
Glenn F. Catlow
112 Dartmouth Street
Boston, Massachusetts 02116
Phone: (617) 536-0138

Hall Electric Supply Company, Inc.
(HESCO)
Earl K. Hall, Jr.
33 Brighton Street
Belmont, Massachusetts 02178
Phone: (617) 489-3450

M.G.M.S. Associates, Inc.
Louis P. Miele
22 Water Street
Cambridge, Massachusetts 02141
Phone: (617) 868-8360

Supply Distributors
Victoria Ludlam
50 Revere Beach Parkway
Medford, Massachusetts 02155

MICHIGAN

Servall Company
Kenneth Adler
228 East Baltimore Street
Detroit, Michigan 48202
Phone: (313) TR-2-3655

   26500 Grand River Avenue
   Detroit, Michigan 48240

   24312 Gratiot Avenue
   East Detroit, Michigan 48021

   6619 Schaefer
   Dearborn, Michigan 48126

   630 West Kearsley
   Flint, Michigan 48503

   440 Lake Michigan Drive, N.W.
   Grand Rapids, Michigan 49504

   1100 South Water Street
   Saginaw, Michigan 48601

   412 East Elm Street
   Lansing, Michigan 48912

   4936 Allen Road
   Allen Park, Michigan 48101

MINNESOTA

Appliance Parts, Incorporated
Martin A. Frederick
250 3rd Avenue, North
Minneapolis, Minnesota 55401
Phone: (612) 335-0931

   964 Rice Street
   St. Paul, Minnesota 55117

Dey Appliance Parts
Adolph Dey
P.O. Box 5086
525 North Snelling Avenue
St. Paul, Minnesota 55104
Phone: (612) 647-0717

MISSISSIPPI

Appliance Parts Company, Inc.
Bruce L. Coleman
727 South Gallatin Street
Jackson, Mississippi 39204
Phone: (601) 948-4680

   2214 Lee Street
   Alexandria, Louisiana 71301

MISSOURI

Marcone Appliance Parts Company
Norman Markow
2320 Pine Street
St. Louis, Missouri 63103
Phone: (314) 231-7141

Marcone Appliance Parts Center
(Branch-Marcone Appl. Parts-
St. Louis)
3113 Main Street
Kansas City, Missouri 64111

St. Louis Appliance Parts, Inc.
Joe E. James
2911-13 South Jefferson
St. Louis, Missouri 63118
Phone: (314) 776-1445

NEVADA

Cal Sales Corporation
(Branch-Cal Sales-California)
3453 Industrial Road
Las Vegas, Nevada 89109
Phone: (702) 734-1104

Electrical Appliance Service Co.
(Branch-Electrical Appl. Service-
San Francisco)
611 Kuenzli Street
Reno, Nevada 89502

NEW JERSEY

Jacoby Appliance Parts
Jules R. Jacoby
269 Main Street
Hackensack, New Jersey 07601
Phone: (201) 489-6444/6446

   57 Albany Street
   New Brunswick, N.J. 07101

   1242 Springfield Avenue
   Irvington, New Jersey 07111

   923 North Olden Avenue
   Trenton, New Jersey 08611

Westchester Appliance Parts, Inc.
(Branch-All Appl. Parts-New York)
470 U.S. Highway #46
Teterboro, New Jersey 07608

NEW MEXICO

Akrit Appliance Supply Company
Carlyle L. Otto
2820 Vassar N.E.
Albuquerque, New Mexico 87101
Phone: (505) 345-8651

NEW YORK

All Appliance Parts of New York, Inc.
Arvey Jonas
1345 New York Avenue
Huntington Station, N.Y. 11746
Phone: (516) 427-4600

   600-C Middle Country Road
   Selden, New York 11784

   2850 Sunrise Highway
   Bellmore, New York 11710

   113-02 Atlantic Avenue
   Richmond Hill, N.Y. 11419

   1985 New York Avenue
   Huntington Station, N.Y. 11746

Westchester Appliance Parts
1034 Yonkers Avenue
Yonkers, New York 10714

Buffalo Appliance Parts Co., Inc.
Frank L. Jarmusz
1175 Williams Street
Buffalo, New York 14206
Phone: (716) 856-5005

Nichols Appliance Parts, Inc.
(Branch-Buffalo Appl. Parts-N.Y.)
801 South Salina Street
Syracuse, N.Y. 13202

Rochester Appliance Parts Dist.
(Branch-Buffalo Appl. Parts-N.Y.)
189 North Water Street
Rochester New York 14604

Jacoby Appliance Parts
(Branch-Jacoby Appl. Parts-N.J.)
1023 Allerton Avenue
Bronx, New York 10469

   214 Route 59
   Suffern, New York 10901

   1654 Central Avenue
   Albany, New York 12205

NORTH CAROLINA

D & L Appliance Parts Co., Inc.
Ralph Brackett
2100 Freedom Drive
P.O. Box 1317
Charlotte, North Carolina 28208
Phone: (704) 375-7306

   2811 Firestone Drive
   Greensboro, N. C. 27406

   2324 Atlantic Avenue
   Raleigh, N.C. 27601

Moore and Stewart, Inc.
Denton W. Cruse
316 East Franklin Avenue
Gastonia, N.C. 28052
Phone: (704) 864-8334

OHIO

American Electric Washer Company
Alvin Brouman
1834 East 55th Street
Cleveland, Ohio 44103
Phone: (216) 431-4400

   2801 Detroit Avenue
   Cleveland, Ohio 44113

   988 East Market Street
   Akron, Ohio 44305

Appliance Parts Supply Company
James A. Staebell
235 Broadway Street
Toledo, Ohio 43602
Phone: (419) 244-6741

   1408 Cherry Street
   Toledo, Ohio 43608

Dayton Appliance Parts Company
James Houtz
122 Sears Street
Dayton, Ohio 45402
Phone: (513) 224-3531

Dayco Appliance Parts
338 East Spring Street
Columbus, Ohio 43215

Brand Service Center, Inc.
Paul R. Palmer
808 Elm Street
Cincinnati, Ohio 56202
Phone: (513) 241-3701

   6944 Plainfield Road
   Cincinnati, Ohio 45236

Mason Supply Company
Howard T. Yost
985 Joyce Avenue
Columbus, Ohio 43203
Phone: (614) 253-8607

   3929 Apple Street
   Cincinnati, Ohio 45223

Pearsol Appliance Corporation
Melvin J. Ellis
2319 Gilbert Avenue
Cincinnati, Ohio 45206
Phone: (513) 221-1195

Pearsol Corporation of Ohio
Leonard F. Mandell
1847 East 40th Street
Cleveland, Ohio 44103
Phone: (216) 881-5085

V & V Appliance Parts, Inc.
Victor Lazar
27 West Myrtle Avenue
Youngstown, Ohio 44507
Phone: (216) 743-5144

   553 High Street, N.E.
   Warren, Ohio 44481

OKLAHOMA

Greer Electric Company
Glen Z. Greer, Jr.
1018 South Rockford
Tulsa, Oklahoma 74104
Phone: (918) 587-3346

Pritchard Electric Company, Inc.
Wayne H. Youngblood
3100 North Santa Fe
Oklahoma City, Oklahoma 73101
Phone: (405) 528-0592

OREGON

W. L. May Company, Inc.
Edward Cohn, Jr.
1120 S.E. Madison Street
Portland, Oregon 97214
Phone: (503) 231-9398

   3619 Franklin Boulevard
   Eugene, Oregon 97403

PENNSYLVANIA

Collins Appliance Parts, Inc.
Richard D. Collins, Jr.
1533 Metropolitan Street
Pittsburgh, Pennsylvania 15233
Phone: (412) 321-3700

Parts Distributors Corporation
(Branch-All Appl. Parts-New York)
312 North Easton Road
Willow Grove, Pa. 19090

RHODE ISLAND

Appliance Parts Company, Inc.
(Branch-Appl. Parts-Boston)
316 Cranston Street
Providence, Rhode Island 02907
Phone: (401) 421-6142

Twin City Supply Company
Henry Dziadosz
885 Westminster Street
Providence, R. I. 02903
Phone: (401) 331-5930

SOUTH CAROLINA

G & E Parts Center, Inc.
Sam Lancaster
P.O. Box 2466
2403 South Pine Street
Spartanburg, S. C. 29304
Phone: (803) 585-6277

   P.O. Box 1074
   1212 Bluff Road
   Columbia, S.C. 29202

D & L Appliance Parts, Inc.
(Branch-D & L Appl. Parts-
Charlotte)
901 South Cashua Drive
Florence, S. C. 29501

Harris Appliance Parts Co.
Dell Johnson
P.O. Box 611
29 Bypass North
Anderson, S.C. 29621
Phone: (803) 225-7433

   423 Laurens Road
   Greenville, S.C. 29606

SOUTH DAKOTA

Dey Appliance Parts
(Branch-Dey Appl. Parts-
St. Paul, Minn.)
300 N. Phillips
Sioux Falls, So. Dakota 57102

TENNESSEE

Brown Appliance Parts
Company, Inc.
Mack Brown
857 North Central Avenue
Knoxville, Tennessee 37917
Phone: (615) 525-9363

   2472 Amnicola Highway
   Chattanooga, Tenn. 37406

   125 New Kingsport Hwy.
   Bristol, Tenn. 37620

Curtis Company
Jerry M. Brasher
562 East Street
P.O. Box 4918
Memphis, Tenn. 38104
Phone: (901) 527-1611

Napco, Inc.
Virgil C. Belcher
501 South Second Street
Nashville, Tenn 37213
Phone: (615) 242-5597

   5002 Charlotte Avenue
   Nashville, Tenn 37209

   111 Old Hickory Blvd.
   Madison, Tenn. 37115

TEXAS

Akrit Appliance Supply Co.
(Branch-Akrit Appl.-
Albuquerque)
1805 Montana
El Paso, Texas 79902

   2306 19th Street
   Lubbock, Texas 79401

Pearsol Appliance Company
Mort Mandell
3127 Main Street
Dallas, Texas 75226
Phone: (214) 741-4638

Standard Appliance Parts Corp
Glenn D. Peek
4814 Ayers Street
P.O. Box 7488
Corpus Cristi, Texas 78415
Phone: (512) 853-9823

   1214 West Van Buren
   Harlingen, Texas 78550

Texas Parts & Supply Company
Herbert Mathis
P.O. Box 115
1209 South St. Marys
San Antonio, Texas 78291
Phone: (512) 225-2717

   2820 Guadalupe
   Austin, Texas 78765

Washing Machine Parts Company
Harold Evans
704 North Main Street
Fort Worth, Texas 76106
Phone: (817) ED-2-5343

   3314 Ross Avenue
   Dallas, Texas 75204

Central Supply
Div. of Washing Machine Parts, Inc.
Kenneth D. Buvinghausen
1011 Wood Street, P.O. Box 3385
Houston, Texas 77001
Phone: (713) 224-8491

   5365 College Street
   Beaumont, Texas 77707

1604 South Shaver
Pasadena, Texas 77502

7417 Hillcroft
#2C Houston, Texas 77081

2612 McKinney
Houston, Texas 77003

UTAH

**IASCO Distributing Company
(Intermountain Appl. Supply Corp.)**
Dwayne C. Zenger
825 South West Temple Street
Salt Lake City,Utah 84101
Phone:(801) 328-0505

**Ray Jones Appliance Parts Company
(Branch-Ray Jones-Denver)**
3336 South 300 East
Salt Lake City,Utah 84115

VIRGINIA

Refrigeration Supply Company, Inc.
Edward L. Booth
1657 West Broad Street
Richmond, Virginia 23261
Phone:(804) 359-3275

1736 Allied Street
Charlottesville, Virginia 22901

**Booth Supply Company, Inc.
(Branch-Ref. Supp.-Richmond)**
2621 Florida Avenue
Norfolk, Virginia 23513

926 Vernon Street, Southeast
Roanoke, Virginia 24013

8304 Orcutt Avenue
Hampton, Virginia 23605

**Trible's Inc.
(Branch-Tribles, Inc.-Wash., D.C.)**
7273 East Arlington Blvd.
Falls Church, Va. 22042

Wholesale Parts Distributors, Inc.
Victor L. Via
1141 Lance Road
Norfolk, Virginia 23502
Phone:(804) 461-3888

WASHINGTON

Appliance Parts & Service Company
Harold R. Hansberry
400 9th Avenue, North
Seattle, Washington 98109
Phone: (206) 622-0152

West 917 Mallon
Spokane, Washington 99201

3730 South "G" Street
Tacoma, Washington 98408

WEST VIRGINIA

**Mason Supply Company
(Branch-Mason Supply-
Columbus, Ohio)**
800 Virginia Street, West
Charleston, West Virginia 25303

3rd & Eoff Streets
Wheeling, West Virginia 26003

WISCONSIN

A & E Distributors, Inc.
Walter E. Kuhn
1418 North Erwin Avenue
P.O. Box 8045
Green Bay, Wisconsin 54308
Phone:(414) 437-8215

Power Equipment
Frank Morella
2373 South Kinnickinnic Avenue
Milwaukee, Wisconsin 53207
Phone:(414) 744-3210

CANADA

Mossman's Appliance Parts, Ltd.
John Mossman
1465 Gerrard Street E.
Toronto, Ontario, Canada
M4L2A2
Phone: (416) 461-1147

746 Ellice Avenue
Winnipeg, Manitoba, Canada
R3G OB6

Waugh & MacKewn Limited

Myrle Hickey
1025 Elias Street
P.O. Box 2277 STN. A
London, Ontario, Canada
N6A 4E9
Phone: (519) 432-1115

5325 Crowley Avenue
Montreal, Quebec, Canada
H4A 2C6

3913 Manchester Road
Calgary, Alberts, Canada
T2G 4A1

2285-A Gladwin Cres.
Ottawa, Ontario, Canada
K1B 4K9

Appendix C: Metric Conversion Charts

LUMBER

Sizes: Metric cross-sections are so close to their nearest Imperial sizes, as noted below, that for most purposes they may be considered equivalents.

Lengths: Metric lengths are based on a 300mm module which is slightly shorter in length than an Imperial foot. It will therefore be important to check your requirements accurately to the nearest inch and consult the table below to find the metric length required.

Areas: The metric area is a square metre. Use the following conversion factors when converting from Imperial data: 100 sq. feet = 9.290 sq. metres.

METRIC SIZES SHOWN BESIDE NEAREST IMPERIAL EQUIVALENT

mm	Inches	mm	Inches
16 x 75	⅝ x 3	44 x 150	1¾ x 6
16 x 100	⅝ x 4	44 x 175	1¾ x 7
16 x 125	⅝ x 5	44 x 200	1¾ x 8
16 x 150	⅝ x 6	44 x 225	1¾ x 9
19 x 75	¾ x 3	44 x 250	1¾ x 10
19 x 100	¾ x 4	44 x 300	1¾ x 12
19 x 125	¾ x 5	50 x 75	2 x 3
19 x 150	¾ x 6	50 x 100	2 x 4
22 x 75	⅞ x 3	50 x 125	2 x 5
22 x 100	⅞ x 4	50 x 150	2 x 6
22 x 125	⅞ x 5	50 x 175	2 x 7
22 x 150	⅞ x 6	50 x 200	2 x 8
25 x 75	1 x 3	50 x 225	2 x 9
25 x 100	1 x 4	50 x 250	2 x 10
25 x 125	1 x 5	50 x 300	2 x 12
25 x 150	1 x 6	63 x 100	2½ x 4
25 x 175	1 x 7	63 x 125	2½ x 5
25 x 200	1 x 8	63 x 150	2½ x 6
25 x 225	1 x 9	63 x 175	2½ x 7
25 x 250	1 x 10	63 x 200	2½ x 8
25 x 300	1 x 12	63 x 225	2½ x 9
32 x 75	1¼ x 3	75 x 100	3 x 4
32 x 100	1¼ x 4	75 x 125	3 x 5
32 x 125	1¼ x 5	75 x 150	3 x 6
32 x 150	1¼ x 6	75 x 175	3 x 7
32 x 175	1¼ x 7	75 x 200	3 x 8
32 x 200	1¼ x 8	75 x 225	3 x 9
32 x 225	1¼ x 9	75 x 250	3 x 10
32 x 250	1¼ x 10	75 x 300	3 x 12
32 x 300	1¼ x 12	100 x 100	4 x 4
38 x 75	1½ x 3	100 x 150	4 x 6
38 x 100	1½ x 4	100 x 200	4 x 8
38 x 125	1½ x 5	100 x 250	4 x 10
38 x 150	1½ x 6	100 x 300	4 x 12
38 x 175	1½ x 7	150 x 150	6 x 6
38 x 200	1½ x 8	150 x 200	6 x 8
38 x 225	1½ x 9	150 x 300	6 x 12
44 x 75	1¾ x 3	200 x 200	8 x 8
44 x 100	1¾ x 4	250 x 250	10 x 10
44 x 125	1¾ x 5	300 x 300	12 x 12

METRIC LENGTHS

Lengths Metres	Equiv. Ft. & Inches
1.8m	5' 10⅞"
2.1m	6' 10⅝"
2.4m	7' 10½"
2.7m	8' 10¼"
3.0m	9' 10⅛"
3.3m	10' 9⅞"
3.6m	11' 9¾"
3.9m	12' 9½"
4.2m	13' 9⅜"
4.5m	14' 9⅓"
4.8m	15' 9"
5.1m	16' 8¾"
5.4m	17' 8⅝"
5.7m	18' 8⅜"
6.0m	19' 8¼"
6.3m	20' 8"
6.6m	21' 7⅞"
6.9m	22' 7⅝"
7.2m	23' 7½"
7.5m	24' 7¼"
7.8m	25' 7⅛"

All the dimensions are based on 1 inch = 25 mm.

NOMINAL SIZE (This is what you order.)	ACTUAL SIZE (This is what you get.)
Inches	**Inches**
1 x 1	¾ x ¾
1 x 2	¾ x 1½
1 x 3	¾ x 2½
1 x 4	¾ x 3½
1 x 6	¾ x 5½
1 x 8	¾ x 7¼
1 x 10	¾ x 9¼
1 x 12	¾ x 11¼
2 x 2	1¾ x 1¾
2 x 3	1½ x 2½
2 x 4	1½ x 3½
2 x 6	1½ x 5½
2 x 8	1½ x 7¼
2 x 10	1½ x 9¼
2 x 12	1½ x 11¼